Casting the Net

*"This is the Net of Light that will Hold the Earth
During the Times of Change that are upon You."*

— Great Council of the Grandmothers

SHARON MCERLANE

BOOK 3 of *The Grandmothers Speak*

Net of Light Press

Published by Net of Light Press, 3/1/15
www.grandmothersspeak.com

ISBN-13: 978-0978846824 (Net of Light Press)
ISBN-10: 0978846826

Cover art: Joyce Huntington (joycehuntingtonart.com)
Book design: Timothy W. Brittain

Printed in the United States of America by Net Pub Press
Copies of this book are available through Net of Light Press at
www.grandmothersspeak.com

To the One Love in all of its magnificent forms.

CONTENTS

INTRODUCTION

"When the wisdom of the Grandmothers is heard, the world will heal"

—Hopi prophecy

Quite a few years ago, while walking and minding what I then thought of as *my own* business, I found myself surrounded by a group of old women. Mysterious, charming, and practical women. This is how the Great Council of the Grandmothers entered my life, and these wise women have been with me ever since—each day prodding, teaching, and stretching me further. More than eighteen years have passed since they first appeared and in that time I've changed a great deal, while my understanding of the world has changed even more.

When they first began to teach, the Grandmothers pointed to the future and described **"the times of change that are approaching."** Then, a couple of years ago they no longer spoke of the future but instead, spoke of the present, saying, **"the times of change that are upon you."** Times like none we've ever known are here, and today, more than ever, we need the wisdom of these wise teachers.

When the Great Council showed up that day I walked the dog by the beach, they altered the landscape of my life. Before I met the Grandmothers, I thought that visions, teachers from other dimensions, out of body experiences—everything in the so-called psychic realm—only happened to special people. Gifted people, or inherently wise ones. But I was wrong. They happen to regular people. People like you. People like me.

Once I got over my shock at being 'chosen' to work with them, real learning began. These wise women put me on a fast track; making sure that every day I discovered something new about myself, about the earth, and about humanity's purpose in the great cosmos in which we're held. They taught it all and didn't slow down for anything. And like a sponge that had been without water for far too long, I soaked it in.

The Grandmothers say, "**The present imbalance of energy on Earth has placed all life in danger. Earth has suffered too long from an excess of *yang* and insufficient *yin*. It is time to return to balance, and for this, women must lead. Women must be empowered,**" they declare. "**This is why we have come.**" When they first began to teach me, I thought their work was only for women but, as time went on and men also began to show an interest in this return to balance, men were included in their message. At this critical time, the Grandmothers have come to awaken the presence of the Deep Feminine and bring women, men, and all life back into harmony.

At the same time I was receiving their lessons, the Grandmothers urged me to pass them on to others. No sooner would they demonstrate a teaching, than they directed me to turn around and teach it to others. "**There's no time to waste,**" they said, and so we didn't waste any. When I climbed aboard that fast-moving train with them, I was forced to say good-bye to my patterns of hesitancy, say good-bye to fears of speaking out about these strange (to me) truths I was learning. No longer could I give in to shyness or holding back. No more telling myself 'I'm not worthy' or asking 'Why me'? "**Get on with it!**" the Grandmothers said, and so we did.

It's now many years later and I'm many years older, but their lessons still come thick and fast. No sooner do I think I understand a concept they've taught than they bring forth another one, or piggyback a new layer onto the first. We are not wasting time.

I say 'we,' because now women and men all over the world have become part of sharing these lessons with others, living the Grandmothers' message, and passing on their Empowerment into the energy of yin. And because we form a community, linked by the Net of Light that holds the earth, the Grandmothers' teachings are spreading farther and faster than before. Being on the ride with these wise elders is gratifying and thrilling. With them, there's never a dull moment.

Once these wise women entered my life, they were relentless in sharing their purpose. They taught and I was eager to learn. *A Call to Power: the Grandmothers Speak* and *Our Love Is Our Power: Working With the Net of Light that Holds the Earth* recount their methods and lessons. Ever patient, droll, and to the point, these wise teachers never gave up on me. Nor will they. They won't give up on anyone they call to themselves, and if you are reading this now, that includes you.

"This is the Net of Light that will hold the Earth during the Times of Change that are Upon You."

—the Great Council of the Grandmothers

A few months after they first appeared, the Grandmothers began to demonstrate what they called 'the Net of Light,' and, being the excellent teachers they are, they taught about this Net in increments. Looking back on this time, I see now that they went slowly so they wouldn't overwhelm me with too much information and little by little, they helped me find my way to the truth of the Net of Light.

They began by likening it to a great fishing net that covers the earth and then asked me to find my place on it. From this 'place' on the Net where two of its strands come together, we are to hold light steady for the earth and all beings. **"As you work in this way,"** the Grandmothers said, **"the Net of Light will lift and bless everything it touches— including you.**

"The Net of Light is lit by the jewel of the heart. "It is the radiance within your own heart that lights the Net, and the radiance in the Net of Light that, in turn, pours light into your heart. At all times there is a two-way flow of love and light moving between the Net of Light and those who work with it. And the more often you work with it, the greater the flow."

Later, the Grandmothers showed us how the Net of Light permeates everything. It is not only horizontal as I first thought, but vertical, diagonal, and all encompassing. It holds the microcosm and the macrocosm, penetrates the cell beds of our bodies and all the stars in the universe. It permeates all landmasses and bodies of water on Earth. I remember coming up out of a sound sleep one night and feeling the Net of Light inside my body and all around me. It was flowing within my bloodstream and at the same time I was rocked and cradled by it. This delicious sensation taught me in the most intimate way how completely the Net of Light supports us. How much at one I am with it and how at one it is with me. From that moment on, I knew that whether awake or asleep, whether it was day or night—the Net of Light is there—inside and all about.

In the autumn of 2013 scientists 'discovered' a form of life they say is the largest living thing in the universe. Astronomers believe that this network of filaments, made up of dark matter, forms the basis of the universe, and they named it the 'Cosmic Web.' This Web, they say, penetrates all life and, reaching through the smallest unit of life as well as throughout the entire universe, *it connects everything*.

In the spring of 2014, my husband and I went to see a film in Los Angeles featuring Hubble telescope photos. The photographs of outer space were soul stirring, and then we saw an image of the 'Cosmic Web.' Here was a visual portrait of the Net of Light, the matrix of love and light the Grandmothers had been teaching us for the past eighteen years! I choked up when the image flashed on the screen and as I sat there, I was probably the only person watching this movie who was crying.

What had once seemed a 'tool,' a teaching technique that the Grandmothers had given us to demonstrate how to connect lovingly with one another, is real. Real in every way. The Net of Light is a spiritual construct, a mental construct, and it's also a physical construct. The Net of Light or Cosmic Web connects everything. It holds, up-lifts, and blesses all that it touches. Welcome to *Casting the Net*.

In Gratitude

Many people have contributed to *Casting the Net* and the reader will find some personal contributions in the last chapter of the book. But there are thousands of others as well—too many to name.

Having said this, I would especially like to thank Peggy Huddleston for her many creative contributions and her editing of this book, Billy Carter for generously contributing his photographic and artistic talents, along with Lin Evanko and Sandra De Graaf, and Tim Brittain for laying out the book and designing the cover. None of us at Grandmothers Speak can thank Pat Cottrell enough for her endless work and patience. Whatever needs to be done, if Pat can do it, she does. The Dutch and Belgian Grandmothers team is a dynamic source for us—Jenneken, Babs, Lilium, Sandra, Catharina, Henya, Carla, Marion, and Anne. We thank Christine and Carolyn who inspire and co-ordinate the Grandmothers teams in Australia, and Debbie who is joyously spreading the Grandmothers' message in the United Kingdom. Each Grandmothers' Beacon—from Greece to Lithuania, from Brazil to Canada—is a precious gift to this work, part of the family of light.

We are also grateful to Joyce Huntington for the use of her beautiful painting for the cover of this book. "The painting just came to me," she says. "I didn't know what it meant." We are grateful to Joyce for being the instrument for this beautiful image that perfectly expresses *Casting the Net.*

CHAPTER ONE

The World Needs Mothering Now

"You have been forced to live without a mother, to rely solely on the Masculine Principle."

One summer day when I was feeling overwhelmed by the negative news I'd been hearing, I called on the Great Council of the Grandmothers. I'd just returned from the east coat where it was green and beautiful, but intolerably hot. "Heat and smog," I said to the Grandmothers, "and the ghettos! The suffering some people are enduring is more than I can comprehend." The poverty, the sense of hopelessness I'd seen, along with the rising temperature on the planet had truly shocked me. "Where, Grandmothers," I whimpered, "is the sense of unity we need at a time like this? Our brothers and sisters are suffering and dying and I'm sitting here dumbstruck. I don't know what to do to help them. Grandmothers," I said, "What can I do?"

Tears pooled in my eyes as I recalled the poverty and degradation I'd seen, and as the Grandmothers took me in their arms, they said, **"We know, we know."** Again I asked what I could do to help and then I fixed my eyes on them, thinking, "I won't move until they answer." So I quieted myself and waited.

"The times of change are upon you now," they said. **"This is what you saw that upset you so—the times we have been telling you about are here. So hold steady,"** they said. **"Hold steady and be a beacon. A beacon broadcasts light."**

"Grandmothers," I said, "you always say something like this and I always try to do it—I really do—but sometimes I'm not very good at it," I admitted, shamefaced. They simply smiled at my response, nodded absently, and regarded me in a disinterested way.

"For thousands of years, life on earth has tried to 'make do' without a Mother. It is this that is causing your *real* discouragement," they said and my eyes grew wide. "What you witnessed on this trip was upsetting, but the cause of your upset is greater than you think. Life on earth is out of balance, so out of balance that today the entire planet is missing its Mother. All of you feel the lack of the Feminine Principle, the holder and nurturer of life. Without its Mother, humanity is suffering and lost.

"For eons you have been forced to live without a Mother. To rely solely on the Masculine Principle for everything. It doesn't work that way," they shook their heads. "The energy of yang cannot by itself supply all that humanity needs. However," they shrugged, "you've had no choice. You had to turn to the Masculine Principle for everything because the Feminine Principle was no longer present. It's been absent from the earth for so long, that people living today have little or no understanding of the beauty and power of yin. For too many years humanity has had to live without a Mother.

"The Great Mother was driven from the earth when, long ago, people were told false stories about Her. Eve eating the apple for instance," they shook their heads in disgust. "Stories that depicted the feminine as weak, duplicitous, even conniving. Those are stories, not truth.

"But the Mother is returning now," they said, brightening at the thought, "and we, the *Grand Mothers*, have come to usher Her in. Those whom we call to this work will help speed Her return, and the more of you who work with us, the sooner She will come. The world needs mothering now," they said, and when I heard this, more tears came to my eyes.

"We have shown you how to work with us to speed this monumental change that must take place. *A Call to Power: the Grand-mothers Speak* and *Our Love is Our Power* demonstrate how to do this. Use our books. Study them and discuss our teachings with one another. By so doing, you will naturally begin to live our message.

"Gather together, cast the Net of Light and magnify its power for your planet. We have come to teach you of the power of the Feminine Principle of creation, to teach you how to *live* this power. The Feminine Principle is your birthright. No longer need you live in a motherless world, cut off from the Power/Beauty of your own nature. We have come to awaken you to who you are.

"Walking this path with us will not be difficult. Our path does *not* lead to suffering, though the path your world is on now does." Holding their gaze on me, twelve impassioned Grandmothers choroused, "Wake up! You are needed! Hear our message and receive what we have come to give. Accept our gift of empowerment into the Feminine Principle and pass it on to others. Study our message. Live it and spread it. Your world is starved for the love of the Mother, and we assure you that She is returning. We, the *Grand Mothers,* are bringing her back. So get cracking!" they laughed and gave me a playful shove.

"Grandmothers, how do I do this? I asked, and they cocked their heads, seeming to study me. I looked back at them, confused. "Wasn't it your grandmother who gave birth to your mother?" they asked and I nodded mutely. "Well?" they said, raising their eyebrows and starring at me, "the same is true here. We are the Grandmothers," they patiently explained, "and as such, we have come to return the Mother to humanity. Therefore, we ask you to ready yourself to receive Her.

"Gather together and study our lessons. Share our message and pass it on. We have come for all. We have told you we will do the work of rescuing your planet and that we'll do it with or without you. So, you don't *need* to join with us, but if you miss the opportunity to be part of this work, you will *kick yourself.*

"Wake up!" they said again. "We are here! Now is the time! Call us. Begin today to live our message. We have shown you how, so come along on the ride with us," they beckoned playfully, "and together we will lift your planet." And looking a bit puzzled, they asked, "What are you waiting for?"

I kept remembering the way they had looked at me when they motioned for me to hurry. They had been reminding me to not waste my life, not to get caught in the ups and downs of living, but to keep on moving forward with their message. This of course was what I wanted to do. It was how I wanted to live my life and yet, for some reason, now and then I seemed to waver and lose my grounding. I'd often wondered about this. Why didn't I hold steady all the time? After so many years with the Grandmothers why did I still go through moments of feeling lost and overwhelmed? As I thought it over, I realized that I tended to waver when something triggered an old familiar feeling of being alone in the world. And though there was no logical reason to feel alone like this, occasionally I still did. Obviously this was a belief from the past, a carryover from childhood—one that now and then still haunted me.

"You have been brainwashed."

The next time I went to my wise teachers I didn't say anything for a while but instead just sat quietly with them and drummed in a measured cadence. It was lovely to be with them again and the drumming must have put me into a trance, because I was taken by surprise when I heard my voice break in. "Please give me power, Grandmothers," I heard myself say, "physically, emotionally, mentally and spiritually—so I can do this work." **"We will give you power,"** they answered. **"Take it."**

I looked up to see them regarding me with serious looks. "Okay, Grandmothers," I said, "I claim it, I claim the power you're giving." No sooner were the words out of my mouth than my spine straightened all by itself, the center of my body seemed to fill out, and I coughed. "Well," I said, "something's moving. That's for sure." My body was feeling strong and unusually straight and then I got a look at myself. It was! I was sitting up tall, almost ramrod straight and at this moment there wasn't a bit of worry in me—only alertness. As I continued to observe this 'self' I had become, I heard myself whispering, "Power, power, our love is our power."

Now my body began to stretch and expand, growing both wide and deep, and as I observed my changing self, I noticed how startlingly long my neck had become. It looked like a tall, tall pedestal. And my shoulders had dropped way down. "This is a new way of being," I said to myself.

"I think I'm becoming a tree," I ventured and it wasn't long before I heard myself cry, "I *am* a tree! Anchoring, anchoring," I marveled as I observed the roots of my tree self, spreading wide and deep. I moved my head back and forth a little and watched as a slight, swaying motion moved through me. A breeze was lifting my leaves.

I was enchanted by this metamorphosis, thoroughly enjoying the sensations that were part of my new tree consciousness, when it came to me that I could *not* be toppled. I was so steady that nothing could threaten or upset me. I was *rooted*. This tree I had become existed somewhere beyond the knowledge and reach of man. Clearly I was *something else*. Shaking my head in wonder at what had happened, I shrugged and said, "I just am."

Next I heard myself say, "I'm drinking in power from the Source," and felt my roots drawing in nourishment. Then birds and small creatures began to run up and down my branches, nesting and playing in my hair. "I like this!" I laughed in delight. 'These creatures are occupying the tree with me. Here I stand," I announced. "I'm planted. Nothing can move me or affect my peace in any way. Come to me," I sang to the birds and animals. "You are most welcome here."

The tree I had become was a home for these creatures. To them I was a source of comfort and generosity—a resting place. And to be a 'home place' for them gave me happiness. "Come to me," I sang again.

"Let what you call the active part of your mind run about as it will," the Grandmothers said and I looked at them in bewilderment. They pointed to the creatures that were scampering about in my branches and said, **"Let this aspect of you do all the things it wants to do. And while you allow it to do what it wants, stand back and observe it with love."** I began to watch then, observing the animals playing in my branches, these creatures the Grandmothers were comparing to my mind.

Scurrying about, the animals busily flitted from branch to branch, and as I watched them, I began to notice how very like my mind they were. Here was the active part of myself—what Eckhart Tolle calls 'the little me,' the part that flits from thought to thought, from activity to activity. From what the Grandmothers were saying, this active part of my mind had its own part to play in the drama here on earth.

"Yes!" the Grandmothers said, responding to my thoughts. **"Let this active aspect of the mind play its part. You needn't get overly involved with it, but simply watch. Just stay as you are while you observe. You have a very active mind. Your mind needs to be busy,"** they said, **"so let it."**

I was beginning to see that my busy mind too had its place on earth. For many years I had tried to control this busy mind of mine, tried to channel and silence it. I'd meditated, chanted mantras, visualized—all to no avail. My mind was as active now as it had ever been. So when

I observed how accepting the Grandmothers were about what I had thought of as 'this annoying mind of mine,' I felt a sense of relief. Their suggestion to just observe, to let it do whatever it wanted, was somehow reassuring, and I began to watch it with the same benevolence I felt toward the squirrels and birds playing in my branches.

"Grandmothers," I finally asked, "will you help this small part of me, this active mind part, plan for and perform the next tasks for your work?" It had come to me that as long as my mind was bound to be busy, I might as well give it something useful to do. **"Of course we will,"** they said, **"haven't we always?"** "Yes," I answered, "you've always given me direction and I really thank you for that." Then I tilted my head so I could see them better, and said, "Well, what do you want this busy little me to do next?"

"Send this message out," they answered. **"Share how humanity has been brainwashed, taught to believe that women are the lesser sex, inferior, and supportive at best. Share how women have been conditioned to be afraid of men, to placate and appease them in order to avoid conflict,"** they said, shaking their heads wearily.

"In addition to this, both women and men have been told that they must 'make' something of themselves. *Make* **something!"** the Grandmothers said, looks of horror on their faces. **"As if you aren't already something, as if you're lacking in some way. As if you're inferior."** They threw their heads back at that and laughed. **"This sort of thinking is absurd, and these are just a few instances of the brainwashing you've been exposed to."** They rolled their eyes and added, **"But they are enough for now.**

"Thought patterns like these cheat you. They turn men and women into adversaries, even enemies. At their worst, these patterns of belief encourage men to be cold and unfeeling—to operate only from their heads while they plunge women into anger and despair, driving them into victim consciousness." The Grandmothers shook their heads at this bleak picture and said, **"We have come to awaken you from this nightmare.**

"You are neither masculine nor feminine," they explained. **"This is true because the core of your being, what you think of as your soul, is beyond the limitations of gender. However,"** they pointed to me, **"*you, Sharon,* are now living inside a female form. At this time**

in history there's a reason why you incarnated as a woman and this is true for every woman who is drawn to our message. The Mother is returning," the Grandmothers said, "and you have a part to play in Her return. You chose to be born in female form because at this point in history there is no more important work than this, and women are the ones who will do most of it.

"You were born for this opportunity. Today the earth is in dire straits—it is desperate for the Feminine Principle. This is why we're asking you to enlist with us, to study our message, and call on us." Giving me a penetrating look, the Grandmothers said, "We will transform your life if you let us.

"At the core of your being, you are already one with the Divine," they explained, "and because this is so, it makes it easy for you to join with us. You may choose to work with us or you may choose not to, but whatever you choose, we will do this work with you or without you. It will be done.

"No matter what you may have been taught in the past, we are not separate from you, nor are you separate from us. For eons humanity has been unconscious of the inner presence of divinity. You've fallen into such a deep sleep that you've forgotten this truth. We notice that even after some of you learn about us and after you receive our Empowerment, you still continue to drift in and out of this sleep. Wake up!" the Grandmothers cried. "Do you want to waste your life sleeping? Or would you rather be about your Mother's/Father's business?

"The transformation of your planet can only take place in and through human beings. *This is the law: On earth, the Divine must work through human hearts and hands.* Since the Great Council of the Grandmothers is part of the Divine," they explained, smiling sweetly, "we have come to work with you. We cannot violate human will. Therefore, we can enter in with you by invitation only. So if you want to be part of returning the Mother to earth, you must call on us. And if you call on us, we promise to give you all the power you need."

I'd begun this journey asking them for power, and at last the Grandmothers had answered my request. They'd also jolted me. I felt more awake now than I did before. I was also more aware of how easy it was to lose my focus, to fall asleep at the switch and I didn't want to do that any more. I never again wanted to waste time doubting the Grandmothers or myself. I was determined not to forget this lesson. "Awake and alert," I said to myself. "Awake and alert."

"Rips in the Net of Light."

A week later I returned to my wise teachers. We were sitting quietly and I was looking at them, admiring their beauty, feeling awash in their love, when they fastened their gazes on me and gestured to the Net of Light. I looked to where they were pointing and noticed that today the Net didn't look like its usual self. Something about it was off. I squinted at its glowing strands, and saw that today the Net of Light wasn't uniform in appearance, but instead shone brighter in some areas than in others. Jutting my head forward to see better, I peered again, and when I came to part of the Net that covered the Middle East, I gasped. There was a tear in the Net of Light! A large one!

My mouth flew open and I turned to the Grandmothers, but they motioned for me to quiet my thoughts and continue my inspection. Now I began to see other rips in the Net—smaller than the one over the Middle East, but there seemed to be a lot of them. So many, in fact, that in some places the Net of Light gave off only a faint glow.

"Grandmothers," I whispered, "What is this? What's wrong with the Net?" But all they did was smile vaguely and shake their heads. "The Net of Light can't be weak and wounded like this," I said. "It's perfect! It's divine!" But although my words sounded confident, I wasn't feeling so confident. What I'd seen had shaken me.

"The Net of Light IS divine," the Grandmothers replied. **"It IS perfect. However, the Net of Light interfaces with humanity, and humanity has not yet realized perfection. The rips and tears you see in the Net were created by the actions of human beings; they were caused by humanity, and therefore must be mended by humanity. We have a job for you,"** they said. **"Call people together to work on repairing the Net of Light. This is important,"** they emphasized, and from their look, I understood that it was *very* important. **"We will give each of you an assignment,"** they said, and I fastened my eyes on them, waiting to hear more.

"Grandmothers?" I quested, hoping they'd give a fuller explanation, but they only shook their heads. **"Call them,"** they said.

"We will take you to a situation on earth that needs loving care."

I did as they asked and because the tears in the Net I'd seen were so sobering, I wasted no time. Since the Grandmothers had 'commissioned' this job, I was confident that they would show us how to do it. So, when twenty women and one man showed up at my home on a Saturday in July we spent the day on this project. By early that afternoon, each of us had her/his assignment—a specific part of the Net of Light to tend.

The Grandmothers had said, **"Do this work together because group energy will multiply the good for you and for the planet. The power that goes out when two of you are gathered together is greater by far than two times one. Because group work multiplies power, working like this will give you more potent results. The Net of Light needs strengthening,"** they said. **"It must be strong to do the job for which it was designed—lifting, steadying, and holding the planet and all the life upon it.**

"Just before you begin this project," they said, **"pray, sing, or meditate to lift the vibration of your group. And be clear that the reason you're coming together is to connect with the Net of Light in a healing way. After you've done that, call on us and ask what you can do to mend the wounded places in the Net.**

"We will take you to a situation on earth that needs loving care and show you your work and you will find that this project resonates with you in a personal way. This is because the specific wound or weakness in the Net of Light you work with will relate to a wound you also have. The work you perform will mend you at the same time it mends the Net of Light. 'Two for one,'" they chuckled.

"We remind you that work like this is selfless and what we mean by 'selfless' is, such work is done by and for the ALL. That includes, but is not limited to you, so in performing this service, you will grow in wisdom and understanding." Eyeing me over the tops of their noses, they added, **"Your compassion for those who suffer will also grow.**

"**Ask us to show you how to lovingly care for this particular place or situation in the Net of Light**," the Grandmothers said, "**how to cradle it in your mind and heart. Ask to be shown the greatest possible good for this place or situation, and then watch, as it is flooded with love. Be sure to also observe what happens inside you as you do this work. Pay attention to what you see and feel. This is how you will learn.**

"**You can accomplish this mending work in about ten minutes**," they said and when they saw the surprised look on my face, added, "**that's all it will take. When you're finished, take paper and illustrate what you learned about this formerly wounded place in the Net. Put your drawings up on a wall where everyone can see them and then share your visions with one another. Share what you learned**," they said. "**Whenever you work together to do a piece of work like this and then share it, what each of you learns is amplified many times over. This is another great advantage to working in a group.**

"**When you finish sharing what you've learned, sit quietly and meditate on the Net of Light. Ask that its power to hold, bless, and steady life on earth be increased many times over. And as you pray like this, be aware of how, at that very moment, the Net of Light is holding, blessing, and steadying you.**" As I listened, I remembered what they had repeated to me so many times. "**You cannot help another without also helping yourself, and you cannot help yourself without helping another.**" I looked at the Grandmothers and as I felt the love between us surging back and forth, my heart overflowed with gratitude.

We learned so much by working together that day—about each other, about our world, and about how to interface with the world in a more meaningful way. We learned about ourselves too, and each of us strengthened our connection with the Net of Light. When the day was over, I felt full—full of light and full of good.

I didn't know it at the time, but the Grandmothers would teach this process over and over again—in Arizona, in Rhode Island, in Belgium, and in many other places. And to this day, the tending and the mending goes on.

CHAPTER TWO

The Damage Man has Done, Man Must Undo

"The run-away energy of yang is so dominant that it's destroying all you've held dear."

Shortly after this mending work, it was again time to send out a message from the Grandmothers. We aimed for a newsletter each month, but the interval sometimes stretched to one every two or three months. For each message I went to the Grandmothers, and this one came not long before the U.S. presidential election. I had asked them to speak about why their work was so important and requested that they use strong language in order to really get our attention. I wasn't sure if people were aware of the criticality of the times we were living in. What the Grandmothers ended up giving us was so potent I was a little leery about whom it might offend, but it was their message, so I sent it out.

"Your country has been swept by a dark tide of lies and corruption," they said, and chills ran up my back. **"The run-away energy of yang has become so dominant that it's destroying all you've held dear. Not just your country, but everything in your world is out of harmony, and will continue in a downward spiral until and unless you wake up, step up, and claim the long-absent power of the Feminine Principle.**

"We, the Great Council of the Grandmothers, have come to earth at this time to return the Feminine Divine," they said, twelve serious faces looking back at me. **"For many years now we have offered our guidance, yet some whom we have called to this work, are still unconscious. We are calling, but are you listening?"** they asked, their frustration showing. **"What, we ask, will it take to wake you?**

"We are urging you to step into your power. Not tomorrow or 'some day' as the mass-mind consciousness of your times whispers, but NOW!" they said, and smacked a fist into a palm. "Do it NOW," they said, giving me a fierce look. "We will not give up on you. We will stand waiting until you hear us.

"This is no time to equivocate and pretend that things are not as bad as they are," they said, their hands on their hips. "We tell you THEY ARE! We have shown you how to take this step into power, and we are happy to give our empowerment to everyone who wants it. It will blow the spark of yin inside you to full flame, making you a force to contend with, a force for good in a world starved for good.

"We remind you that women are the natural reservoirs of yin for this planet," they said, looking me over, "that women store this energy, not only for themselves, but for everything that lives. At this point, the energy of yin on your planet is so depleted that every woman who allows this spark within her to blaze into flame will become a blessing for the earth. The earth is calling you. Take this step," they urged me/us. "Do not wait another day.

"Call on us, and if you call, we will answer. Read our messages and study our lessons. We are here to serve, but we, and every form of the Divine, must work *through* human beings so we will work with you and through you if you will allow us. Engaging with us will not make you famous or rich," they smiled at the thought, "but you will help your planet.

"Please wake up. Commit to restoring the Feminine Principle to the earth. Read our lessons, receive our Empowerment, share our message, and take this opportunity to serve. Do not miss this chance," they said. "It will not come again."

I sent their message out and immediately heard from people around the world who resonated to it. Only a few asked to be dropped from the mailing list. The Grandmothers' language had not offended as many as I'd feared.

The 'Old Ones'

A week after this Bear came to me in a dream, but this time he showed up as a little blonde cub, so cuddly and darling that I was treating him like a pet. I had received some packages of cheese and other delicacies in the dream and as I was opening them, he snatched one out of my hand, and in the process, bit me. Since I'd been thinking of him as puppy of some kind, I tried to get him to let go of me by playfully prying his mouth open. But his powerful jaws had locked down and those massive incisors had passed right through my hand.

"Uh oh!" I moaned as I struggled to get his fangs out of me, "there's going to be a lot of blood." And tugging and sweating, I woke myself up. My heart was racing crazily and I lay there piled up in the covers in a state of panic until I realized it was only a dream. Quickly I recalled that whenever Bear showed up in a dream like this, scaring me awake, he did it to make sure I wouldn't forget that he'd come. "Ah..." I said to myself, "Bear has a message for me. I'll go to him first thing in the morning." Then I rolled over and went back to sleep. But as soon as I awoke in the morning, I called on the Grandmothers, stepped into their Circle of Stones, and journeyed to the lower world to find him.

"You came in my dream last night," I said as soon as I saw him, and shaking my head in wonder, added, "Bear, you really got my attention with that bite. That was pretty dramatic. What is it you want to teach me?" By now I really wanted to know.

He swayed back and forth while he hummed something to himself and I stood there watching him. When I realized he wasn't going to say anything, I continued. "I want to learn from you, Bear, so whenever I'm aware that you've come to me, I'll journey to you. I'll do it every time," I declared. But he still wasn't saying anything, and as I wondered why, he tilted his head back and gave me a look from under his brows, as if to say, "You don't impress me." Then he flicked a paw in a dismissive gesture, and turning his head slightly, smacked me lightly on the back.

He wandered off a little way, and then dropped down onto all fours and, with a jerk to his head, motioned me to follow him. I didn't understand why he wasn't speaking, but trailed behind him just the same, and because he was moving at a good clip, I had to push myself to keep up with him. He kept glancing over his shoulder to be sure I was still behind him and when I noticed this, I murmured, "I want to follow you, I want to follow you, Bear," as I scuttled along behind. When he heard my words, he stopped in the middle of the trail and took me on his back. "Oh! I see," I said to myself, "he wants me to remember to follow him."

We hadn't gone far when he paused and stood very still, looking out over a cliff on the left side of the trail, and because I was sitting on his back, I too was able to look. Here the canyon walls dropped far down into a valley, and at the very bottom of the canyon was a river. The expanse that stretched before us reminded me of something I'd seen on another journey—one I'd taken a while ago. That place had looked very much like this one, and I remembered that this was where I'd watched a pack of wolves racing as they followed the River of Life.

Now I began to wonder exactly where Bear was taking me, and why. "Bear," I asked again, "what do you want to teach me?" Standing still, his shaggy head unmoving, he held his eyes on mine and growled, "**I want to teach you.**" "Oh please do," I begged. "I have so much to learn and I want to learn. So much!" I added. "**Ummph,**" he grunted, and then he reached over my head and absentmindedly, straightened my spine.

As my spine aligned itself I took in a deep breath and when I did, my eyes passed over the canyon again. I was admiring its red rock patterns when my up-coming trip to Arizona came to mind. It was the red of those rocks—so like the rocks of Sedona. "I wonder if I'm here today with Bear because of the work we're going to do in Sedona," I said.

"**Listen carefully,**" Bear growled and then he began to make repeated bobbing movements. Bobbing his head lower and lower, at last he bowed low to the ground and I heard him whisper, "**the Old Ones.**" When I saw the reverent look in his eyes and his carefully bowed head, I understood that by "the Old Ones," he must mean the original people of this place. And with that thought, something in the atmosphere shifted and I became aware of the presence of ancient beings peering out of the rocks at us. These must be what Bear meant by 'the Old Ones.'

They seemed to be familiar with Bear and appeared to be interested in what I was doing with him in this place. As they studied me, I noticed that their faces, etched deep by the desert sun, were much larger than human faces. Their bodies too were different—almost square in shape. The Old Ones looked somewhat human, but not exactly human. They seemed to be part human and part rock.

I too bowed deeply to these ancient beings, impressed by their great age and by the veneration Bear was showing them. Thanking them for allowing me to be with them, I spoke of how honored I was to be in their presence. Then I asked for their support for the up-coming

Grandmothers workshop in Sedona. "I don't understand why we're meeting in Sedona," I admitted. "We're gathering there to work on mending the tears in the Net of Light, but I don't know why we're meeting there. I'm pretty ignorant of all this" I confessed at last. "This workshop was prompted by the Grandmothers who told us to go to Sedona and mend the tears in the Net of Light." When I mentioned the Grandmothers, I saw the Old Ones nod to each other.

"Here there is a vortex," they said and when I heard this, I replied, "Yes, there is a vortex here. Sedona is famous for its vortexes." But they gave me a look that said, "What do you know?" shook their heads, and said, **"NO. Here there is *a* vortex."** "*A* vortex?" I asked, repeating their words. Had I heard them right?

They nodded 'yes,' and pointed to several formations that jutted up from the land where we were standing. Each of them seemed to be separate and distinct from the others, but when the 'Old Ones' showed me how to observe them from below ground level, I saw that they were all part of one massive phenomenon. 'A' vortex indeed.

Now a whirling energy rose up from the canyon floor and began to spin its way toward us, and as it whirled and twisted, the Old Ones began to communicate in a sign language I was somehow able to understand. After the sea receded, it was this energy that had created the rock formations that lay before us. This spinning energy had formed the colossal rock outcroppings in Sedona. These had been brought into existence from a force deep within the earth, created according to a specific pattern that was reflected in the rocks there. They said that all these formations are part of the same vortex or energy generator and though they may look separate and distinct, they are not. "Why," I wondered, "are the Old Ones explaining this?" and then they pointed to the mighty generator/vortex underneath the earth and said, **"This is where we live."**

I blinked and shook my head. It seemed that the Old Ones were caretakers or guardian beings for the powerful generator of power within the earth here. **"Yes,"** they nodded and then they stood quietly, staring at me expectantly. "I see," I said and, taking in a breath, I took the plunge, trying again to explain why we were coming to this place.

"The earth is in grave danger," I began, and quickly corrected myself when I realized that it might not seem like grave danger to beings that have been in this place for time out of mind. "Seemingly grave danger,"

I said. "There is so much suffering on earth," I told them, "and with all our hearts, we wish to help...." I saw their impassive expressions then and stopped speaking. Those ancient faces were telling me, **"We've seen it all; we've heard all this before."**

"Okay," I sighed, defeated by their blank looks. I would have to re-think what I wanted to tell them, not say too much, and certainly not go into the horrors of the times I was living in. "They have been here forever," I reminded myself, "so what seems horrendous to me, is nothing new to them."

I tried again. "Dear Old Ones," I said, and a catch in my throat made me aware of just how much I wanted them to understand. "If you would teach us how to help," I said, "we would be so grateful. If there is anything we can do for the earth, for all living things, we want to do it," and at that point one of them, an old, old female with a dwarfish appearance, took my hand in hers. When I looked into her eyes I felt how young and unknowing I was, but then she squeezed my hand and instantly I felt how ageless I was.

The way she was able to change my consciousness with just a touch made me aware of how wise the Old Ones were and how potent this place was. "The vibration of the Old Ones is steady and enduring," I said to myself. "They aren't rousted about by the dramas of the moment. No, not that. They're utterly steady. Witnessing everything," I marveled. "This place and these beings have experienced all that's ever happened, and they've endured it all." I shook my head in wonder.

Somehow I knew what I was saying was right, and as the truth of it came home, my head, the center of my body, and all my limbs began to quiver. When I started shaking in earnest, my eyes flew open and I looked to my ancient guide. She nodded to reassure me, and then drew me along with her until at last we came to a stop before the other Old Ones. As we stood in front of them, a feeling of timelessness came over me. "Time is nothing here," I said to myself. "All the changes on earth may come and go, but this place will remain. Always. The Old Ones have occupied this place before what we think of as time."

I breathed this changeless quality into my body and noticed how the energy here felt dynamic and at the same moment peaceful. Beyond what we think of as calm, the current here vibrated with force and steadiness, and as I registered its specific qualities, my body fell into harmony with it. Suddenly I too had moved beyond calm. An electric humming thrummed in and around me and, encased in this power, I was able to view my 'self' from somewhere far away. Then I heard my voice. "The energy here is fundamental," I said, and immediately the word, 'fundament' began to run in my mind. "Fundament, fundament, fundament."

I didn't understand why I'd become fixated on that word but I was fixated. The next day, when I looked up 'fundament' in the dictionary, the definition I found for it was *'underlying ground, theory, or principle.'* "Yes," I said then, "the energy generator in Sedona is like that. It holds that. It IS that."

As I stood among the red rocks with the Old Ones, this fundamental energy pulled me into a state of harmony with them and with the land. I became as steady as they were, and shortly after this, a tremendous heat began to rise from the generator/vortex in the earth. Its radiation was so intense that I began to vibrate with it in earnest. Now I was becoming incredibly hot, so hot I could hardly bear it.

The intense heat started to scare me. "Is the work we're supposed to do here, the work on mending the tears in the Net of Light, going to be too much for us?" I wondered. "Will the people coming to this workshop be able to hold steady while power like this pours through us and into the Net of Light?"

"Yes," the Old Ones answered my unspoken questions; **"you will be able to do this here. Such work is only for certain ones,"** they explained, **"and the right ones will come."**

When I heard their reply, I relaxed a bit and felt myself aligning with them even more. My body was shifting again and now, like the Old Ones, my shape too was becoming squared off. "Actually," I said to myself, "I'm more rectangular than square." Then I noticed that this new body of mine was moving down and attaching itself to the earth—very deep. My new, squared-off shape was walling in what I had always thought of as 'myself,' but as I observed walls rising around me and turning me into a rectangle, I was surprised to note that I didn't feel confined by them. As far as I was concerned, this rectangular shape I'd taken on was just another form for me to occupy. I remember being really surprised by my response.

It wasn't long before I felt myself becoming a caisson, a rock-like anchor, plunged deep into the earth, and as I continued to occupy this strange form, I became aware of the importance of the red color in the rocks of Sedona. That red was nourishing me now, strengthening the rectangular formation I had assumed. I shook my head in helpless wonder, continued to observe my metamorphosis, and again noted how dispassionate I was.

This feeling of dispassion lasted only a short time, however, and then "Whoa," I heard myself groan. My consciousness had shifted. I was beginning to feel overwhelmed by all this change. "What's happened?" I cried. "What's happened to the 'me' of me? Where's myself? Where's the one I'm accustomed to?"

My head began shake then. Really vibrating. 'Wham-a, wham-a, wham-a wham.' It was impossible to focus my thoughts, and though I wasn't exactly in pain, the continuous vibration and noise in my head was scaring me. "This shaking I'm feeling must have to do with the energy here," I said as I tried to calm myself, to be 'reasonable,' and make sense of what was occurring.

Then I became aware of the Old Ones sitting quietly together, watching me. They didn't seem at all concerned about the jackhammer in my head and as I took note of their placid faces, I breathed in deeply, hoping to pick up some of their relaxed energy. Maybe this would relieve the pressure in my head.

I would ride this out, I decided; I would withstand this relentless quaking inside my body. "Be brave," I told myself, but when, instead of easing off, the shaking increased, I didn't feel brave at all. "Old Ones! Help me!" I cried. "Help me withstand this energy! It's more than I can hold!"

They heard me and looked up, but they didn't do anything—just sat there, observing. Now I started to get angry. I knew there had to be a lesson in what I was going through but this was too much! I began to mutter under my breath, "To them the life of a body is nothing—unimportant. Who cares?" I gestured. "*They* don't! These Old Ones exist beyond the confines of form; they aren't really physical anyway, so when I ask them to help me hold this energy in my body, they look at me like, 'Huh? What's the problem'?"

I glanced at them again and when I saw their complacent looks I really got mad. "How dare they treat me like this!" I cried. "Have they no mercy?" Fuming and sputtering, at last I called out, "You've *got* to help me, Old Ones! *I can't do this!* And I won't be able to carry on with this work if I get sick."

They eased the energy off a bit when they heard this, but still showed no emotion. Impassive as ever, they simply sat there and observed. "Why are you putting me through this ordeal?" I asked [at last. "Why are you giving me an experience with such intense power?" I had come to the limit of my patience and wasn't willing to take any more.

"Because it's the truth of this place," they answered, **"and you are coming here."** "Oh…." I said softly, the anger draining out of me. "The truth of this place…," I repeated, "I think I understand."

It wasn't that the Old Ones didn't care about human beings. They weren't cruel; it was that they didn't feel emotion. They simply were who they were and that was not human. They were helping me now as much as they knew how to help, and they would help all of us who came to Sedona to work with the Net of Light, but they wouldn't 'help' in the way the Grandmothers would or as a friend might. "The Old Ones are elemental spirits," I reminded myself. "*Of the earth,* so by their nature they are very different from human beings. But in their own way they are willing to work with us. They love the earth," I said at last, "and we too love the earth. We love the same thing."

"Thank you, Old Ones," I said; "I understand better now and I'm grateful to you. Thank you. We will call on you and ask you to work with us when we come to Sedona." **"Yes,"** they nodded benignly, their faces still impassive.

Thirty women gathered in Sedona to mend the tears in the Net of Light and the work we did together flowed beautifully. We connected with the Net of Light and asked the Old Ones to pour energy from the great vortex/generator in the land there into the Net so it could more powerfully do its job. The Old Ones were present the entire time we worked. They anchored power and distributed it throughout the strands of the Net of Light, but never said a word. Seated silently in the room with us, they quietly observed.

"Trapped energies."

A few weeks after this, I was on my way to Rhode Island for another Mending the Tears workshop. I had just taken my seat on the plane when the thought came that perhaps the Grandmothers were expecting more from this workshop than I'd considered. "Whoops!" I said to myself, "I'd better find out."

"Grandmothers," I closed my eyes and called on them, "what is the *full* purpose of this trip to Providence? Is there more this time to the work of mending the Net of Light?" Smiling, they glanced knowingly at each other and said, "**Listen to us. You think you are going there to teach the same thing you taught before, to spend time with Jane, and meet some wonderful women.**"

"Yes, Grandmothers," I replied, my voice meek, "I've been thinking that. But if I'm wrong, please enlighten me." Quickly, I added. "What's the *real* purpose of this trip?" and by now I was a little afraid of what they might answer.

"**We will show you,**" they said, and turning slightly, they gestured to a map of the east coast of America. "**The purpose of this trip is to return this area to its origins,**" they said. "**Providence, providential,**" they pronounced, playing with the name of the city. "**Words are important.**"

I had never before considered the meaning of the city's name, but now I leaned forward in my seat, my eyes fastened on them. "I want to know the real purpose of this trip," I repeated.

"**We have called you east to anchor more power,**" they said, "**to anchor it on the east coast and balance the power that has already been anchored in the western part of your country. You will have a smattering of women from different New England states at this event, and because of this, their states will also be affected. Many beings will work together on this project—more than you'll see with you in the room. Native peoples and seekers among the Europeans who settled here long years ago will gather in strength to support this work,**" they said. "**The ancestors will participate in a healing and blessing of the land.**"

"**Think of the benefit of this gathering going deep into the earth, the Net of Light holding strong throughout the American northeast. It will happen,**" they promised, their hands on their hips. "**Rivers of light will flow forth from this gathering,**" and as they spoke, I saw light flooding outward in every direction, branching out, and seeping throughout the land of New England. These rivers of light were aligned with the physical rivers in the Providence area—the Providence, the Pawtuxet, the Warren, and others. "**The rivers are important,**" the Grandmothers said; "**their waters will carry our message. Trust us, and watch the work go deep. Watch what happens on this weekend. Observe our hands at work.**"

I made a note then to follow their instructions to the letter, to be aware of everything that happened, from the moment we touched down at the Providence airport. So, as soon as we arrived at Jane's house, recalling what the Grandmothers had said about words being important, we pulled out her dictionary and looked up 'Providence.' This is what we found.

"Providence. Divine guidance or care. Good conceived as the power sustaining and guiding human destiny.

Provident. Marked by foresight

Providential. Occurring by or as if by an intervention of Providence. Fortunate."

I wasn't sure how these definitions would play out, how they would fit the Grandmothers' purposes for the weekend, but I liked the meanings.

Thirty-five women and one man jammed themselves into a room in the old part of the city and since some of us had worked together before, the atmosphere was not only cozy, but genial. I shared what the Grandmothers had told me about the purpose of this gathering, and then we went to work with the Net of Light.

We focused first on the land around Providence, calling on the ancestors of the native peoples who had inhabited the area, the ancestors of old New England, as well as the ancestors of our own family lines. The first time a Grandmothers' group had worked with the ancestors like this had been at the Mending the Tears workshop in Laguna Beach and we'd been thrilled by how the presence of the ancestors had amplified everything we did. No sooner had we called them, than they were there, showing us in no uncertain terms what we had been told so many times—that there really IS no death. And because the ancestors participated with us in repairing the Net of Light, we were able to accomplish much more than we'd thought possible.

So, just as we had done in Laguna Beach and again in Sedona, we began the work in New England by calling on the ancestors. But this time we didn't get far before we noticed something was wrong. Several women were looking distressed and when we saw their faces, we stopped what we were doing to find out what was going on.

Five of them told us they were feeling afraid, and when we pressed them to find out why, they said they were having flashbacks from earlier times—not from their childhoods, but from former lives. We certainly hadn't expected this and we were concerned by their responses. So we tabled our 'program' for the moment and turned our attention to them.

As it turned out, they were reliving terrors related to the New England witch trials in the seventeenth century. History records trials, tortures, and executions of women in Massachusetts and Connecticut for the 'crime of witchcraft' and some historians suspect that these trials took place in other colonies as well. Three women in our group had become so paralyzed by fear that we had to comfort and calm them, and two others said they had become fearful of speaking out, afraid to share their feelings in front of other women. "It's not safe," they said, and when they said this, they looked as puzzled by their reactions as we were. "I don't know where this is coming from," one woman said. We didn't know either, but we could see that those feelings were real.

We sat together then, called on the Grandmothers, and asked them to take over the workshop, to guide and help us. Immediately the Grandmothers encircled and embraced us and as they held us, they began to show us the nature of the fears that had begun to rise up in our group. As it turned out, these fears were part of a block of terror that had become locked within the land of New England. **"This is an old fear,"** the Grandmothers explained, **"it's not their personal fear. Don't worry about it,"** they added, making a dismissive gesture. **"As you work together, you will lift this fear. We will help you."**

We breathed a sigh of relief when we heard this, and then quickly pulled our focus back to the task at hand. Together we called on the Net of Light, asking it to lift all this fear, and in a short time, the ancient terror had cleared. Once it was gone, we were able to get back to the purpose we'd come for—mending the tears in the Net of Light in New England and all over the planet.

Now that we'd seen the damage that a block of fear, created more than three hundred years ago, could do to our group, we were really motivated. We reasoned that if we could be taken by surprise by an old terror like this one, so could anyone. So we set to work with a will to mend all the tears we could.

Because we had come together to work with the Net of Light in order to heal old wounds, and because we had enlisted the help of the ancestors, our group had been given a large task to perform—a very large task. The hidden pain of the witchcraft trials had taken us by surprise, but by uncovering it, we gained a greater understanding of the importance of the work we'd come together to do. In the process, our compassion for one another had increased, and we learned that whenever emotional states came up in any one of us, they didn't necessarily belong to that individual. This one for instance had come from a group fear from long, long ago. Working with this issue had also made us more conscious than we'd been before of the compassionate ancestors who were now standing side by side with us.

The experience in Providence taught us about blocks of negative consciousness that are locked in the earth at different points on our planet. **"Locked into the elements of earth by the negative actions of man,"** the Grandmothers explained. **"Whatever damage man has done, man must undo. We will help you with this,"** they said, **"but it is human beings who must perform this work."**

I would encounter trapped energy like this at many different places in the world before I came to understand that not only is energy present everywhere on earth, but it exists in every possible variation. Some of it feels beautiful and full of light while some is quite unpleasant and not at all full of light. I had a great deal to learn about the subject of old, trapped energy and though I might not always enjoy these lessons, they were important. The Grandmothers would continue to teach me.

CHAPTER THREE

Human Beings Are the Instruments

"We are on fire with purpose. So will you be."

After returning from Providence I had a lot to think about, and as I reflected on what had happened in Rhode Island, it dawned on me that at that meeting, the Grandmothers had opened a door I hadn't known was there. When I recalled how things had unfolded, once again I saw how little control I had over any endeavor with these wise teachers. "When the Grandmothers are present, anything can happen," I told myself, "…and does." I was also beginning to suspect that there was more to these Gatherings of the Grandmothers than I'd previously thought. They weren't just get-togethers for loving, compassionate people.

"Grandmothers," I said when I next went to them, "You say our meetings, workshops and gatherings '*are so important*,' and I think I understand this more than I did earlier. I know the growth that takes place in us when we meet like this is valuable, but why else do you say they are so important?"

"**You look at '*important*' differently than we do,**" they replied. "**When we use that word, we aren't just referring to events of the moment. It's more than that. We are building a foundation for the times that are coming,**" they said, giving me an intense look over the top of their noses, "**and we use these meetings, study circles, and gatherings for that foundation. At this point many have joined in this work, and when they feel themselves part of our family, it brings them joy. There's a forward momentum at our gatherings. People's hearts open, the divine presence within them awakens, and goodness flows into every corner of their lives. This takes place at every meeting, but even *this* is only part of the picture.**

"What we've just explained occurs only *on the surface of life*," they said. "What you aren't aware of is what takes place beyond your own personal experience. These meetings, workshops, and gatherings are holding tanks for the energy of yin," they explained. "From the sites where you meet, yin pours into your planet. And because these meetings are now taking place all over the earth, the energy of yin is able to sink in everywhere. Each time you gather, you work with the Net of Light. Calling on the Net lifts the entire planet, especially the areas where your meetings take place. Many sites in Europe will especially benefit from this amplified connection.

"The mending work you did with the Net of Light in Rhode Island is still going on," they said, "and the northeastern part of your country greatly benefited from what you did that weekend. Sedona, Arizona also needed this mending, although in a different way. Many draw from the great power source in Sedona, taking from it what they need. It's not wrong to do that," the Grandmothers said, "as there *is* great power there, but at the Mending the Tears workshop, you worked *with* that power source and replenished both yourselves and it. The Net of Light both gives and receives light, so by linking it to the massive generator in the earth of Sedona, you 'fed' both of them and amplified power throughout the planet. And from now on, when people go to Sedona to work with the 'vortexes,' they will automatically link with the Net of Light. This connection will benefit the entire earth.

"Our gatherings, circles, and workshops do not occur by happenstance. At some level you already know this, but we remind you of it again because you still get caught in feeling overly responsible for things. This is *our* work," they reminded me. "*We* set it up, we draw the right people to it, and….," they chuckled, "we delight in surprising you. We are always, always at the wheel." "Yes, Grandmothers," I agreed.

"Many brave European women and men will come forward to be part of our work now. It's time for the righting of many wrongs on that continent. Truth has been sacrificed to special interests everywhere on earth," they shook their heads sadly, "but it's time to correct some wrongs in what you refer to as the old countries of the world. We would right those conditions.

"Let the call go out to those who wish to help mend and strengthen the Net of Light that is holding the earth. We invite everyone to join us in this work—whether they do so individually or in groups. The great changes on your planet that have been predicted for so long are upon you now, and it is an untold blessing to participate in sacred work. We are on fire with purpose," they grinned, "and so will you be."

"Awakening the deep-down love within the land of Ireland."

Shortly after this, I got a phone call from a woman who asked me to come to Ireland to present the Grandmothers' message. This came as a total surprise and though the thought of taking the Grandmothers' message to Ireland was exciting, before I could throw myself into exploring it, I had to talk to the Grandmothers.

"My beloveds, my teachers," I said as I bowed to them, "I love the work you've given me, and now I'm being invited to take it to Ireland. I never expected this," I said and looked up to see what they thought of it. "I know this has to be your doing," I said, "since it sure wasn't mine."

The Grandmothers listened and when they didn't comment, I continued. "They want to have a Gathering of the Grandmothers in Cork City and the woman who called wants to know exactly what we'll do at this Gathering. I don't know what to say to her, as I don't know what this is really about. So I can't answer until you tell me—what do you have in mind for this work in Ireland, Grandmothers?"

"We are happy to be sending you to Ireland," they said. "Yes, Grandmothers," I replied. "Thank you for this wonderful opportunity, but please tell me—what is its purpose?"

"Awakening," they said, and repeated, **"awakening. Awakening the deep-down love within the land of Ireland. There is a force field there, and a reservoir of love, good wishes, good will, and blessing in the land. Eire is overflowing with generosity,"** they said and pointed off into the distance. I looked too.

Spread over the hills and imbedded in the land of Ireland was a cornucopia of love and blessing. Sun sparkled on the rocks, trees, and fields, while countless glistening bays, lakes, and inlets backed up to rolling hills. **"There is great beauty lying in the land there, and in the hearts of the people too. The people are the instruments for the power within their land, and when you come together in Cork, you** will awaken this power. We are *very* happy that you are going," they said and I gazed at them, hardly able to believe what I was hearing. "*You* will be very happy too!" they laughed, and when they said this, I had to clamp a hand over my mouth to stop myself from crying.

"We know you're intimidated by the thought of working with the spirits of the land there," and I nodded, 'yes,' "but we assure you that you will simply be working as our instrument. We have called this Gathering into being, and the potency of our purpose, as well as your well-established connection to the Net of Light, will do all the work. We remind you that *the Divine needs an outlet* where it can plug its current, and your presence there will allow this connecting to take place." Smiling to reassure me, they said, "We will guide you every step of the way."

"Working with sacred sites isn't something I know much about, Grandmothers," I admitted. "We're aware of that," they laughed; "and that's why we've called you. *Because* you have no experience in working with sacred sites, your mind won't be able to get in the way of what needs to be done."

"Really?" I asked, but their heads were nodding so firmly that I knew they were serious. After a minute I started to giggle at the absurdity of it—how in this case my ignorance could actually be a blessing, and when the Grandmothers saw me laughing, they laughed too. "Yes," they nodded. "It is precisely because you have nothing lodged in your mind that we have chosen to work through you."

"Okay, Grandmothers," I said, "okay. It seems kind of strange but I think I get it. Still, I need to be able to explain to these people why we're gathering."

"Let them know they will be reconnecting with the ancestors, the ancestors of their bloodline, the ancestors from all their past lives, as well as the ancestral spirits of Ireland. The ancestral spirits of the land of Ireland have worked hard and long to hold that island in harmony. And, in spite of the dark deeds that have taken place there, they've managed to do it. There is a prototype of light within the land of Ireland that is still pure. It has not been diminished over time; it has not even been muted. The presence of this prototype will make it *very* easy to re-activate the blessing power of the land," they said, their faces lit by smiles.

"At the Gathering in Cork City, you will journey back in time, moving into a consciousness that existed before the advent of patri-archy, touching into a time when harmony and balance were valued. **When harmony and balance were a way of life!**" they crowed, and I began to cry.

"I'm so grateful, Grandmothers!" I said, "so grateful to be part of such a thing." "**The people who come to this event will have pure intentions, and because of this, they will do great, great good. We will call them, and no one will come unless we call. You can relax,**" they said, patting and cradling me, "**and know that this is so.**

"**This Gathering will be a sacred event. And it is all is our doing,**" they smiled happily. As I regarded them with awe, I asked, "Is there anything else I should tell these people?"

"**Tell them to get ready, tell them to read our books. Much will happen in the days you spend together, and they need to be ready for it.**" Rocking their heads back and forth, they looked bemused for a moment as they seemed to peer into the future and then they said, "**Together you will perform enormous service.**"

The Grandmothers stood silently and after a while, the spirits of the land began to speak. "**We are waiting for you,**" they called. I turned when I heard their voices, and there they were! "Tara's here!" I called, my voice catching in my throat, "and there are others too! I see the little guys!" I cried in delight as leprechauns, in tiny hats, coats, and aprons began to scamper about. Somersaulting and playing leapfrog, gleefully they jumped over one another while others danced and skipped. Songs and shouts filled the air and then I heard another sound.

"It's the heart of the Mother!" I whispered, my voice barely audible. "I'm hearing Her and I'm feeling Her heart beat. Her heart is beating right here in the land! I can hear Her," I gasped, and then I caught a glimpse of a vague-looking form rising up from the land. A graceful form, an enormous form. "It's the Mother," I whispered, awe stricken, my eyes fastened on her. I had seen Her once before—the first time I took the Grandmothers' message to Lithuania—so *I knew* it was the Mother.

"**She wants her own,**" the Grandmothers said; "**the Mother is call-ing.**" And when I heard their words I understood that *She* was the force behind this meeting in Ireland. *She* was the reason we were coming together. "**Yes,**" the Grandmothers nodded. "**People will come to this Gathering. They will come.**"

Everything was quiet for a few minutes and then the Grandmothers said, "**Tell people to read our books and messages to get themselves up to speed, so they understand who we are and why we've come. That way they'll have a better idea of what they'll be doing with us at the Gathering. We love them dearly,**" they said; "**we love them deeply, and we've arranged all this,**" they smiled brightly. They embraced me to their breasts then and said, "**We've called the right people to organize this Gathering and we will call each person who comes to it. The time for this event is now,**" they beamed. "**Come!**"

"Now and then humanity is given a chance to increase the power of light on Earth."

A few days later I felt the Grandmothers calling again. They wanted to send out a message, asking people to work with those of us who would meet in Ireland. Whether these people were able to attend the actual Gathering or would work with us inwardly on their own, the Grandmothers wanted to give as many as possible the opportunity to participate in this Gathering. A month before I left for Cork I sent out their message.

"**Now and then humanity is given a chance to increase the power of light on earth,**" they began, "**and today, amidst all the destruction on your planet, a shining opportunity has arisen.**

"**There is a reservoir of luminescence and spiritual power stored within the land of Ireland that Mother Earth needs now. This source, once it is connected to the Net of Light, will help lift your planet,**" they said, and pointed to hundreds of glimmering lights coming from inside the Emerald Isle. "**These flickering lights within the land are waiting for you,**" they said. "**They must be gathered into the Net of Light, gathered in and held there. Because they are not yet plugged into a network, they appear to be separate and small. And though their potential is enormous, at this point it is still only potential.**

"**We are summoning you to Ireland to call these scattered lights home to the Net of Light. The Gathering of the Grandmothers in Cork will be a true *Call to Power*,**" they declared, their heads nodding wisely, "**and because this is so important, we have carefully chosen the time and place for it. The date for the Gathering (September 11) is no accident, nor is its location. The Net of Light has come forward** at this moment to hold the earth steady, and this radiance within the land of Eire will feed the Net, helping it support your planet. *This is an opportunity for an important connection to take place,* and those who take part in it will provide the circuitry."

Shifting into teaching mode, the Grandmothers said, "**You call these lighted places on earth 'sacred sites' and you think of them as separate sources. However,**" they said, "**now is the time to *connect them to the Net of Light*. Once these seemingly separate sites are linked with one another and with the Net, they will charge the Net to far greater capacity. To make a connection like this, human beings are required;**" they explained, "**as only humans can make this link for the planet.**

"**From age-old times poets and bards have sung of the special qualities of the Emerald Isle. Long ago they recognized the source of power lying within this place, and now we will show you how to work with it. Together we will call forth these ancient reservoirs of light. It is time.**

"**In order to activate the power imbedded in the land of Ireland, one needs a pure focus point,**" they explained, "**one untainted by institutional drag, thought forms, and the human ego. The Net of Light is this pure focus point.**"

"**The service you will perform in Cork will be more valuable than you can imagine. The purpose of this work is pure and this task is greatly needed. Each of you who takes part in it will not only benefit the Net of Light, but will increase her and his own capacity for light. You will blaze forth with light. The moment of giving is always the moment of receiving,**" they said, "**and in this case, your receiving will be tremendous. You will become a nexus of radiance.**"

I sent out their message.

What stunned us was how grateful the spirits of the land were!

Not only people from Ireland, but also English, Dutch, French, and Americans showed up at this Gathering. Many had never heard of the Grandmothers before, but when news of this event crossed their radar, they scrambled and got themselves to Cork.

Together we discovered how to move the energies of yin and yang from static/fixed positions into flow, and as soon as the energy of yang was embraced by yin, both energies began to move together like one river. We were practicing these movements together, dancing with yin and yang, when a man at the back of the room called out, "I've never felt so good in me life! Didn't know I could move like this."

After I explained to everyone who the Grandmothers were and why they'd come at this time, a woman with an expression of intense pain in her eyes came up and asked, "Is it true? Is all this about the Grandmothers true?" she demanded, her eyes fixed on me. And when I answered, "Yes, every bit is true," she broke down sobbing. "I've had no joy in my life," she explained, "none at all, so I'm overwhelmed by all this love."

Everyone in Cork was moved by the devotion of the Grandmothers' group leaders from the Netherlands who had flown over to support this work in Ireland. After the Dutch shared stories of all the good that had come from their Grandmothers' groups in Holland, an English woman stood up and announced that what she'd seen in the Dutch leaders had so affected her that she was going home to start a group of her own. She'd do that, she said, as soon as she returned.

Working with the spirits of the land moved many of us to tears. The work itself was potent, but the waves of gratitude that flowed from the land back to us really affected us. The spirits of the land were *grateful to us*! The Irish power sites were so happy to have this opportunity to plug into the Net of Light that they enfolded us in kinship with them, with one another, and with the land. A wave of *communion* moved through our group and into the Net of Light—flowing to us, through us, and from us.

As this occurred, we understood how, just as a person with a tremendous talent has no greater joy than to share that talent, the sacred sites in Ireland were overjoyed to be able to use their beauty and power in service to the earth. I had never before worked in partnership with the land like this, nor, I think, had anyone else. We were awash in gratitude. Gratitude and joy.

CHAPTER FOUR

Two in a Thousand

"We don't communicate in fancy or mysterious ways."

After the experience in Ireland and the flurry of activity that followed, it wasn't long until a familiar feeling of frustration visited me once again. This had happened many times before, and now, on the heels of this Irish 'success,' came a series of disappointments. First, two women who I'd thought were dedicated to the Grandmothers' message stopped leading their groups, then a woman in Russia and another in Poland, both of whom had asked to translate the Grandmothers' books, changed their minds, and someone who was going to make a Grandmothers' video disappeared. Over the years, one theme in my work with the Grandmothers had been this 'two steps forward, two steps back' dance of people coming and going. And although the rhythm of the dance might vary from time to time, I'd gotten awfully tired of this two-step. I wanted things to move forward, not backward. To move only forward, and at a faster pace. Needless to say, it didn't seem to be working out that way.

"I'm not having much effect, Grandmothers," I mumbled the next time I journeyed to them. "Your message is so pure and so needed, and yet it isn't spreading very far or fast. I'm not seeing the results I thought I would," I continued, "and I'm working really hard. I'm trying," I said, "I really am, but ...," and I shook my head as I struggled to make sense of the discouragement I was feeling. "I guess what I need to know, Grandmothers, is whether or not to continue on with the work. And if I should continue on—why?" I asked, swallowing hard. "I need to know this for my sake and for everybody's sake. I've been trying hard—maybe too hard—for a long time, and I'm tired."

The Grandmothers looked on sympathetically but didn't say anything. "Please show me your perspective on this," I said to my teachers. "This work with you has given my life meaning, but I don't want to do it just to make myself feel better," and then I surprised myself when I broke down sobbing.

The Grandmothers took me in their arms and pulled me onto their laps. **"There are different lenses to look through,"** they said, and as they showed me a microscope with an array of lenses, they pointed to a large group of people. I put my eye to the lens and peered at the men and women before me, but something seemed to be out of focus. I ran my eyes over their bodies again, but as soon as soon as I began to look up at their heads, their forms got fuzzy and seemed to float off into space. "Oh!" I exclaimed as I looked again. "This is really odd! Their necks are stretched so long that their heads are lifted extremely high. They look like they're up in the clouds." Then I put down the microscope and looked instead at the Grandmothers, bewilderment written large on my face.

Again they pointed to these long-necked people and I watched them as they scuttled from place to place, their feet running and their bodies and heads following after. Because of the strange disconnect between their heads and the rest of their bodies, they moved awkwardly, often banging into one another. Their heads didn't seem to know where their feet were. "Uh oh!" I said as I watched them careening about. "Um, Grandmothers," I asked, "are you showing me something about myself here? This head in the clouds stuff—is this me?" **"No,"** they answered, and I breathed a sigh of relief.

Now I began to pull on those floating heads, trying to get them down, out of the ethers and back into *this* reality. I yanked and yanked until at last I was able to haul one toward the ground, but no sooner did I get it down, than it snapped back up. "I'm not having any luck!" I called to my teachers as I struggled to haul another one below the cloudbank. The oddity of the scene was starting to wear on me—the elongated necks, the fuzzily defined, floating heads, and me, pulling on them to get them down. "This is absurd," I whispered and then I started to giggle. "It makes for an interesting image. I have to admit that," I said to the Grandmothers, "all these floating heads, but it's crazy," I decided. "And what in the world does it have to do with the issue I came with today?" Now I was getting annoyed.

"We'll explain," the Grandmothers said and patted me softly to calm me down. **"Because our message is practical, it doesn't fit every-**

one's image of what *spiritual* is," they said. "Often *spiritual seekers* are searching for something grandiose, something mysterious, and elaborate. We don't communicate in *fancy or mysterious* ways. And our teachings of the energy imbalance of yin and yang and of the power of the Net of Light are new to many. Most people have no notion of these concepts so they don't know what we're talking about. Many of them don't understand what we've come to give them because what we're saying is deceptively simple. These people are looking for *'the truth'* to show itself somewhere *out there*. So, as you've witnessed today, many of them *do* have their heads in the clouds.

"It doesn't matter whether or not people respond to what we've come to give," they shook their heads. "Their lack of understanding doesn't invalidate our mission. Out of a thousand people, perhaps two will hear what we have to say, will take in our message, and pass it on to others. But those two will seed the future."

I listened intently and realized that they were repeating what they'd told me when they first appeared. **"Only a few will be drawn to our message,"** they'd said the day I walked the dog beside the beach, but neophyte that I was then, I hadn't believed them.

"Keep on writing," they said. **"Our books will last long after you are gone and the messages you send out on the Internet—those too will go far and wide. Remember,"** they emphasized, **"perhaps two out of a thousand. You are seeding."**

Giving me a look of loving understanding, they said, **"This is lonely work, but remember that when you said 'yes' to us, you signed on for the long haul. So prepare for the long haul. Don't expect this work to support you financially or to support you in other ways either. At this time, expect no allies,"** they grinned while they shook their heads. "Whew!" I exhaled and, as I caught their meaning, I shook mine too.

"You wanted to serve with all your heart," they reminded me. "Yes," I nodded, recalling that this was why they'd come in the first place. "Yes," they agreed, **"you asked and so we came. We have given you important work to do, but we know it's not easy. We could only give it to someone who wanted to serve *very much*. A person without a strong desire would have given up long ago."**

I listened to what they were telling me, my attention trained on them. They were right of course. I *had* asked for work—hard work. I remember telling them that I wanted to cook on *all* my burners, not just some of them. I had begged for work like this.

"Grandmothers," I pleaded, "help me to not give up. Sustain me so I don't lose faith." **"Yes,"** they said, **"we will do that. That's our job,"** and as they spoke, I felt them coming in underneath me. With their bodies they formed a sling that cradled and lifted me. Here they rocked me back and forth. **"This will hold you steady,"** they said. **"Certain ones hear and immediately understand our message—the group in Australia, in Seattle, in Slovenia, in Holland. Just remember the numbers we gave you. Two in a thousand—one or two in a thousand. We are seeding; seeding for the future. The Mother is returning and you have a part to play in Her return."**

"I'm grateful for the part you've given me, for the part you've given all of us," I said and I meant it. **"You are moving forward against thick resistance,"** they replied, and as they gazed into the distance, I followed their eyes and noticed a figure there, slogging through what looked like mud. Then I saw that the figure was I.

It was slow going as I trudged along, but beside this 'me' figure ran a trickle of water, not yet a stream, but pure, flowing water nonetheless. **"You are moving forward through the mire,"** they said, **"but you *are* moving forward. And the people you saw earlier, the ones with their heads in the clouds...,"** they paused before they continued, **"are not able to anchor light. They can't *use* the light in a practical way yet because they aren't grounded. They are good people, but because their heads are stuck in the clouds, their awareness is foggy.**

"Go forward anyway," they said, gesturing with their hands; **"go forward. We know it's difficult. We see you and know that yours is a lonely job. We wouldn't have given it to anyone but you,"** they said, and when I heard this, I began to sob.

"I get it, Grandmothers," I said. "It's because I don't give up, isn't it?" **"That's right,"** they said, **"that's right."** "I understand," I replied. "Please send me whatever assistance you can, and thank you for all the grandmothers in Lithuania, in England, and here in California."

"Our message is pure and it is simple. Deceptively simple," they said, **"and the simplicity of it throws people off. There are hordes of spiritual teachings *on the market* now and many of them are good. However, some are grandiose, some are frightening, and some, because they promise prosperity and riches, find an eager audi-**

ence. However, many of these spiritual messages have been weakened, compromised by buying and selling. But what you share at your meetings is simple and has not been compromised." They gave me a meaningful look. "You offer our message and Empowerment as service."

"Yes, Grandmothers," I said, and then I shrugged my shoulders and laughed. "And from what you're telling me, we won't be winning popularity contests with your message any time soon." Ruefully they shook their heads too and we laughed together. "Thank you," I said, bowing to my wise teachers. "Thank you with all my heart."

"Separation from the Divine lies like a cloud over the earth."

That journey to the Grandmothers put things into perspective. Saying that at this time I wasn't going to find much support for their work actually helped. Now I understood that things were going along pretty much the way they were supposed to. I just hoped that my new understanding would stop me from trying so hard to *make things happen*, hoped it would help me relax and enjoy whatever *was* happening. *Accept what was.* That was it. I wanted so much to approach everything in life in this accepting way—my family, friends, work, finances, myself—everything just as it was. I realized that my difficulty in accepting how slowly the Grandmothers' work seemed to be spreading mirrored my difficulty in accepting everything in my life. And now that they'd made this clear, I wanted to accept it all.

A few days later, I journeyed back to my wise teachers. "We are doing this work together," the Grandmothers said before I could ask them anything. "You are one with us, and the women we call, and the men too, are also one with us. But most of them don't know it yet.

"They've been conditioned to see themselves as separate from the Divine, taught to revere *and fear* the Divine. Fear of God!" they ejaculated, looks of horror on their faces. "You've been taught to believe that you should fear God!

"What does a '*teaching*' that tells you to fear God do except separate you from God?" they cried, throwing their hands in the air. "Crazy," they declared, gazing at me in disbelief. "You've often wondered why people don't step up and take leadership in our work. Well, this is why. They're afraid. And they feel unworthy.

"Sometimes you become frustrated when people don't step forward to pass on our message, discouraged when they lose faith and commitment, and drop by the wayside. But this fear we are speaking of is endemic." Their faces were serious as they said, "**Fear creates cowardice, scattered energy, lack of confidence, and depression. All of these are symptoms of separation from the Divine.** "Separation from the Divine now lies like a cloud over the earth. All diseases and forms of unhappiness spring from this," they said, "and nothing else.

"We have come to lift this pall, so we will always enter in with those who hear our message and go on to work with the Net of Light. Each one who practices our teachings and begins to live our message will become a radiating force of light on earth. Such people will automatically broadcast light. They will hearten one another, and strengthen the Net of Light that holds your planet.

"You long for comrades in light," the Grandmothers said. "We understand this longing, and so we have come to be with you. We are always with you," they said and smiled such sweet smiles that I felt my heart melting. "Come sit with us awhile," they said, drawing me close to them, "and as we broadcast light together, let yourself experience how light pours out from you in every direction—out the front and back of your chest and out the sides of your body too. A downpour of light will flood into and out from you at the same moment," they said, and I felt it.

A tide of light began to pull and then push at me, so that no sooner did light come flushing out of me, than I filled with it again. And as soon as I was again full of light, I automatically relaxed and released it all. This surging flow was not only endless, but effortless.

"Light will flow into the fibers, nerve endings, and cells of your body," the Grandmothers said, "strengthening everything," and I watched as it began to do just that. Radiance was flushing into me from below and from above, while the vibration of light began to pulse in every part of me. "You are a fully lit bulb now," the Grandmothers said, smiling at the stunned look on my face, "and your wattage is growing as we speak." "Yes, Grandmothers," I whispered. The forces moving through me were almost taking my breath away.

"Don't blame yourself when others don't respond to your light with a similar wattage," they said. "Their behavior has nothing to do with you. You are not the cause of their lack of commitment. They hang back because of fear. It's the old lie in action again, the one about being separate from God. That's why people have trouble responding to light. They think they're separate from it. But," they smiled broadly, "the consciousness of separation that has blanketed the earth for so long is thinning now. The old beliefs in separation are weakening as the light that so many of you are holding and magnifying dissipates them. And today," they announced, "some of you are beginning to recognize that you *are* the light.

"Call on us often," the Grandmothers said, "you can't overdo it. Sit in circle with us. You are not lower than we are. You are not smaller or less than we are. You are one with us," they said, giving me a look full of understanding. "We ask everyone to take their proper place now and sit in circle with us, and once you have taken your place, then let light flow as it will. You are a divine being," they smiled brightly, "so enjoy your birthright. Hold the light, be held by light, and all the while let us hold you."

"Many things will try to frighten you, will try to veer you away from your path."

Now and then as I moved forward with the Grandmothers, I was hit by waves of fear and doubt. As far as I could tell these weren't triggered by anything in my environment but seemed to pop up out of the subconscious. I'd be full of confidence one moment, trusting in the trajectory of the work I was doing, when from out of nowhere a worry would arise to nag at me. Anxiety might float to the surface of my mind, or a general malaise set in. Mostly these waves of fear were sneaky—or at least they were at first. I'd hardly notice them, but if I didn't pay attention, soon they'd wrap themselves around me and if I still wasn't paying attention, they'd try to pull me under.

For a day or two I'd been aware of an uneasy feeling bubbling up inside me, pestering me, when I finally remembered to pay attention to it. "Okay," I said, "I want to know what this is about," and when I went to bed that night, I asked the Grandmothers what I could learn from this nameless fear. "Please teach me how to handle fear when it comes up like this," I prayed. I thought that maybe they'd give me a dream to cast some light on the subject, but when I woke in the morning I didn't recall anything. No dreams, no messages. But while sitting at the breakfast table, who should pop into my mind but Bear? Then I remembered. He had come in a dream.

Quickly I put down my cup and hurried upstairs to journey: and lying down, I called on the Grandmothers and stated why I'd come. Then I stepped into their Circle of Stones and, fixing my mind on Bear, plunged downward to the lower world. I made my way through the now-familiar bushes that grew beside the river, and there he was— massive and darker than he'd appeared in my dream. "Bear," I said, "I asked the Grandmothers for help before bed last night and instead of them coming, *you* came. Did you come to help me?" Grunting, he reached down and lifted me onto his shoulders. Then he turned and ambled down the trail.

He didn't seem to be in a hurry today, and when I realized this, I scooted down from his shoulders and settled myself comfortably on his back. "I'm so grateful to you, Bear," I said, breathing a sigh of relief, "grateful that you came to my call. There are times when everything I'm doing with the Grandmothers seems so serious, and sometimes," I said as I gave him a squeeze, "I don't think I understand it very well. So right now I just want to be with you."

"Today I am going to teach you," he said and having made this declaration, he stepped off the path and began to weave his way through the trees, moving toward a meadow. When he reached an opening in the trees, he plopped himself down in the sun and I slipped off his back to sit beside him. "Ahh," I sighed as the warmth of the meadow and the scent of grass and flowers washed over us. "Verdant, mummmm… lush," I murmured as I slowly gazed around, admiring the graceful trees that bordered the meadow. "Oh!" I cried and then, and a yip of pleasure escaped me. "I'm seeing the elemental spirits!" I cried. "They're in the plants and the trees! Fairies, devas, and tree nymphs!" I cried, beside myself with wonder. "For years I've heard about them, Bear," I said, "I've read about them, but I've never seen them before." And completely entranced, I began to peer around the glade with eager eyes.

But just then, a wind gusted through the meadow, and Bear wrapped a paw around me, pulling me up against his side—so close that I could smell his warm, bear smell. "Ummmm," I crooned as I scooted closer still, but then something in the air seemed to shift and though I was still snug up against him, a chill ran down my spine. All sounds hushed and I pulled myself up, spine straight, eyes wide and alert. Bear too was alert. Listening carefully, senses switched on, I became aware that we were waiting for someone or something. Then a terrifying picture flashed in my mind and I gasped. "But, but....," I stammered, "that can't be real."

From far back in the forest something began to make its way toward us. A hulking darkness, an animal-like creature, was lurching in our direction. Snapping branches and strange rumbling sounds marked its approach. "I don't recognize it," I whispered to Bear as it came into view. "This is no animal I know." Dark brown or black in color, it seemed to stagger forward on its back legs while its enormously long front paws dragged on the ground. The monstrous thing lumbered closer and closer until it got to about fifteen feet from us and then, hunching over, it fastened malevolent eyes on us and stared.

My heart was pounding so hard that all I could hear was that pounding, but Bear didn't seem to be concerned about this creature. In fact, he looked perfectly calm. When I saw this, I scooted closer to him, and leaning into his familiar body, made myself as small as I could. The thing began to roar then, and what a noise it made! The hairs on the back of my neck stood up, but still Bear didn't flinch, but remained unruffled, observing and interested. And when I realized that Bear's response had to be a deliberate one, I did my best to mimic him. So now there were two of us sitting quietly and watching, and as we continued to give calm attention to the monster, its roar seemed to lessen.

Soon it began to look puzzled and stood there slobbering, staring at us, its great head bobbing from side to side. It seemed to be studying us, and as I watched it, I realized that probably no one had ever reacted to it in the way we were. The beast was clearly accustomed to creating an uproar, accustomed to everyone fleeing from it. But, carefully following Bear's lead, I continued to sit and observe and now, I noticed that in addition to Bear who was on my left, the holy man was sitting on my right while the Grandmothers were encircling all of us. Bear and I were being protected, and when I became aware of this, tears sprang to my eyes. Then the Grandmothers spoke. **"Nothing can harm thee,"** they said and to this, the holy man added, **"She has my blessing."** And when the dark, lumpish thing heard that, it shrugged its massive shoulders, and shambled off.

"**Many things will try to frighten you, try to veer you away from your path,**" Bear said, "**but don't worry,**" he shook his shaggy head. "**Stay the course and all that comes at you to distract you from your purpose will fall away.**"

"**You are on a GREAT adventure!**" the Grandmothers cried. "**You are voyaging into the unknown and you will continue this voyage for a long time. Never be frightened,**" they said. "Thank you," I said to all of them. "I will try to remember."

This journey heartened me no end. "How," I later asked myself, "can I let myself become distracted by sneaking fears that come bubbling up from the subconscious when I am able to face down a monster like that one? Thank you, Bear," I repeated, over and over again. "Thank you for this lesson, for showing me how powerful it is to simply *watch* a monster. Not react, just watch. That's what I'm going to do," I said. "And the Grandmothers are right. This really *is* an adventure."

"Reclaim the Motherland."

Shortly after the encounter with the monster, my husband and I took a vacation to Europe. Our plan was to join our Dutch friends in Milan, attend the Slow Food conference in Turin, and drive around northern Italy together. And after this part of our trip was over, Babs, Lilium, and I would put Roger on the plane in Milan and we three women would drive on to Grandmothers' Gatherings in Switzerland, Belgium, and Holland.

We began our holiday by exploring the Piedmont region of Italy, its rustic landscape and remarkable food, staying the first week at small inns in the countryside. One day we drove into the city of Bra, where the Slow Food movement had started. We were taking our time, meandering through the old town, when suddenly I felt sick and, using my tiny bit of Italian, was able to find a toilet just in time. "What," I worried out loud, "caused that?" I hoped I wasn't going to become sick and spoil everyone's holiday.

We were on our way back to the car when Babs and Lilium spotted an old church and ducked into it. After several trips to Europe, Roger had decided he'd seen enough old churches to last him a lifetime so he didn't go in. I too had made up my mind to stay out of ancient buildings. I'd learned how sensitive I was to sites that held old, trapped energy, so, though I might admire them from the outside, this time I wasn't going inside. Besides, at the moment, I was uncomfortable enough.

As we waited for our friends, I noticed what looked like another church across the street. This building had an unusual flat face and above a statue of the Madonna on the front side, there was a symbol of a triangle with an eye in the middle of it. "I've seen that symbol somewhere before," I said as we crossed the street. "It's old. Possibly Egyptian," I ventured, and as I examined it, I became transfixed by the building.

Babs and Lilium still hadn't returned, and Roger had begun to window-shop, but I couldn't move. Mesmerized by the energy of that building, I stood in front of it and waves of grief and fear rose up around me. What I was feeling was old fear, not a fear personal to me. But as it continued to build, I heard the ancient Mother of that place crying out. Then strange scenes began to flash before me. Statues of the Mother were being carted away from where they'd stood for time out of mind. Priests and dignitaries were carrying them away, removing them so they could use the power of these ancient sites for their own ends.

By now I was rooted to the sidewalk. All I could do was observe a horror that had occurred in the past and when the Mother's cries for help and my own seeming impotence overwhelmed me, I began to sob. When Babs and Lilium found me, I could barely find words to tell them what had happened, what I'd seen taking place. I had never felt more helpless in my life, nor had I heard of or imagined scenes like the ones I'd just witnessed.

Though with all my heart I wanted to do something to lift the pain of that place, my knees were knocking so hard I could barely stand. But with a Dutch sister on either side of me, together we called on the Net of Light and prayed. Then Babs spotted a plaque on the building written in Italian and, deciphering a word here, a word there, we figured out that this was not a church after all, but had originally been a hospital—run by the Knights Templar.

We wrapped our arms around each other then and prayed on, calling on the Grandmothers, the ancient goddess of this place, and Mary, the Blessed Mother. "The painful period you went through is over now," Babs said to the weeping Mother. "Today is part of another time and you are no longer alone for now we are all here together. That horror happened in the past. It's over," she said. "The Grandmothers have come and it's time for the Mother to return to earth."

The next day we drove back to our hotel in Turin and, in the middle of the night, the holy man appeared in my dream. **"The work you are doing is beautiful,"** he said and then he showered me with love. Each time I recalled that dream a great happiness spread over me, filling me with confidence. This feeling would bear me up in the days to come.

Just before we left for Milan to take Roger to the airport, I asked the Grandmothers about the work we three were to do. **"This is where your blood lines come from,"** they responded. **"Europe is the Motherland for you, and most of the pain that western women carry (whether they live in Europe or in other parts of the world) comes from here."** They paused a moment and then they corrected themselves. **"Much of the pain that women in *both* the western and eastern hemispheres carry comes from Europe. That is why you need to do the work here."** This was a big statement and I wanted to ask them more, but they motioned me to be silent and just listen.

"Cast the Net of Light to the places in Europe that are sacred to the Mother but that have been 'capped off' by patriarchy," they said, and when I heard this, my mind flew to that church/hospital in Bra. It must have been sacred to the Mother at one time—that would explain why the goddess who appeared there to me was in so much distress.

"There are more of these capped off sites in Europe than anywhere else on earth," the Grandmothers said, **"and as you cast the Net of Light to them, you will free the energy of the Mother to flow everywhere Europeans have settled."** As I listened to them, it came to me that all people with European ancestry, no matter where they might live now, will benefit from the un-capping of these ancient sacred sites. Nodding, 'yes,' the Grandmothers said, **"Cast, cast, cast.**

"You will be traveling through Germany on your way to Belgium," they said. **"While you're there, remember that Germany was sacred Motherland long before it was declared 'the Fatherland.' Cast,"** they repeated, giving me a penetrating look. **"Cast to the sacred places you know as well as to the ones you don't know. Reclaim the Motherland, and as you do this, you will help men and women everywhere.**

"You will be able to do this work quite easily," they said, eyeing me carefully. **"You'll feel and sense the sacred places on this continent, because you have 'outsider' senses."** My jaw dropped and I turned to them, bewildered, but again they waved away my questions. **"You are not as culture-bound in Europe as were your ancestors,"** they explained. **"Because you were born in America and your bloodline has been removed from the Motherland for several generations, it will be easier for you to see what is here.**

"Now the sacred part of the trip begins," the Grandmothers said and gleefully rubbed their hands together. **"Keep all your senses open. What you have come here to do is the work of *en-couraging*. Fill-ing with courage, calling forth the courage that (of necessity) went underground in the women here. Again, because the cultural bind-ings around you relating to this continent are looser and fewer, it is easier for you to do this work than it is for them. However,"** they said and held up a finger, **"courage runs deep in the blood of the people of Europe. It is who they are, so as soon as you pass our Empowerment on to them and their ancestors, this often buried courage in them will spring forth."**

I closed my eyes when they said this. Then I turned my awareness inward, and called on my own ancestors, and no sooner did I call them than they in turn called forth theirs. And so it went—back and back for many generations. I was touched that my husband's mother who died several years before I met the Grandmothers wanted to be given the Empowerment and as she stepped forward to receive it, with her came her mother, her grandmothers, and her line—far, far into the past. Now there was a vast crowd at my back. **"This is how to work on these sacred sites,"** the Grandmothers said, **"with the backup the ances-tors provide."** "Yes, Grandmothers," I agreed, my body humming with power. The force elicited by this team of ancestors behind me was huge.

"The planet itself is awakening as its people awaken."

Ever since 1996, when the Grandmothers first showed up, people had asked me, "Why *is* there an imbalance between yin and yang on earth? How did this happen in the first place?" Early on with the Grandmoth-ers, I was so busy trying to understand their messages and pass them on that I didn't have time to think about this question. I don't know what finally brought it to the front of my mind again, but suddenly, one day there it was. So at long last I journeyed to them to ask.

I was on my way to them when I thought, "I'd better hurry and ask this question before I get distracted by something else." And right after that thought came, I heard the Grandmothers say, **"We're already here"**—and there they were! I didn't need to journey after all. I didn't even have to ask my question. They were ready for me without me having to do a thing, and this made me wonder if perhaps the process of journeying was becoming unnecessary. Maybe I no longer needed this formalized way of making contact with them.

"Grandmothers," I said to their expectant faces, "when you first appeared, back in 1996, you showed me how grossly out of balance the energies of yin and yang were and in the years that followed, many of us worked with you to correct that imbalance. But now it would be helpful if you shared with us what happened to cause these energies to get *so far out of balance in the first place.* I know that Divine will is behind everything that happens," I said, "so this imbalance couldn't have occurred just by accident."

When they continued to regard me silently, I went on. "We are limited in our knowing, Grandmothers," I said, "very limited, but if we had an understanding of this it would help us a lot."

"This subject is difficult for you," they replied. "Yes," I nodded. "I don't understand why this happened and I don't think anyone else does either." **"We know you don't,"** they said and they continued to regard me.

"I've been told it's not good to ask the Divine 'why,'" I said, "but I don't know what else to say. Because of this yin and yang imbalance, so much suffering has gone on for so long... so I have to ask you... why?" I said again. And as soon as I pronounced that word, everything went blank. First there was just silence, then darkness, and then there was nothing....no thing. No Grandmothers, no me, no thing. Nothing at all. I had never experienced such emptiness, such blankness.

After what seemed a very long pause, the Grandmothers said, **"This is beyond your understanding."** "Ummmph," I groaned, "I thought that might be the case, that maybe this issue was beyond human understanding."

"What you are asking about has to do with the expansion of love and compassion," they said, eyeing me from the side to see if I understood. (I didn't.) **"It has to do with the reach of love,"** they said, trying again. I must have still looked confused, because at last they asked, **"You see what is happening in America now?"** "Yes," I nodded, "I see.

We just elected a new government and there's a surge of hope in the country." "Yes," they said. "The situation in your country went down so far, that America is making a sharper turn to hope and compassion than it would have been able to make had you not had those dark years. Now, think about how this situation relates to what you just asked.

"Your question has to do with the flow of yin and yang," they said, "the way they push, one against the other. The flow of energy on earth is changing now and there is an upwelling of yin. Yin has begun to flow into the crevices on your planet, to pour into the hardened hearts of the people on earth and to infuse the atmosphere of the earth with love. Enjoy this change," they said; "you've waited a long time for it.

"This change in energy is part of the divine play. Today love is able to grow, expand, and fill every inch of the universe in a way it couldn't before. And," they smiled, nodding encouragingly, "as its people awaken, the planet itself is awakening. Each of you who opens her or his heart is making a place for the energy of the Great Mother, a place for She who loves, supports and cares for life. *This* is the return of the Great Mother. She is coming back now, returning within each of you who opens to receive this message. She is returning to those who are part of this generous giving and receiving, giving and receiving," they repeated, and they swayed back and forth as they spoke.

"It's time to let yourself receive. Don't worry about the past. If you screw your head on backwards and peer behind you to examine what *has been*, you will only confuse yourself. Instead, come forward with us. Wouldn't you rather have this joy now than spend your days trying to figure everything out? Figure it out so you can parse it, box it up, and tie the bits together to store away somewhere?" they laughed.

"Soon the world will make a turn toward compassion, integrity, and generosity. Yin and yang are on their way toward balance. And with this harmonizing and balancing, you will see a return to dharma, a return to living in the right way.

"We have told you many times of the qualities of the Great Mother," they said, "but we remind you again that the Great Mother loves *all* her children and seeks the highest good for life everywhere. The time we are now entering into is Her time. You are part of Her work, part of Her mission. Enjoy yourself," they said, beaming, "and give thanks."

"Progression toward union with the Divine always moves forward—always forward."

While my work with the Grandmothers continued, at the same time, for more than a year I had been bombarded by huge changes in my personal life. It felt like I'd been swept down a river of loss—flooded by sickness, sadness, death, and separation of every kind. Both my mother and my best friend were in the process of dying, and as I dealt with these losses my health began to falter. One day when it seemed that all the starch had been leached out of me, I went to the Grandmothers for help. "Grandmothers," I begged my wise teachers, "how can I maintain faith and stay grounded at this time while the very earth under my feet is shifting?"

"We are holding you," they said and drew me close. "We are holding you. Feel us underneath you, behind you, and at your side. We are holding you and *will* hold you through all the changes that are coming. Lean back and rest on us," they said. "We are here and we will never leave you. You will never be alone again, nor will you have to go through these changes alone."

They looked hard at me and then shook their heads. "You are still looking for help to come to you from outside yourself, looking for *us* as if we were outside you. Waiting for us to show up. You often call on us as though we are somewhere far away," they said, marveling at the consistency of my backwardness.

"When we first came to you, we appeared from 'outside' yourself. We let you 'see' us. We had to do that to get your attention because at that point you wouldn't have listened to our message had we not 'appeared' in some form. Had we come to you as 'presence' or an inner knowing, you would have denied your experience."

"Yes," I said, "you're right. That's exactly what I would have done." They looked me over then, and seeming to size me up, said, "But you are no longer at that point in your life. You have evolved well past the place where you must look outside yourself to confirm the presence of the Divine.

"Remember," they said, "**progression toward union with the Divine only moves forward—always forward. It doesn't go backward nor does it stand still. Because of this law you cannot have the same relationship with us now that you had ten years ago. It would be impossible because within that ten-year period you have become so much more than you were earlier.**

"**Whenever you forget how far you've come, whenever you forget that you are** *in fact* **one with us, you will find yourself slipping into fear and doubt, and each time the mind tips you into fear, your faith will become shaky. This will happen for a while yet,**" they said, shrugging their shoulders. Then they fastened their eyes on mine. "**The times you are living in** *will* **shock you and** *will* **challenge your faith. The daily dramas you are living through now will pepper you with fearful thoughts and test your resolve to be at one with God. Many people are experiencing losses at this time, and the feelings of sadness and fear that arise with loss can shake one's faith.**

"However," they said, wagging their fingers in my face, "**you will become stronger by weathering these so-called losses, and** *you need to become stronger* **if you are going to move forward with this work.**" I gulped when I heard this. "**We will hold you throughout this difficult time. We will never let you go, but remember that you asked to be of service in this radically changing world, and we assure you that what you are going through now is preparing you for greater service. Be brave,**" they said. "**Let loss be your teacher and turn to us—***turn within.* **We are here, and we will never fail you.**"

"You are shedding another skin."

A few days after this I returned to them with desolation weighing on me like wet cement. I couldn't talk to my mother or my dying friend about how devastated I was to be losing them. In the process of dying, both of these precious women had turned inward and were no longer available to me.

My mother was too drugged, and Mahri was overcome by pain and shock. There was no way I could burden them with what I was going through and I didn't know what to do with my grief. "All I can do is move within myself, Grandmothers," I said as I stood before my compassionate teachers, "and feel the presence there. That's the best I can do and really, it's not bad. Only it's awfully lonesome living like this. I really miss…the loving connection that we shared. I miss it a lot—that kind of joyful sharing," I said. "But the joyful part isn't there any more. In fact, the sharing isn't there either. They're already gone from me. I'm vibrating differently too, Grandmothers," I said. "I'm in a new state now and although this current vibration inside is tentative, I can feel the difference."

"You are shedding another skin," they replied and regarded me with compassion. **"The shedding you are experiencing occurs whenever you grow beyond a state of seeming separation. Skins protect,"** the Grandmothers said, **"but skins also separate one person from another, one being from another. At this time you are growing beyond separation."** My mind was terribly dulled by sadness, almost cloudy, but when I heard their words, I felt the beginnings of a lifting taking place.

"I *am* growing," I admitted to them and to myself, and when I said this I became aware of a sense of oneness I was feeling with the women in the Grandmothers' groups in Europe, those whom I'd been hearing from recently. It was like these women were actually present. "They're here," I said to the Grandmothers, wondering how I knew this. "And I'm there," I added. "And….and," I stammered, "I'm in India too.

"God!" I exclaimed, "I'm everywhere!" Amazed at being able to be in so many places at the same time, I said, "I don't feel like myself at all. Not like my old self anyway. In fact I can't even feel my old self now. It's not here any more. That skin *is* gone," I said to the Grandmothers and then I really looked at them. "You're right," I said to my wise teachers.

"You are growing a new skin," they said, giving me a gentle smile of reassurance, **"and this skin is a *One skin*. A unity skin,"** they explained. **"This new skin covers everything. It will bind you to the whole of life, not to separate individuals, but to the whole."** "Yes, Grandmothers," I replied and sighed in relief.

After a few minutes of silence while I thought it all over, I said, "Grandmothers, it seems like this message is a good one for others to hear too. I know I'm not the only one who has been suffering like this." **"Yes,"** they agreed, **"shedding the miserable prison of separate consciousness in order to identify with the whole of consciousness is something that eventually will come to each life. It is the difference between watching the same disappointing black and white movie** over and over again or experiencing the whole of life in all its colors and variations."

"How can I start doing that?" I asked, and corrected myself, "how can *we* do that? How can we start watching the whole of life in living color?" "There's nothing you can do or need to do to make this happen," the Grandmothers replied. "Gradually you will become tired of the repetition of the same dramas in life, also tired of your old attachments and roles. Not everyone will become tired like this or get fed up at the same moment," they explained, "because not everyone is evolving at the same rate, nor should they be. Certain ones, however, will become disenchanted with the predictability of their states of anger, their feelings of despair, fear, and disappointment. They'll tire of their fleeting attachments to one sensation or another. You're one of them.

"When you ride the roller coaster of life long enough you start to wonder, 'is there anything beyond this roller coaster?' That question loosens your fascination with the small, isolated self you've thought you were and then you become interested in something beyond the seeming separation from others, something beyond the seeming separation from all that is. Losing that fascination is all it takes," they laughed, "because of course the answer to 'is there anything beyond this roller coaster?' is *'yes.'* And as you become interested in what that is, it reveals itself.

"This awakening we're speaking of isn't something that happens in one moment. Rather it's a growing in consciousness. A great part of our mission," the Grandmothers said, "is to help you grow beyond the limits of that sense of separation you have for so long accepted as *reality*. To move you beyond the old dance of duality," they chuckled, "where you feel you're never quite enough and where you spend your life in sadness and anger." They threw back their heads then and laughed heartily. "*You are enough!* You are more than enough."

Reminding me of the question I had come with today, they said, "You don't feel the same now as you did earlier in your life because you are *not the same* as you were then. And the places, people, ideas, and identities within your life are shifting too. That's as it should be.

"Let yourself float, untethered in this new state for a while and just observe. We understand that you feel insecure, but although this state is unfamiliar and therefore uncomfortable for you, you are coming into the true security of your being. You are coming to the truth. Another way of saying this is: 'You are growing into your own greatness.' And no matter what changes you go through as these shifts occur, no matter what drops away from you, we are always here. We are here with you now."

When they said this, I felt them. They *were* with me. At that moment it felt like together we were rolled up into one being. Together, the Grandmothers and I formed one skin, and now I became aware that I could see out the front, the back, and the sides of this one skin they were teaching me about. "Now here!" I exclaimed as I began to observe life from this vantage point, "is a new way of being."

"Going yang" again.

The loss of my mother and my friend was affecting every part of me. Even my heart was getting into the act—racing and fibrillating like crazy. I often felt dizzy and light-headed. This became obvious the last time I drove to my mother's place when I had to pull the car into the slow lane of the freeway—just in case I started to faint. I knew that although much of the stress I was feeling seemed to originate in me, some of it didn't. I now 'felt' my mother's confusion; I 'felt' Mahri's pain.

For a long time I'd known I had a tendency to take on other people's issues and load them into my body. In fact, more than one person had told me I was a 'psychic garbage collector' and as much as I hated the term, there seemed to be truth in it. I suspected it was this tendency to take on what wasn't really 'my' business that was making my heart go crazy. "If this is how I'm feeling now," I wondered, "what's going to happen to me when I go to the next Grandmothers' Gathering in Europe where the crowds are so big? Am I going to pick up *everybody's* stuff there too?" I was becoming leery of taking on emotional states that weren't mine—especially where hundreds of people gathered to work with the Grandmothers.

I knew I needed to get some clarity on this issue. All I really wanted was to go forward with my life, to go forward with the work I'd been given. I wanted to keep it simple—to love people and help them whenever I could. That was it. I wanted to accept whatever I was given and simply move forward with it.

"Grandmothers," I said the next time I went to them, "please help me with this. How do I let people feel whatever they're feeling, let them go through whatever they're going through, and just *be* there? I do want to love them, but I don't want to take everything on."

"We will teach you how to do this," they said and when I heard that, I sat myself down with a plop. "I'll wait for this as long as it takes," I muttered, but as it turned out I didn't have to wait long at all. After regarding me thoughtfully, the Grandmothers took me by the shoulders, turned me around, and showed me 'myself.' This 'self' they showed me was sitting in a circle with them, and the first thing I noticed about her was her furrowed brow—her deeply furrowed brow. She/I was leaning toward them and concentrating; in fact, both energetically and physically this 'me' was leaning in so close to the Grandmothers that 'I' was infringing on their space. "Oh!" I exclaimed when I noticed what I was doing. "Look at that! I've moved out of my own space into theirs."

As I continued to observe, I noticed that leaning forward like this not only looked awkward, it felt wrong. So I quickly corrected myself and returned to my own space. My corrected posture lasted for a second or two and then I did it again! And this time when I leaned in close to the Grandmothers, I saw them teetering a little. "Oh no!" I cried, "I'm so far into their space that they have to fall back in order to regain their balance."

Now a scene from my career as a teacher popped into my mind. I had been working at a school for troubled adolescents and one day when the school psychologist observed me, he remarked on my body language. I'd been leaning toward a boy while listening intently to him, and the psychologist said, "I've never seen anyone more empathetic than you. Your body language and everything."

"Oh God," I moaned as this memory returned. "Yukkk! That's where all this came from. Ever since he told me that, I've prided myself on being so 'empathetic' and look at it! That's not empathetic! That's not helpful! When I move into somebody else's space like that, I end up putting the attention on me—*in essence I make myself too important and them not important enough.* And then they lose their balance," I shook my head in disgust. "Yuck!!"

Now I saw myself doing it again—this time with my own children and then with my friends. Leaning forward, essentially violating their space. I watched this action replay itself over and over again. "Grandmothers," I said, "this is sickening…just awful. But," I said, letting out a sigh, " Thank you for showing me because now I can see the trouble it's causing. Not only does it not help others, but I'm putting more energy into these situations than the situations can handle. I'm striving so hard to '*understand*' and '*help*' that I'm wearing myself out. Oh my God!" I cried, "It's the energy of yang again. I'm going yang!" and at that the Grandmothers laughed uproariously. But I was so horrified by my behavior that I could only stare at them until at last the ridiculousness of the scene struck me and I laughed too.

"It comes down to not trusting you enough, doesn't it, Grandmothers?" I said at last. "I'm still thinking I'm the one who's doing everything, still believing it's my job to do it 'right.'" Now the situation looked so silly, so innocent, so stupid, that I threw my hands in the air. "I give up, Grandmothers," I said. "I give up. I'm a dope. I'm really a dope because I still haven't gotten it. I just keep running in the same groove. Please show me how to drop this behavior once and for all. Teach me how to trust you fully, how to trust you with everything. That's what I want."

"**Turn within,**" they replied. "**Turn within, turn within, turn within.**" "Yes," I said, breathing a sigh of relief, "I will."

I was more aware of this pattern after this experience with the Grandmothers and just a few months after that session, my beloved friend died. Mahri would come to me many times after this in my dreams and meditations but I didn't know that when she died. So I cried for my small, human self who believed she would never again hear Mahri's voice or see the light in her eyes, and I cried tears of gratitude that she had at last been released from her suffering.

CHAPTER FIVE

Stretch your Hearts—You are Ready

"When a person does something counter to what you deem as right, there's a tendency to close your hearts to them and shut them out."

I had a lot to integrate as I weathered the loss of my friend and it was several months before I again returned to the Grandmothers. Throughout this difficult time they supported and held me up each day, but I hadn't had the energy to go to them for more learning. Not until now.

"Grandmothers," I said as at last I stood before them, "I got the feeling that you wanted to talk with me about something," and no sooner were the words out of my mouth, than the dogs began to bark and I heard the toilet running. The Grandmothers shrugged their shoulders and laughed at my dilemma. **"The interfacing of ordinary and non-ordinary reality,"** they said, throwing up their hands, **"perfectly normal."** "Thank you, Grandmothers," I said, and jumping up, I shushed the dogs, and fixed the toilet.

"Okay," I said when I returned, "what do you want to tell me? **"Your friend, Mahri, is working with us.** "Oh!" I cried, and then I saw her. Mahri was sitting with them and when I spied her, I laughed out loud because I could tell by the look on her face that she loved being with the Grandmothers. **"She is a real friend,"** they said. "I know, Grandmothers, I know," I answered, surprised that I wasn't breaking into tears. **"The two of you will interface non-ordinary and ordinary reality together, you'll be a good team."** My heart leapt in my chest when I heard this and yet somehow their words didn't surprise me.

Mahri and I had been so close; we'd lived on the same wavelength.

And even though her physical body was no longer with me, I'd known that somehow she would stay in my life. For a long time I'd been aware that death was not what we'd been told it was, and seeing her again like this was proof. She and I had worked together in life and now we would work together again. The veil of separation that we humans call death was in fact thinning. I grinned at the Grandmothers and at my friend as I thought about how miraculous this meeting was. Tears came to my eyes then and through their glow, I saw how beautifully the Grandmothers and Mahri sparkled.

"Tell her about the men," Mahri said, eager to get to work. She smiled knowingly at me, and I recalled how committed she'd been to working with men in the last years of her life. This had become a focus for her shortly after Jesus came to her in a dream and said, **"Work with the men."** "Tell me about this, Grandmothers," I said. "I want to hear it. I know that men need help. Mahri understood this way before I did," I said, "but *how* can we help?"

Smiling, the Grandmothers put their arms around both of us and drew us into their circle with them. **"Consciously think of opening your hearts to men,"** they said. **"Think that thought and hold it. Sometimes you feel the impetus to close your hearts to men, especially when you learn about their bad behavior. But we are asking you to *open* your hearts to them and keep them open.**

"When a person does something counter to what you deem as right, there's a tendency to close your hearts and shut them out. This is how prisoners are treated. This is how the so-called enemy is treated, and this is how people of different races and backgrounds are treated. Hearts close and when this happens, no energy goes to them. This is wrong," the Grandmothers said, shaking their heads, **"and today humanity is being challenged to become greater than it has been in the past. These times are ripe for expansion, and closing the heart prevents expansion."**

I listened carefully as they spoke and I remembered my friend, Peggy, telling me how many indigenous people handle this issue. When people in so-called primitive societies perform criminal acts, their families and friends circle round them and 're-mind' them of all the wonderful things they are and have been. They remind them of the good things they have done in their life and this 'remembering' helps put them back together again, helps return them to their 'right mind.' These people believe that the power of love transmutes all negativity, even criminal behavior. I looked up at the Grandmothers and they smiled.

"**Now we will speak about male and female relationships,**" they said. **Most women think they** *have* **opened their hearts to men, but deep within women are reservoirs of fear, hatred, disgust, and terror. These exist in response to events that happened between women and men in the past. Many of these traumas have become wedged within women.**

"**Historically women have been treated badly by men and even today they aren't treated fairly. Because you are not welcomed as equals,**" they eyed me pointedly, "**you hold a reservoir of fear that can cause you to shut down emotionally. So even when you think you are opening your heart to men, you're only opening it a little bit and even then in a superficial way.**

"**We don't blame you for this. Shutting down your heart is a habit, one that came about from not being able to trust men. But in order to step into your** *own* **greatness, you must open. You cannot step into greatness when you're closed, holding back, and self-protective. You must open your arms and heart and say 'Y-e-e-e-s-s-s.'**

"**You** *can* **do this,**" they said, their voices strong. "**You can do it because you are more powerful now than you have been in millennia. Do it!**" they cried, "**and as you open your hearts, everything on earth will change. Once again we are calling you to greatness. We have called you like this over the years. In the past we have asked you to open yourself in increments, but now we ask you to step into a degree of magnificence you've never before imagined. And we promise that you can do it,**" they said. "**Call on us and we will teach you how—how to open, how to soften and stretch your hearts. You are ready.**

"**We have a great deal of information for you today,**" they said, and quickly I sat up tall, wanting to hear every bit of it. They came in close then and seemed to be examining me. This made me nervous and the nervous feeling intensified when I heard one of them whisper, "**Is she ready?**"

What did she mean? But before I could ask, I saw something hard and round hovering in the air in front of me. It looked a bit like a globe, but more like a fist than a globe, and as I studied it, I saw red and black colors swirling in and around it. It *was* a fist—a dark fist of anger. "This is male energy," I said to myself as I studied it, "and it's been boxed in for some time. What does that mean—'it's been boxed in'?" I asked myself and immediately my mind started playing with words—*box, boxed, boxing, boxing gloves*. There was a feeling of punching in this fist, punching or hitting out. It was one angry fist.

"This is interesting," I muttered to myself as I stared at it, "but what does it mean?" I continued to observe it, but couldn't figure it out, so I asked my question again. "Grandmothers, you wanted to talk with me about something today. What is it?"

"The raging anger in this fist has to be expressed," they said, **"and women fear it. You fear it because often you have been the brunt of it. This is that raging, terrified bull we pointed out to you many years ago."**

I recalled the bull they were talking about. They'd shown it to me shortly after they first appeared. The bull was a wild and crazed creature that had been run to the end of its tether and I remembered that it was at the same time terrifying and terrified.

"The fist you're seeing here, like the bull we showed you earlier, stands for yang energy as it is on earth today. This energy feels confined. It wants to express itself, and when it can't express," they said, throwing up their hands, **"it strikes out. And,"** they added, peering at me from under their eyebrows, **"when it strikes out, it often does so at women."** I looked at them with a question in my eyes. "At women? Why at women?" **"Women are the holders of yin,"** they explained, **"and the unbalanced energy of yang is desperate for yin.**

"If you were to observe the way the energy in this fist lashes out, it might remind you of a baby throwing a tantrum," they said, and I saw what they meant. Then I felt it. The pent up energy of yang was coming on strong now. It was pushing hard and I could feel its vibrating tension. In fact, my body was beginning to shake. **"It doesn't know what to do with itself. You're feeling the tension build up in your own body now,"** they said, confirming what I was experiencing, **"and because you are, you can better understand what this unbalanced energy of yang is like.**

"Those who are consumed by this vibrating force don't know where to put it," they explained, shaking their heads in sympathy. And because of what I was feeling in my body, I understood what they meant. "What often happens with this build-up is this: the 'baby' turns on its mother, blames her, screams at her, and strikes out at her. You see people with unbalanced yang doing this all the time. Both women and men, but men who do this lash out mostly at women. Of course they also lash out at children, at society, and at each other. You'll sometimes observe them when they're caught up in this energy, when, like a hardened ball, they crash into and bounce off one another. This energy is red hot," they said. "Hot, and extraordinarily intense.

"But this energy can also be used in positive ways. When an opportunity presents itself and this unbalanced energy can be put into humanitarian pursuits, it often expresses itself as heroism. *This energy can serve humanity*," they said. "Its striving quality causes it to thrust forward in full yang style and when it shoots outward, it forms a projectile with a force so strong that it's able to pull others along with it. When this force is motivated by a desire to serve, its previously repressed energy creates a potent forward momentum. At such a time, it becomes a vehicle for positive change.

"Without a heroic goal before them, men still feel the power of this surging force within themselves, but they're confused about what to do with it. The energy wants to express, but without the right goal, it lacks a channel. And without a channel, this force ends up going random and damaging others."

"Grandmothers," I said, "what you're sharing here is new information for me, but it fits with what I've observed." After I thought it all over a little while, I said, "Okay, I think I get it. So what can women do?"

Expanding before my eyes, the Grandmothers grew taller and taller until at last they towered above me. "**First**," these mammoth women said, "**anchor yourselves to Mother Earth. Drop down into the foundation inside yourself and stay there. You are reservoirs of yin**," they said, eying me fiercely. "**You are great, you are deep, and you have the power to hold.**"

I wasn't sure what all this meant, but then, out of the corner of my eye, I glimpsed several objects—cupped structures of some kind. Bowl-like, they were receptacles inset deep into the earth. "**Yes,**" the Grandmothers said, "**what you are seeing here is just that. Each of you who have stepped forward to hold the energy of yin is helping to form these structures. **You are creating vast holding tanks of yin within the earth."**

My eyes opened wide and the Grandmothers nodded. **"Dropping into the depth of your being will anchor you, anchor you even during the most bizarre and difficult of times. Anchored like this, you will be able to withstand every radical shift of energy that comes your way. Your steady holding will counteract the unbalanced energy of yang. You will be able to ground yang so it doesn't shoot out randomly and create havoc."**

I gazed at them in amazement. "You, Grandmothers," I said to these magnificent beings, "are creating a network of power, a grandmother/ sisterhood/brotherhood of elemental power. A network that will hold everyone and everything secure. And the men who join with us and plug into this network too will support everything that lives.

"I can see it!" I suddenly cried. Before me now was a reservoir of yin that lay deep underneath the earth, and as I stared at it, I saw people rising up from it. "I see men coming up from this holding place," I said, "and as they step up and out of it, I can tell how steady they are. They're powerful. These men are awesome!"

"The deep holding that only women can provide will give men the structure they need to live strong, meaningful lives," the Grandmothers said. **"And as men come into this state of balance, women and men will be able to work harmoniously with one another. Together they will provide a foundation for a new way of life on your planet."**

As I observed these women and men interacting, I noticed that the women formed a curved, embracing shape, somewhat like the letter 'U,' while the men formed a right-angled shape, like a rectangle. And as I continued to watch, the rectangles were drawn in and held by those curved 'U' shapes. "Oh!" I whispered; "This is the power of yin.

"There's an interlocking action as these 'U's and rectangles come together. The way they're harmonizing with one another reminds me of the pattern fish scales make—each scale interfacing with and embracing the next one. There are rows and rows of them," I marveled as I examined their shimmering design. "They're so iridescent that together they set up a cellular glow." I noticed that the interlocking pattern of the harmonized 'U's and rectangles—shining ever more brightly as yin and yang came together—seemed to be having an effect on all life. Everything was now beginning to relate to everything else.

Glimmering light filled the space around me as this blending and harmonizing continued, and from all the interlocking and connecting that was taking place, a honeycomb structure began to form. It was luminous inside the massive comb—full of gold of every hue. Green gold, yellow gold, rose gold, and shades of amber. Even the atmosphere was becoming golden and I felt myself softening, longing to fold myself into it. I sighed deeply and let myself bask in the golden light and as I rested there, a low humming sound built in the air around me. This droning went on and on, intensifying, until I heard myself gasp, "It's a bee hive! And I'm in the center of it!"

My body was undulating with the humming, moving rhythmically with the swarming bees that were now fanning the air around me. Swarms began to cover my skin with feathery touches while others hovered in the air above me. And instead of feeling fear at their touch, frightened of being in their midst, I was ecstatic. I was becoming part of this living gold. I was part of the hive too, and being at one with the hive was bliss!

"Hold to this beauty," the Grandmothers said. **"Stay in the richness of this golden glow and let yourself rest here. Stay in this place,"** they repeated. **"It will feed you, rejuvenate, and restore you."** "It really *is* a hive!" I stammered, amazed that this was really happening to me. **"Yes, it is,"** they replied.

For a long time I stood in the midst of this beehive of loving connection. It was spreading over the earth now so that all life was held within the vibration of the hive. "It's healing everything it touches!" I whispered, "restoring it and building strength and stamina. All over Earth, goodness is flowing in full supply." As I spoke I basked in the honey-like glow in the air, which was so warm and sweet that I could almost taste it. "Oh, Grandmothers," I said, gazing at them with eyes full of happy tears, but they quietly shushed me. **"This is enough for now,"** they said.

"There will be a parting of the ways."

After this journey I felt so complete that all I wanted to do was float around in what I'd received. What the Grandmothers had given me had truly buoyed me up. They had filled my heart, and after the experience was over, I continued to spend a lot of time in that honeycomb, sitting in the midst of all that gold and letting myself be healed. But after a few weeks of resting, I realized it was once again time to send out a message from the Grandmothers. Time for me to learn a bit more and pass it on.

"Grandmothers," I said as I came before them, "Many people I know have a lot of apprehension about the times we're living in. They're afraid of what may be coming up next. I've been hearing from so many of them lately," I explained, "that this subject is much on my mind. **"We understand what you're talking about,"** they nodded patiently. **"There will be a parting of the ways."**

They looked down when they said this, and pointed to the ground underneath us. When I followed their eyes and looked too, I saw a sheet of clay lying there that looked like it had been rolled very thin, so thin that the beating sun had peeled and cracked all of its edges. **"Sloughing off,"** the Grandmothers said, **"the edges are falling off.**

"This," they explained, giving me a meaningful look, **"is happening everywhere."** And from their look, I knew they weren't talking just about dirt and clay. They continued. **"Power systems on earth that were set up long ago, systems that were created by those who sought to benefit themselves, by those who wanted control of society, who wanted wealth and influence, are beginning to fail now,"** they said. **"And like this dry clay, they too are cracking and will soon fall off.**

"Dust," they said as they brushed their hands together; **"it's all crumbling."** Giving me a stern look, they said, **"You must no longer place your faith in societal systems and institutions. Even now, your hallowed institutions are being exposed for what they really are. Self-serving,"** they said, and no sooner were the words out of their mouths than before me there appeared rows and rows of men in suits—bankers, businessmen, investors, clergymen, and politicians.

"There's something odd about these 'suits,'" I said. And, as I examined the suits as well as the men wearing them, everything began to shrink. Bit by bit, cloth began to rip and shred while the men shrank down and folded in on themselves. This strange metamorphosis continued for some time until everything dwindled down to an insignificant pile, at last collapsing in a wizened heap.

I watched it all crumble, and as the suited men collapsed, everything in the scene began to slide. Roadways and structures cracked, buildings swayed, shook, and trembled. "It's an earthquake!" I cried, and I bolted upright, but it wasn't the kind of earthquake I was used to in California. This one was different. It was an earthquake of institutions, a breaking up of constructs. Investment houses, governmental, and religious systems— all the established hierarchies of our time—began to crack apart and fall to the ground. The sacred cows of my lifetime were collapsing before me and my eyes grew round as I watched them go down. Everything was flaking and shattering, shifting and disintegrating, until the ground before me was littered with dust. I couldn't believe what I was seeing and when I turned to the Grandmothers, all that came out of my mouth was a squeak.

They drew me to themselves then and patting me gently, said, **"Don't be frightened by all this destruction. These institutions need to fall. These systems, dogmas, and theories evolved in earlier times for a variety of reasons. Most of them were established to serve the powers of their creators, although a few of them came into being to help humanity. However, today even those operate only for their own sakes—to feed their own well-established hierarchies. At this point, these institutions are no longer useful to humanity or to the world. So you are beginning to see them exposed for the tottering structures they've become."** I was incapable of speech, but nodded to let the Grandmothers know that I understood what they were telling me.

"Keep your life simple," they said. **"Do the things that mean something to you and don't waste your time on things that don't. Don't be fooled by establishment fixtures you were taught to value, institutions you were told were the bedrock of society, permanent and fixed, but that now appear extraneous, even foolish. Instead of attaching yourself to such antiquated constructs, look instead to the living things of this world."**

As they spoke, before me there appeared forests, waterways, lakes and rivers, mountain ranges, grassy plains, and flocks of birds and animals roaming free. Then I saw the people I especially love and care for. The healing presence of nature girdled and wrapped around them, and as I too felt nature's embrace, I sighed. **"These heartfelt connections are real,"** the Grandmothers said, and gave me a loving smile. **"The others are not real at all.**

"Place your faith in the truth that lives deep within your own heart and in the truth that lives in the hearts of others. *Look* **at one another,"** they said. **"***See*** **each other. It's time to let go the habit of rushing through life, passing, perhaps saying hello, but** *not really* *seeing* one another. Running, running from event to event, from meeting to meeting, yet not *connecting* anywhere."

They looked up, glanced at one another, and began to giggle. **"You've been taught to behave like machines,"** they said, **"to keep your life 'running,' to keep it full—always 'full.' Fill that machine,"** they pantomimed, laughing harder. **"You've lived like *a thing* for so long that you've forgotten what you are. You are *human* beings,"** they said, their voices full of passion. **"And because you are, you are divine. You were born to love,"** they spread their arms wide. **"You were not born to race around. Has this so-called 'race of life' made you wiser? More compassionate? More full of joy? Ummmuhhh,"** they groaned and shook their heads. "No, Grandmothers," I agreed, shaking mine too, "it hasn't."

"Each time you slow down enough to look at one another, to speak to her or him from your heart, *you feed your own soul*. When you do this, you stop living only from your mind and start living from your soul. When you relate like this, your soul is able to speak through you, able to hear through you, and able to love through you. Every cell in your body longs for this sort of communication," they said, watching to be sure I understood. **"This is why you were born. To be part of the living, breathing tapestry of life. Person to person.**

"Living in perpetual motion is a kind of madness that has in recent times become instituted, even glorified," they said, weary looks in their eyes. **"But this life on the run that your society is so fond of has created a societal mental illness—a sickness within your entire culture. Such a frenetic pace is self-destructive. It leaves a trail of destruction behind it, harming everyone. Madness always does that."**

Now the Grandmothers fell silent. They seemed to be thinking of something and after a while they spoke. **"Again we remind you to *keep it simple*. Do not involve yourself in anything you do not understand. For example, do not buy health programs, mortgages, investments, appliances—anything you do not understand. And do not 'buy' ideas you do not understand either. Never assume that someone else knows what you do not. Instead, trust your inner guidance.**

"Many people are just going along for the ride. They don't understand what they're doing or why they're doing it—they're simply going along, following where others lead. This mindless following is

not their fault, as they, like most people, have never experienced the power that lives inside them. In a society with no anchor, people are inevitably left adrift. And this aimless drifting has been going on for a long time.

"In your world, you are encouraged to listen to *the authorities* and give way to *the experts*. However," the Grandmothers said, rueful smiles playing about their lips, "**the** *experts* **on how to live, how to prosper, what to think, and what to do are being exposed for the less-than-truthful pundits that they are. A pattern of life that encourages abdicating one's inner radar is finally coming to an end.**

"**This is a rare moment in time, a moment of fundamental change, and at this time we encourage you to withdraw from all bogus activity and instead seek the real. Simply live. Live simply. Do the things that are meaningful to you and avoid the others. We promise that when everything you once thought of as** *so important, so vital* **falls away and the cracking off is complete, you will wonder why you were ever involved with it in the first place.**"

"There is no battle to be fought.
There is no adversary to be faced."

It was the end of October of 2009 and the Gathering in Belgium was coming up soon. I decided it was time to journey to the Grandmothers to ask what specifically they wanted from this event.

"**Those who are coming to Bruges need to know what it is to live in peace, what it is to live in a sea of love. Giving and receiving love,**" they said, "**instead of being bombarded by fear and anxiety. Instead of guarded and closed, feeling safe and open to receive. The experience of reception. These people are tired. We will fill them.**"

"Thank you, Grandmothers. We will follow your guidance. I also want to ask you about the purpose of this work in Europe. What, for instance, needs to be done to re-activate the power and presence of yin there? I know that the Great Mother was once revered in Europe."

"**Yes,**" they replied, "**and this is something for Europeans to reclaim. Long ago the Mother was worshipped on that continent and there are artifacts that prove it. This can be a source of comfort to Europeans. Especially now as we move into the coming age.**

"**The brutal way the Feminine Principle was repressed in Europe** explains why many people in this part of the world feel so much fear and distrust. Long ago the core of life and love on that continent was driven underground, and though some of this was done in ignorance, all of it was done brutally. Many actions that were taken against the Mother were purposeful. The trauma that the people of Europe suffered when the Mother was banished can still be felt in the land there. This has engendered fear in the people, especially the women. When you see how hard the women there must struggle to step into power and confidence, you will understand how dominant this fear from the brutal suppression of the Feminine Principle was."

The Grandmothers nodded thoughtfully. "At the same time, on the continent of Europe there is a lot to build on. The foundation of the New Age, a foundation of balance and cooperation, where Father God and Mother God sit in harmony together, is already present there. Although the ancient Mother sites on that continent were usurped and desecrated by patriarchy, they existed in the past and their template still exists. Nothing is ever wasted. The power of these sites can yet be called forth because the original blueprints are there. The blueprints didn't die," they laughed. "Such things cannot die. It is true that there are overlays now—misuses of power and deviations of purpose—that lie on top of those ancient sites, but the sacred pattern is set in the land. We will call on that!

"Don't worry," they waved their hands in a dismissive gesture, "if buildings are sitting on these sacred sites now. Don't worry either about who may have committed what atrocity at those places. Yes, yes," they grimaced, "all of that occurred, but the original intent is still present in the land. Together we will reactivate that intent. Just as the template for the Net of Light is being reactivated throughout your planet, just as the blueprint for Beauty/Power inlaid in the cell beds of your body is deepening as you come into full bloom, together we can and will call forth the original blueprint for harmony and balance on the continent of Europe.

"There is no battle to be fought, no adversary to be faced. Those sorts of ideas spring from a yang view of the world, and such ideas will no longer work. Yes," they said, "many terrible things happened on the continent of Europe. The Feminine Principle was denigrated, countless Mother sites were destroyed, and women were tortured and murdered. Yes, it all happened, but it is history now. Done," they said and brushed their palms together. "**The template for the true way of relating to one another and for the true way of relating to the earth is still alive. It is as present as we are, and at this Gathering, we will reactivate it.**

"**Call on us as you gather in Bruges and we will surround you. We will drop a hoop of light into the earth, and create a protected space for this work to take place. And from this sacred space, together we will call on the Net of Light.**

"**Beat the drum when you meet,**" they said, and I heard its slow 'bom, bom, bom.' "**Each beat will reactivate the original pattern within the cell beds of your body and within the body of Mother Earth.**" Again I heard that slow 'bom, bom, bom.' "**Beat the drum like that.**"

"**As soon as you begin, we will come in, and with us will come legions of angelic beings. They will fan the air with their wings and spread healing all over the continent,**" the Grandmothers said, and again I heard the drum.

"**Wherever you may live in the world, all of you work with us in similar ways. You call us, you pass on our Empowerment, and you share our messages and amplify the power of the Net of Light. Everyone does this, whether they live in North America, South America, Australia or Europe. Because of the consistency of the work that you all do with us, wherever you gather, you share a common understanding. There is also something else that happens when you gather. The work you do each time you meet becomes harmonized with the site where it is done, and from that place light pours into the earth. Light soaks into the land and feeds the need of the place where each meeting is held.**

"**Many sacred Mother sites in Europe already hold the presence of the Feminine Principle,**" the Grandmothers said. "**The balance between yin and yang, feminine and masculine, once strongly existed on this continent, and this balance is beginning to return. We ask you to join with us now, and in so doing, benefit yourselves and everything that lives. As the presence of the Feminine Principle awakens on the continent of Europe, the Mother will once again grace that land. And as this takes place, all the lands on Earth will be blessed.**"

Many women came forward at the Bruges Gathering, volunteering to start Grandmothers' groups in both Belgium and Holland. This made us very happy, and having men show up to join with us also made us happy. Having so many men participate was a first, and the men who came to the Gathering seemed to really 'get' the Grandmothers' message! Responding full-heartedly, they threw themselves into everything we did.

As soon as we began to work on mending the tears in the Net of Light, a few women became paralyzed by fear. This was now familiar—very like what had happened in Rhode Island. Similar fears were now rising in Bruges. But this time, because of the language difference, it was more difficult to help these women move out of fear's grasp. However, we had a translator with us, a Belgian group leader with a firm understanding of the Grandmothers' message, who explained to them what was happening and helped us move through this difficulty.

By the time we got to the end of the weekend, the Grandmothers had us up on our feet, dancing and singing. Our wise teachers had accomplished their mission; the Net of Light was firmly anchored in the land. It was also anchored in each of our hearts, and the downside to that was how difficult it was for us to say good-bye to one another.

"There's a lot of drama during the holidays. Watch out for it."

I arrived home from Belgium about a week before Thanksgiving and within a few days found myself dealing with a member of our local group who was going through an emotional upheaval of some sort. I never figured out what caused Helen's upset, but whatever it was, it plunged her into so much anger that she began to act it out on me. She was irritated, even downright mad, and I had no idea why. Having to cope with her personal thunderstorm was a bit shocking, especially because it came on the heels of that heart-filling event in Belgium. Her angry outbursts were about the last thing I had expected, but there they were.

"Okay," I said to myself after the first onslaught hit, "remember what the holy man said—**"Fame and blame are all the same."**

"Fame and blame are all the same, fame and blame are all the same," I repeated to myself and this became my mantra. I kept my focus on it as much as I could to avoid reacting to her anger and then one day it dawned on me. Why was I trying to do this by myself? I'd forgotten to call on the Grandmothers! As soon as I realized this, I called on them and on Bear too, to ask for guidance, but this time it was Bear who showed up.

"Bear," I said, when I came face to face with him, "What is the lesson in this onslaught of negativity?" He looked at me but didn't say anything. Then he motioned for me to climb onto his back and quickly I swung a leg over him, taking a grip of his fur and giving him a hug in the process. "Bear, you are so dear to me," I crooned, and as I felt my love for him swelling inside me, I hugged him even harder. "Thank God for you, Bear," I said, "thank God." He grunted in reply and then he began to run, racing through a forest, and then onto a seemingly endless plain where I watched the light change from daylight into night.

At last he slowed his pace, made a rumbling sound in his chest, and came to a standstill, and, giving a satisfied grunt, he plopped himself and me down on the ground. **"Sit here,"** he said and ambled off to gather leaves and twigs that he brought back and piled beside me. When the size of his mound seemed to satisfy him, he scooped a nest into the middle of it and motioned me to lie down there. I snuggled into the bed he'd made and he blanketed me with still more leaves. Gently, he packed more foliage in around me, and then he covered this leafy nest with a coating of warm mud.

He'd made a cocoon that held me close and it gave a delicious sense of safety and comfort. After he'd tucked me in, he sat himself down beside me and rested a paw on my chest. "Mummm," I sighed. I felt so cozy, so cared for, that I snuggled in even further and, before I knew it, I had drifted off. The last thing I remember was hearing Bear's soft snuffling.

I woke from my nap when he began to scoop the mud and leaves off me. Then brushing me front and back, he said, **"Old...not good,"** referring to the energy the leaves and mud had pulled out of me.

"Don't worry," he said, **"it's nothing,"** and he began to explain a particular type of energy that's present during the holiday season and exerts a magnetic pull on us—drawing us to the past. **"Easy to get pulled to past pain,"** Bear said, and from this I understood that as memories surface during the Holidays, not all of them are good ones. These painful recollections can create a push/pull effect on us and when we find ourselves both attracted and repelled by memories, we become confused.

Bear nodded as I sorted this out in my mind, and as I watched his head bobbing up and down, it came to me that this was what had happened to Helen. I'd arrived home from Europe at the beginning of the holiday season, which in America, starts with Thanksgiving. "Bear," I said, "is this what caused her anger? Did she get caught in this push-pull you're telling me about?" I knew there was a history of jealousy and estrangement in her family so maybe that was it. Rumbling low in his throat, Bear growled, **"Not happy,"** and shaking his head from side to side, added, **"foolish."** He stomped a foot then, letting me know that I needn't understand any more than this. This was enough

"Thank you, Bear, I think I get it," I said and immediately he began to draw circles in the air around us. As his great paws swooped around his head, then circled downward, he showed me how negative energy from the past forms a downward spiral. I watched as the energy pulled in the direction of the earth and the closer to the ground it got, the tighter and smaller Bear's circles became. And as his paws made smaller and closer swirling motions, I saw that they were moving in a counter-clockwise direction. Energy was contracting.

Then he said, **"Happy movement is up and out,"** and circling his great mitts in the opposite direction, he began to draw loops that kept expanding. With every swipe his circles got bigger and bigger until his entire body was following his motion. And as I watched him drawing these enormous circles, a feeling of happiness grew inside me. Here energy was being freed up and expanded. I was feeling that expansion inside my body.

Bear nodded, as if to say, **"This is good,"** and I reflected on how different the contracting and the expanding energy circles felt. Long ago I'd made a decision that I was going to live my life in expansion—not in contraction. What he was showing me was something I was determined to be conscious of during the holiday season. Now I was aware of how nostalgia and regret from past memories could haunt us and make us contract and I wanted none of it. **"Drama,"** Bear said and shook his shaggy head. **"Watch for it, and choose the way you want to go."**

CHAPTER SIX

For the New to Come, the Old Must Pass

"You Are Desperately Needed."

Early one April morning the Grandmothers woke me and were so insistent that I quickly piled out of bed and listened to them. **"Send this message out to as many people as possible,"** they said, **"and send it right away."** I did as they directed, and as soon as I posted it, like the loaves and fishes, it multiplied.

"We ask you to cast, anchor, and hold the Net of Light steady for the Gulf of Mexico," the Grandmothers said. **"The crisis of this Gulf oil spill is affecting the entire world, and *humanity is asleep.* Animals are dying, plants are dying, and your Mother is writhing in agony. If you hold the Net of Light steady at this time, you will help stave off further catastrophe.**

"You have been lulled into a false sleep," they said, **"told that others would take care of this problem. This is not so,"** they said, **"nor is this the time to drop into oblivion. Determine to stay awake now,"** they said, **"and once you have made that commitment, think of, cast, and hold the Net of Light. Hold it deep and hold it wide.**

"Amplify its reach so it can penetrate the waters of the Gulf and dive beneath the crust of Mother Earth. Anchor it at the earth's core, and as you hold it there, ask it to unify with the mineral kingdom of this planet and harmonize with the solid and liquid mineral states on earth—including oil and gas. The Net of Light will call these minerals back into harmony.

"For many years men have wreaked havoc and abused the kingdoms of life on earth, but this time their destruction has reached crisis proportions. Whatever human beings have damaged, human

beings must correct," the Grandmothers said. "*This is the law.* We repeat: *This is the law.* You cannot sit back and ask God to fix the mess humanity has created. Each of you must throw your shoulder to the wheel and work. We are asking for your help now. Several years ago we gave you the Net of Light so you could help the earth at times like this. Step forward *now*," they commanded. "*This is the Net of Light that will hold the earth during the times of change that are upon you.*

"Move into your heart and call on us," the Grandmothers directed. "We will meet you there. *The Net of Light is lit by the jewel of your heart,* so move into this lighted place within you and open to the Net of which you are a part. Then bask in its calming presence. The Net of Light holds you at the same time that you hold it.

"Now think of magnifying your union with us. We, the Great Council of the Grandmothers, are with you, and all those who work with the Net of Light are also with you. There are millions of people now connected in light," they said.

"As you think of your union with them, also call forth the power of the sacred places on earth. These sacred sites will amplify the potency of our joint effort. Then call on all the divine beings that work with the earth, those who have come now to prevent this catastrophe that threatens to overwhelm your planet. We will all work together," they said, nodding slowly.

"Think of, cast, and magnify the presence of the Net of Light in the Gulf of Mexico. See, imagine or think of it holding the waters, the land, the plants, sea life, and the people. Holding them all!" the Grandmothers said. "The Net of Light is holding them steady and returning them to balance. Let the love within your lighted heart continue to pour into the Net of Light and hold, hold, hold. Calmly and reverently watch as the light from your heart flows along the strands of the Net. Light will follow your command. It will continuously move forth, so as soon as you think this thought, it will move into action. We ask you to practice this for only a few minutes at a time, but to repeat it throughout the day and night.

"We promise that this work with the Net of Light will do untold good. We are calling you to service. You are needed," they declared. "Do not miss this opportunity."

After this message went out I was inundated with mail from every corner of the earth. People threw themselves into this work—holding prayer circles, ceremonies, sacred singing, and coordinated meditations with the Net of Light.

"When you clutch at pain as it arises, you hold onto it. Pain isn't permanent."

After the Gulf oil spill debacle I had a hard time getting my mind off the state of the world. I was working diligently with the Net of Light, just as the Grandmothers had asked, but my concern about the world of nature and the havoc humans were wreaking on the kingdoms of life was constantly on my mind. I thought about it *all the time* and the more I thought about it, the less energy I had. My body had begun to tighten up in pain and I was sinking into despair when it finally occurred to me to take this problem to the spirits of the lower world. The compassionate animal spirits had helped me many times in the past, especially with physical pain.

"Please have pity on me. Help!" I prayed to the animal spirits. "I'm worrying about the world non-stop and it's making me sick." And as soon as I said this, I dropped through the entrance to the Lower World and held onto my prayer until at last I came before Bear. Today he was not alone, but stood with a council of animals. I'd caught a glimpse of this council as I began my journey and when I landed in their presence, I prostrated myself before them. "Please help me," I said. "My body hurts all over, I can't stop worrying, and I seem to be feeling everybody's suffering."

Bear nodded and I saw that Wolf and Buffalo were standing beside him. The great apes were present too and then I saw Lion, Elephant, Crocodile, Deer, and Gypsy, our beloved dog from many years ago. "Gypsy!" I cried and then I saw that Sadie, Willie, and McBear—all our old pets—were also there. The beloved animals moved to encircle me and as they did, I heard a drum beating. "Birds are here too," I said in surprise, "flocking around and above me. There's so much love!" I cried, my voice choked with emotion. "This great love that they're giving, their enfolding love, is steadying me," I said as I noticed that my body had started to relax.

"**You never feel safe**," the animals said as they came in around me.

"You anticipate suffering, and it is this that has caused the grief, disturbance, and inflammation in your body." Gazing at me with compassion, they added, "We are your family and we will never leave you."

They crowded in then, so close that I closed my eyes felt their breath on my skin and heard their gentle moans and growls. "Oh, to be enfolded like this," I sobbed. Lion stood at my back where I'd had pain for so long, and when I felt his warm breath on my back and heard him growl low in his throat, I cried harder.

Then one of the animals began to suck at the back of my neck, drawing something out of it. I felt a warm mouth on me, pulling, pulling on something while beside me the great apes swung their arms and rocked back and forth. I saw their dear faces, noted the looks of compassion they wore, and as I did, I understood that I'd taken on suffering from this world and that I'd taken it on specifically from the animals.

"No, no, no!" they cried then, and Horse emphatically shook his head. Then the cows chimed in. "Give it to us, give us this pain," they lowed. "It's too much for you. Give it to us," the animals chorused together and so I did as they asked. "I give it to you, I give you the pain," I said to them.

"It is not as you think," they said, their big heads nodding from side to side. "There is a fraternity here. A fraternity made up of all forms of life—people included—and there is a sanctity in this fraternity."

I got a glimpse of what they were talking about when they pointed to the Net of Light Underneath us and spreading outward in every direction was a beautiful pattern of connection. As I examined it, I saw that this pattern or tapestry lay under all the conditions, actions, and beings on earth. All forms of life were linked together and as I looked on, I saw that even humans' cruel actions towards the animal kingdom were held in this fabric of connection.

"Whoooohh," I moaned and then I began to sob. "Lift up out of your self-imposed suffering!" the animals said and I started at their words. Was I inflicting this pain on myself? "Yes!" they said, nodding emphatically and answering my unspoken question.

"Help me please," I cried. "Help me to let go of all this," and immediately the clay sculptures I'd been making appeared before me. Some were of human forms and some were animal forms and as I looked at them now, I noticed how the figures seemed almost alive—affirming this fraternity the animals were talking about.

"**Sacred connection**," they said. "**Making a sacred connection is goodness itself!**" As I reflected on, "Making a sacred connection is goodness itself," I tasted sugar in my mouth. This was surprising, and, even more surprising was, that with this sweetness came a change. Things looked softer and brighter. The figures of the animals now stood out from the background. They looked more defined, more detailed, and as I registered this change, I became aware that my sadness had left me. "**Far seeing**," the animals said, nudging and patting me. "**Far seeing.** *Now* **you are seeing far.**

"**Stay in connection like this with the fraternity of life and keep on making the beautiful things you make**," they said. "**They are objects of worship, objects that testify to this fraternity.**

"**As you move closer to the times of change that are coming to earth, all sorts of pain will arise. The horrors will become more and more evident and, as they do, you will need to maintain your link to what is real, to what is changeless. As evil behaviors become more pronounced, turn to the Net of Light that connects every living thing. Stay connected with us through the Net of Light and you won't be swept away by the shock of the moment.**

"**Much is changing on earth at this time and you must allow it to change. Don't fight it. It's supposed to change**," and they repeated, "*supposed* **to change. It's part of the 'play,'**" they said and I reflected on the word. "Yes," I responded. Now I realized how the drama of what they were calling 'the play' had drained my energy. "**Life is supposed to change**," the animals said again. "**Let it. In order for the new to come, the old must pass away, and when it is time, we too will pass. We will pass into another form**," and they gazed at me with impassive faces as if this were the most natural thing in the world.

I must have looked distressed when I heard this, because they said, "**You've forgotten about it being a play. You think everything that happens on earth is real.**" Shaking their heads, they reminded me, "**Nothing ephemeral is real. That which is real is changeless and that which is not real, is always changing. Life on earth is always changing**," they said, and when I looked up at them, they laughed good-naturedly.

"I know what you're saying is the truth but I forget it," I admitted. "I get sucked into the drama of the moment and when I do that, I believe that whatever is happening *is* the real deal." As I spoke, I realized I was especially susceptible to getting caught like this when there was suffering. Whenever animals or people were suffering, I lost my sense of equanimity. **"Give it to us, give it to us,"** they said again, waving their paws and hoofs at me, **"give us your attachment to suffering."** I let out a big breath then and begged them, "Teach me, please teach me. I want to give everything to you, but I don't know how."

The animals moved in close to me and began to focus on my heart— massaging and holding it. One of them was actually cauterizing it. "It's been bleeding!" I cried, shocked by what I was seeing. "I had no idea," I blurted out and then words failed me. Silent, I simply watched them work. "I'm a literal bleeding heart," I whispered at last; "it's no wonder I've been losing strength—really losing strength."

"We will *hearten* you," the animals replied, **"and we know how to do it. Life is supposed to be full of change, especially at this time. The changes you've been told about are here now, so let them come. And as this change comes, give everything over to us. Because you think that everything that's happening in the world is real, you contract whenever these so-called 'losses' occur. You try to prevent them from taking place, and every time you do that, your heart clutches and holds onto pain. Ridiculous!"** they cried. **"All of this is passing. Let it pass. Don't hold onto any of it."**

"We had dinner with friends last night," I interjected, "and when our dinner partners started talking about eating different parts of animals, it was so upsetting, I could hardly sit there."

"Just let it pass," the animals replied. **"That's where these people are, so let it pass. It's only a story after all, and since it's not a story for you, let it flow. Let it go. Whenever you clutch at pain, you hold onto it,"** they explained again. **"Pain isn't permanent and isn't supposed to be permanent, so let it pass. It's supposed to pass."**

"How do I let it go?" I asked them. "I'm so used to clutching. Even now I can feel my neck muscles straining and holding on to something." **"We will help you,"** they said, and one of the great apes came in behind me to massage my neck. Putting his big head close to me he began to softly call, **"Come out now, come out now!"** He was talking to the stuck energy in my neck, and when I realized what he was doing, I burst out laughing.

"Whenever you feel pain like this," the animals said, **"remember that you're holding onto something, thinking it's permanent when actually it's just flowing down the river."** Maybe it was the phrase, 'flowing down the river,' but now I found myself thinking about the oil spill in the Gulf of Mexico. My body tensed at the memory and I caught myself holding my breath. **"Let it flow, let it go,"** the animals chorused.

"All the things you get so upset about—the government, the environment, it's all flowing. Then they began to sway, and, swinging their bodies back and forth, back and forth, they pulled me into rhythm with them. **"We aren't suffering from all this change,"** they said, **"so why are you? We know how to flow and we'll teach you how to do that, too."** "Oh yes, please," I begged.

They looked so happy as they swung back and forth like that—so at ease in their bodies. "They're teaching me as if I were a little child," I thought and then I yawned and said, "I guess I am a little child." **"We're good teachers for you,"** the animals confirmed. **"So relax now and remember that at every moment you are being carried down the river. Carried downstream with the flow, to peace."**

I recognized the truth in what they were saying, but this lesson wasn't an easy one. To remain unaffected by all the drama and trauma in the world was a struggle for me. It seemed to be the way I was wired. I had always been deeply connected to animals as well as to people, so, whenever they suffered, I suffered. I realized that this empathetic connection inside me often did more harm than good, and yet, detaching myself from stories of animals and people that were wounded and in pain was a continuing challenge.

I kept reminding myself of the animals saying, **"It's only a story after all…let it flow. Let it go."** Reminding myself that whatever was changing in the world was not, at the deepest level, 'real' and true. "Take a deep breath," I'd say to myself. "Take a deep breath and let life flow."

Sometimes I actually listened to those wise words. And sometimes I didn't.

"One of us alone is powerful, but standing in formation like this, we are a force."

A few days later I went to the Grandmothers and by now I was feeling so much better that I was able to ask them a question, not just for myself, but for everyone. "Grandmothers," I asked, "what can we do to maximize our strength at this time in spite of the upheaval that's come upon our world?"

"**Listen to us,**" they said and while I waited for them to say more, a totem pole appeared in front of me. Carved animals stood on one another's shoulders and the pole climbed high into the sky. I could see that while each animal embodied its own particular qualities, the animals below supported the ones above. Yet, unlike the way people think about a seeming hierarchical structure like this one, I could tell that the animals lower down the totem pole were no 'lesser' than the ones higher up. Value was not determined by how far up or down the pole one stood. Rather the pole was the strong and beautiful piece of work it was because *each one* stood in its perfect place.

Again I asked my question to the Grandmothers, adding, "I don't understand what you're telling me with this pole." There was a long pause and then they said, "**Stand up straight and feel your body.**" I did as they said and immediately my shoulders dropped and my breath evened out, while my eyes gazed out peacefully on the world. In fact, my gaze was so clear that I could see everything. "I'm a force," I said to myself, "a source of power," and inside myself I felt solid—almost foundational. "This is a potent feeling, Grandmothers," I said, "but I still don't know what it has to do with my question."

"**Watch us,**" they replied and they turned and walked away, their skirts swirling with the speed of their motion. They kept on walking like that until I thought they were going to fade into the distance.

"Where are they...?" I said to myself, but before I could complete my sentence, the Grandmothers turned as one, took a step forward and stood silently in a long line, facing me. "**We are a force,**" they said, speaking slowly. "**One of us alone is powerful, but standing in formation like this, we are a force.**"

"Whew!" I exclaimed and nodded in agreement. A line of majestic women stood facing me now, each one drawn to her full height, her gaze unfaltering. They held their ground like this for a few minutes and seemed to appraise me. "Grandmothers," I said at last, "I don't understand what..." but they ignored my words and began to march forward.

"**Stand together!**" they shouted and when I heard this, I froze and stared at them. "**Stand together,**" they repeated. "**You are not alone.**

You are not a puny individual, one person among many. You are part of a great movement. A moooooovement! Do not forget this. Call on us! Gather together, reach out to one another, and in your great love for the Mother, call out to us.

"What mother will desert her child?" they asked and looked hard at me. "We will *never* desert you," they declared, shaking their heads. "Come together, support one another, and call on us. You are a movement. The time for moving forward is now and you have been called to do it. So stand with us. This is the answer to your question. This will hold you in strength."

I stared at them for a long time, my mouth hanging open in amazement, and then it hit me. I was no longer alone. I was one with the Grandmothers, part of a movement. I was one of many who loved these wise teachers, and was in turn led by, and loved by them. I was part of a family of light, part of the Net of Light.

"We are heartened by this human response. As fear and desperation grow, so is love growing."

Responses to the Grandmothers' request to hold the Net of Light for the Gulf of Mexico kept coming in and I was so touched by the desire of people to help, that one day I went to the Grandmothers, deciding I would lay all these responses before them. "You gave us that beautiful message for the Gulf, Grandmothers," I said, "and so many are listening now for your messages. We are in turmoil as we watch the devastation in that part of the world and unfortunately fear and despair are running rampant."

"We are heartened by this human response," the Grandmothers replied. "As fear and desperation grow, so too is love growing. Selflessness is growing and community is growing. Many times humanity must endure these horrific events in order to come awake, to remember what is truly important. What is important," they said, "is your love and service to one another, your love and service to all life.

"The yang dominance of your culture has separated you from this loving connection with the truth of life, separated you from the things that grow and bloom, that blossom and bear fruit, that bear young. You've forgotten your deep-down link with life," the Grandmothers said, "and when mankind forgets, then the lessons must come. And when the forgetting is deep, the lesson will be equally deep.

"Let your hearts open now," they said. "We understand that to see the suffering—in the Gulf, in Central America, in the Middle East, in Africa—in so many places—" they said, shaking their heads, "is painful. And to see the hardened hearts of those that you call 'the haves'…" they laughed ruefully. "Those people are most pitiable of all. In their hearts they have nothing and though they clutch at everything, they end up grasping at emptiness.

"So," they said, gazing at me, "take the challenge and let your hearts open. Feel what you feel. Let compassion well up in you and then serve wherever you can. Serve with your hands, your voice, and with your listening. But most of all," they said, "serve with a loving heart. Such service will bring you joy.

"Cast the Net of Light," the Grandmothers said. "Hold it and let yourself be held by it. Pray for all the creatures affected by these catastrophes and hold them in the Net. That is your job. The holding, holding, holding of the light.

"You have been conditioned by the energy of yang to expect things to happen fast," they said, "but the shift in energy that you will create when you hold like this will endure a long time. It will do lasting good. By your decision to 'hold,' you will lift these heavy conditions. You will lift the earth itself.

"It is the steadiness, the on-going connection to the Net of Light that lifts and elevates. Don't lose heart," the Grandmothers said, shaking their heads. "When you catch yourself wanting things to happen quickly and are disappointed when they don't, stop and take pity on yourself. You have been conditioned by the dominant energy of yang to behave in this way. That's all it is. Don't blame yourself for the rushing about you sometimes get caught in," they laughed. "You have been conditioned to live that way.

"But make the decision now to hold, and each time you hold like this, recognize the good you are doing. Take joy and pride in it. In this holding you become part of a great family of light. This steadiness is what is needed now," they said, "not the rushing about or the instant fix.

"You are needed to do this work and you are needed *day in and day out,"* they said. "To perform this task, you need the stamina the Net of Light gives, and as you develop that stamina, you will become stronger and able to do more. Living from this steady place inside yourself will give you greater and greater joy.

"Call on the Net of Light right now," they said, "and feel it under you, behind you, and beside you. Rest in it. Send light from your heart along the strands of the Net and notice how it blesses everything it encounters. As you do this, everything that swims, walks, breathes, thinks, loves, and fears will be lifted. Lifted, lifted," they said. "This is all you need to do. *This* is *everything.*

"Each time you feel the Net of Light holding you, you will also feel its calming action. You both receive and send calming energy through the Net, and this happens each time you move into your heart to let light flow.

"Honor yourself," the Grandmothers said, and then they surprised me by making a small bow to me/us. "You are the purveyors of goodness," they said. "You are our instruments."

"You are a subtle warrior."

The week that went by after that was filled with desperate-sounding emails from people worried about the fate of life on earth, a week also filled with family emergencies. "Grandmothers," I said as I came before them, "I have all these things I need to do for the house, the family, and my business. At the same time I want to do this work…." But before I could finish my sentence, they planted my feet firmly on the earth and said, "The work you are doing with us grounds you."

"I don't want to get blown out by my personal dramas, Grandmothers," I responded, and when they heard this, they reached out and embraced me. "There *is* a lot of drama now," they said and from this I understood that they were not only referring to my family, but also to the fear and anger being engendered in millions of people by the various catastrophes on earth.

"Be wary of drama," they cautioned. "The mind and ego love drama because it feeds them. But when your heart is at one with the Net of Light, it is able to reach far beyond any seeming difficulties. Your connection with the Net of Light forms the elemental Fabric of Being.

"*This* is where you are needed," they said, "anchored in and to the Net of Light. When the world attempts to draw you into panic and despair, drop into your heart. Drop into the core of radiance that lives within you, and sitting there, give thanks. Each time you connect like this, light shoots along the strands of the Net, upholding the light within you and upholding light everywhere.

"Many of you are fearful of trusting our call to power. In the past you encountered teachers, gurus, religions, and spiritual systems that disappointed you, and so now you hold back. And some of you are so caught up in the energy of your yang-centered world that you haven't slowed down enough to really listen to what we have come to share.

"We ask you to take your courage in your hands now and turn your attention to us," they said. "Listen to what we are saying. We ask you to do this for your sake as well as for the sake of all life. There is work for you now if you will take it up and do it. The task we are calling you to is simple," the Grandmothers explained. "It's not difficult, although your mind may try to make it so.

"We ask you to read and share our messages, to read and discuss our books and pass on our Empowerment into the energy of yin. We have given you the Empowerment Ceremony, the books, and messages so that you can increase the amount of Beauty/Power within yourself and become a walking blessing upon the earth. We promise you that this will happen," they said, their eyes fixed on me.

"You will bloom more than you can imagine. You see," they said, and smiled their sweetest smiles, "because of the gifts we've given you, you need no longer live an ordinary life. The time for that is over. *You can now live an extraordinary life,* and we are calling you to it. You are a subtle warrior," they said, and hugged me to themselves. "You are *our* subtle warrior."

CHAPTER SEVEN

River of Life

"Always, and at every moment, each one is evolving."

Something disturbing happened at a women's discussion group I'd been part of for a long time and I couldn't get it out of my mind. At our meeting Alice shared that the therapist her teenage son had been seeing was encouraging the boy and his father to reject 'the woman of the house.' When they went to his office for a family therapy session, the therapist told her son and husband to 'take charge' and vent their anger at her whenever they felt like it. He said that to properly step into his manhood, a young man needed to attack feminine 'power' wherever he found it. It was especially important for a young man to reject his mother and it was 'good' for him to see his father put his mother 'in her place.' As Alice shared this with us, I listened with a growing sense of horror. I'd been a psychotherapist for more than thirty years and had never heard of such a thing.

After the therapist's edict, some angry scenes took place in their home. Alice's husband sided with the therapist and she was crushed when he, as well as her son, began to turn on her. As I listened to her tale, I was sick at heart. I was a mother too, so I could imagine the pain she must be going through. Her report shocked me and I couldn't wait to take it to the Grandmothers. So that evening I journeyed to them, explained the situation, and asked, "What are we as women supposed to learn from an experience like this one?"

Looking grim, the Grandmothers responded, **"For a long time women have been treated badly."** "The behavior of this therapist is more than that!" I interrupted. "If these sorts of actions against women are still going on today, what do are we to do? I know that back in history men behaved like this," I said, "but today?" The Grandmothers gazed at me and though they said nothing, the looks they wore radiated compassion. At last their calm expressions helped me get a grip on myself. "I'm a mother, too," I said to them at last. "I have a son and a daughter, so I'm asking this for all of us mothers, Grandmothers. What is the lesson here?"

The Grandmothers took my hands in theirs and drawing me along with them, we walked forward together. It was growing dark and I wasn't able to see very well, to know for sure where we were going, but we seemed to be climbing up over a bridge. However, when we came down the other side, darkness had truly set in, making it impossible to know for sure.

There was muggy murkiness and swirling air around us, and when the Grandmothers again took my hand to lead me further, it felt almost like we were crossing into another world—a world like Tolkien's Mordor. This was a dark land, where everything was obscure—even the air. I didn't understand where I was or what any of this meant, so, not knowing what else to do, I returned to my question. "What is the lesson in this?" I asked the Grandmothers. "What is the lesson?"

"We will show you," they said, and as soon as they spoke I caught a movement off to my left. Something was out there. Then, one by one, animals with strange shapes began to approach us until they had us surrounded. These animals weren't exactly dinosaurs, but as they lumbered in our direction, they looked prehistoric. Massive and ungainly, they swiped at the air as they came forward and when they got close to where we were standing, they stopped still and, swaying from side to side, reared up and roared. I shrank behind the Grandmothers.

Some of them had snouts that made them look like massive sloths. "Ugggh!" I shuddered as the roaring and screeching intensified. "They're monstrous, they're primordial," I moaned, searching for words to describe what I was seeing. "This dark land is their terrain," I continued, "and they're striking out as they move because the air is so cloudy here that they're almost blind." The atmosphere around us was so thick that if something stood more than ten feet away, it disappeared into the general gloom.

Now I began to glimpse spots of color in the murk. Here and there blotches of red stuck out of the darkness. "Oh! ackkkk!" I gagged, "it's their mouths. They're bloody!" Shuddering at those gaping maws, I wrapped my arms around myself and shook my head to rid myself of that image. "Grandmothers," I cried, "what is the lesson here? I don't get any of this!" The monsters roared even louder then, and when the ground began to shake with their roars and stomps, the Grandmothers said, **"Just watch."**

I stood back then and observed the beasts, and as I did, I recalled a journey I'd taken not long after the Grandmothers first came into my life. I don't remember the question I'd asked them that day, but it had brought me to a primitive land where stone-like fish swam. Like the animals I was seeing now, those fish too were an early form of life. Monstrous in size and slow moving, the fish seemed to have no consciousness at all but simply lurked along the bottoms of the waterways, patrolling the rivers and lakes. Then I recalled that their mouths had also hung open, ready to drink in whatever got in their way, and I remembered that I'd found their size, coupled with their mindless nature, menacing. They were not pretty or interesting-looking fish, but blob-like, they seemed to spend their time lying in wait. I'd been careful to avoid them, and the animals I was seeing now reminded me of those fish.

As I recalled this experience, I said, "There seems to be a theme today of pre-emptive striking out. You're showing me a pretty low form of consciousness with these animals, Grandmothers." And when I heard myself speak, I wondered if perhaps the pre-emptive striking out I was seeing also related to the man I thought of as the 'cruel therapist,' the one who had set Alice's husband and son against her. "Grandmothers," I said, "How does what I'm seeing here relate to the question I came with today?"

I waited for them to speak, but they didn't, and as I continued to wait, the animals wandered off and disappeared. Now, just the primordial fish, the ones I had recalled, remained—slowly patrolling the water before us. I was giving them my full attention when I noticed something else in the water with them. Something colorful and, by the way it moved, feminine.

Darting in and out between the hulking fish, a feminine creature gracefully navigated those waters, swimming nearer and nearer to where I stood. When she got to a point directly in front of me, she drew herself out of the water and onto a rock to sun herself. "Sun herself!" I exclaimed, "in the midst of these monsters?" But the slight creature seemed to be totally relaxed, and when she settled herself down in the sun, I heard myself gasp. No sooner did she take her seat on the rock than the sunlight enfolded her, seeming to shine not only on her, but *from within* her. She was glowing! And not only was she full of light, she was casting light all around. And when I looked again, I saw that she *was* the light.

I watched intently and tropical-looking plants began to spring up behind her. Palm trees, grasses, ferns, and flowers appeared, and then I saw a sandy beach. It seemed that we had moved to yet another time and place. The little blonde creature had changed the atmosphere around her and though the monstrous fish were still swimming back and forth, to her they were simply background—part of the scenery.

"Okay, Grandmothers," I said, turning to my teachers, "what is the lesson in this? I'm here with you, and I'm watching all these scenes coming and going, but I don't understand what any of them mean."

Again there was silence and then I noticed that groups of people had begun to gather on the sand. Everything was morphing again and here was yet another scene. Now men in battle gear stood forth—Roman soldiers wearing helmets, togas, and sandals and although they didn't look particularly menacing, all of them carried spears. "Good God," I said to myself as other figures came into view, "there are slaves with them—long lines of them." The slaves moaned as they stumbled along, their hands tied behind their backs, but the misery of their captives seemed to be having no effect at all on the soldiers. They had been ordered to move these people and I watched as they matter-of-factly herded them along.

"Now what does *this* mean?" I asked the Grandmothers, and no sooner was the question out of my mouth than in the midst of the soldiers and slaves there appeared an imposing object. Fixed in the middle of the pathway where they were walking stood an enormous stone head. It looked like the head of a god, and stood fifteen or twenty feet high. I studied it and as I did, I recalled that Roger and I had several like it in Angkor Watt.

As I trained my eyes on the features of this head, it began to breathe, blowing its breath on the soldiers. 'God' breathed on them and as this took place, their spears, helmets, and battle gear began to glow. Their faces came alive too, and in an instant the entire scene moved from tones of sepia, into full color. As light flooded everything, I saw the soldiers turn and look at the captives as if for the first time. The soldiers were coming to life! Now they noticed the captives, and as they did, the soldiers softened and became more fully real. I felt my heart expand as I observed what was taking place and as I was mulling it over, the scene changed yet again.

Now I saw my mother. She was lying in her bed in the room she'd occupied during the last two years of her life. She was in the process of dying. Her labored breaths were coming and going and she looked the way she did on that final day when I'd sat with her, waiting for the end. Once again I saw her working her way towards her death and as I watched her labored breathing, waves of grief washed over me, and along with the grief—awe, shock, peace, reverence—all of it. Giving into these feelings, I wept quietly. I was sitting beside her, watching her and loving her when I heard a voice. **"All are evolving,"** it said. **"Always, and at every moment, each one is evolving."**

"Yes," I answered the voice, and as I thought about it, I understood that *there is no moment in time when we are not evolving.* "All of us," I said and then I cried and cried, marveling at what I was feeling as my heart slowly opened.

Every form of life the Grandmothers showed me on this journey had been in the process of evolution. Starting with the man I had thought of as the cruel therapist, the one who was turning a son against his mother. He was evolving and was acting the way he was because he had come only so far in his own evolution. The monstrous animals and fish too, the lovely feminine spirit in the water, the Roman soldiers and the slaves were also evolving. All of them. When I remembered how color had flooded the soldiers and brought them to life, I understood that I had witnessed an important moment in their evolution as human beings. And my mother, taking her final breaths there in her last hour on earth had also been evolving.

At last the Grandmothers spoke. **"All are evolving,"** they said, **"and all are blessed."** I sobbed in earnest when I heard the truth in their words. "All *are* blessed," I agreed, "all."

"Those who cause pain to others," the Grandmothers said, **"are at a certain point in their evolution and cannot be anywhere but there. Levels of evolution run the full spectrum,"** they explained, "from those slow moving, slow thinking life forms you saw earlier (the monstrous fish and prehistoric-looking animals), **to that blithe spirit who loves the light, and *is* the light. Degrees of evolution run the gamut,**" they said and as I listened, tears continued to pour down my face. "**Don't be surprised when these primitive ones show up in your life.**" I blinked when I heard this, but the Grandmothers gave me a reassuring smile. "**After all,**" they said, "**the primitive ones are still here on earth. All levels of life are here.**

"**The line of evolution for man, for animals, and for the planet itself is very long. Countless degrees of intelligence contribute to this line, and when we say 'intelligence,'**" they explained, "**we include the intelligence, not only of the mind, but of the heart. So within the human family you will find all sorts of people—bankers, teachers, healers, laborers—everyone, and each one is at her/his own level of development. There are advanced souls—like the Mahatma Gandhi, Mohammed, and the Dalai Lama—and now and then an entirely pure being like Jesus the Christ, the Buddha, or Sathya Sai Baba appears on earth. At the same moment you have drunks, drug users, and lost ones,**" they said. "**On earth you will encounter those who suffer and those who create suffering, those who bring joy and those who create misery for themselves and others. Everyone and everything is present on your planet. Present at every moment,**" they said, "**passing in and out of life.**"

After that, all was silence. Then before me there appeared a river, and in it swam countless varieties of fish—the slowest and lowest, the brightest, the quickest, and the lightest. They swam together in every color of the rainbow and I saw that all of them belonged to the river and moved within the same current. Each one was perfect just as it was and, at the same moment, each was involved in the process of becoming. The faster, more graceful ones easily circumvented the slower, heavier ones while others, not so quick, not so graceful, bumped up against one another as they swam. "**We are showing you the River of Life,**" the Grandmothers said. "**It is full of swimmers, swimmers of all kinds. The River of Life has existed for millennia and will go on forever. That is life!**" they said, their eyes lit by their smiles.

"**Notice how the movement for all the swimmers is forward, always forward. The movement is now. It exists only now—this minute. No two swimmers are evolving at the same pace,**" they said, "**nor should they be. Each one is perfect just as they are, perfect within this moment."

Looking me up and down, the Grandmothers said, **"Your job is to be yourself, your job is to love and recognize your own perfection and live it. Not wishing your life away, not bemoaning your fate and thinking you should be somewhere else or someone else. And not expecting anyone else to be different from who and what they are either. After all,"** they said, **"you are swimming together in the River of Life. So shouldn't you respect your fellow swimmers?"**

"Grandmothers," I said, "beloved teachers, I thank you. What you've taught me today is beyond beautiful."

"Bless the man who brought all this up for you. By his seemingly cruel act, he gave you the opportunity for far greater understanding. And..." they chuckled as they kept their eyes on me, **"if you pay attention, you'll find that everyone you meet will do this for you—each one will give you an opportunity for greater understanding."**

"Ahhhh," I groaned, not knowing whether to laugh or cry at this prospect. "Thank, you, Grandmothers," I said, "thank you."

"For women, men are 'the other.'"

At the 2010 California Gathering of the Grandmothers a man who works in maximum security at a men's prison, spoke. Chris had come to the Gathering with his wife and as he participated with us, he found himself deeply affected by the Grandmothers' message and by how sincerely we were attempting to live it. "The men I work with have little understanding of themselves, little understanding of others, and especially of women," he said. "I really hope you women will be able to call up the power of yin and stand steady for these men. They're lost. They don't know how to rein in the raging power of yang and it's almost run them to death. If women can't anchor the power of yin for themselves and everybody else, men like the ones I work with don't have a chance. These guys are so dead inside they can't help themselves. Please step into your power," he pleaded, "do it for yourselves and for the men who can't do it." What he shared with us throughout that weekend touched us deeply and his plea has continued to lie on my heart.

Thinking of him again and then remembering Alice, whose husband and son had 'turned on her,' served as a wake-up call for me. Now I had two painful examples of how damaging out-of-balance yang energy could be. Many times I'd felt the intensity of yang energy coming at me and, like most women, I had been on the receiving end of male aggression. If I was going to be honest I had to admit that not only had this intense, thrusting energy, come charging at me, but sometimes it had come *from me*. Men weren't the only ones whose yang energy could get out of balance. "My God," I whispered to myself, "when yang isn't in harmony with yin, it's *really* not a pretty picture—not for anyone."

"Grandmothers, I said the next time I went to them, I have an important question today," but before I could get out another word, they said, **"Women and men have real difficulties understanding each other."** "Yes," I sighed, "that pretty much covers it, Grandmothers. I've been thinking about the power of out-of-balance yang. What's the best thing we can do to deal with this aggressive energy when it comes at us? Sometimes these attacks aren't obvious and sometimes they're right in our face, but however they show up, what's the best way to deal with them?"

The Grandmothers didn't say anything for quite awhile. In fact, I began to wonder if they'd heard me. I was studying them, asking myself what I should do now, when I saw what looked like an electric flash behind them—a fast, jagged movement in the air. It was that sharp, thrusting energy of yang, and before I knew it, Bam! It came flying at me! But just before it hit me, something intervened.

"Oh!" I cried, as I watched the energy of yin and yang interacting. When the yang projectile hurtled forward, just before it hit my body, the energy of yin, which had expanded at its approach, magnetized yang to itself. This 'yin intervention' prevented the missile of yang from landing in my heart and solar plexus. And because yin had called yang to itself, I experienced no wounding or shock. "Wow!" I said to myself, "That was so effortless. It was like watching a dance movement." Yin had drawn yang into a dance with itself. Then I remembered how Sandra from the Netherlands had demonstrated a similar movement for us at the last Gathering. She had taught us how to 'receive' the energy of yang in an effortless way.

"Grandmothers," I said, "please explain how this works. Not everyone will understand this dancing stuff unless you can make it very clear." **"Yes,"** they said, **"we'll explain, but we especially want *you* to get 'the dancing stuff.'"** "Okay, okay," I agreed and laughing, they said, **"When someone projects yang in that missile-like movement,"** and here they pantomimed the thrust of yang, **"what is needed is a yin receptor. At such a time, yang needs to be held and you just witnessed this taking place."**

"Yes, Grandmothers," I said, "I did. Yin expanded and drew the energy of yang to itself. It actually contained it. I understand that yang needs to be received, needs to be understood. I get that. I've even experienced it. For instance, when I'm feeling 'yang,'" I added, "feeling all charged up with energy, I want to be able to express the feelings I have and I want to be understood. I don't mean that I want things to get confrontational," I explained. "I don't want to get into an argument or a battle with someone. Rather, I just want to be received and understood. And when I feel like that, I'm even willing to have my energy blunted or offset a little if necessary, so I can 'play' with the person I'm relating to. I want us to 'dance' together. I don't want to scare them off. I just want to enjoy our exchange." The Grandmothers had me thinking.

"Grandmothers," I asked, "are you showing me that when men thrust themselves at us in those aggressive ways, they're not trying to annihilate us? They're not heat-seeking missiles?"

"Except in extreme cases, they are *not* trying to annihilate you," they replied, **"because, as you just pointed out, then they wouldn't have anyone to play with. This is simply what yang does. That forward thrust of power is its signature. You need to learn the ways of yang,"** they said, eyeing me seriously. **"Men *are* mostly yang and so it's important for you to understand this. It's their way, and it's very different from your way."**

"I get that," I said, "I really do," and then, to emphasize the difference between the sexes, the Grandmothers began to demonstrate the intricate patterns of connection that women make when *they* come together. First they showed me a group of women sitting together in a room and from observing them I could tell that these women didn't know each other. There wasn't much talking going on and although nothing was actually being 'said,' there was still a lot of connecting taking place. As I stood back and observed these women, I noticed all sorts of looping patterns and energy flows in the room. There were back and forth movements, up and down waves, various weavings, and encircling designs—and all of them were moving between and among the women. Even when these women did begin to speak to one another, most of their communication continued to be non-verbal. "Maybe this is why women are so good at multi-tasking," I mused as I watched the varieties of patterns being woven among them. Woven with seemingly little effort, woven simultaneously, and created on many levels. "Connect/exchange, connect/exchange," I chanted as I observed them. "This way of relating is entirely natural to women. To them it's as easy as breathing."

Next, the Grandmothers showed me a group of men, and now, although less actual connecting seemed to be taking place, there was *something* going on. In place of the multiple exchanges I'd seen with the women, here were a series of forward thrusts. These movements weren't necessarily physical and in some cases they weren't even verbal, but they certainly were potent. "Pow!" they broadcasted as one man shot his energy forth to let the group know who, what, and where he was. Then another volleyed the first one's energy back to him or picked up his thrust and sent it on to someone else. One and then another, one and then another, and as the men parried and sparred, energy rocketed back and forth between them.

The men wore looks of pleasure as they volleyed like this, but as I felt the 'pow-pow-power' of their energy, I began to hear my own nervous laughter. What I was witnessing was making me very uncomfortable. Although these men were clearly enjoying volleying energy back and forth, their interaction was putting me on edge. To them, it was a game and they relished the rivalry of yang's push and pull. They reminded me of football players, smacking and punching one other as they came off the field. "Yang, yang, yang, yang," I sang to myself as I observed.

I began to chuckle then at how different the energies of yin and yang are, and when I looked up, I caught the Grandmothers' eyes. **"Expect men to be different from you,"** they said, **"observe them and don't judge them. We understand that their aggression can feel frightening to you; it's not comfortable to women because it's foreign to them."**

"Yes, Grandmothers," I said, "you're right about that. It makes me nervous." **"We understand. Sometimes their aggression feels like an attack, and when yang becomes too far extended, too far out of balance, it *can* become dangerous.**

"But that's not the usual case. This energy will thrust itself at you because its forward push is one of the aspects of yang. Pow!" they shouted as they threw up a fist, imitating yang's aggressive action and I jumped as it shot out at me. "This is what yang does," they said, shrugging nonchalantly. "**You need to learn how to open to it and receive it. Practice!**" they said, and my eyes grew wide. "**Assume that men will propel this energy at you because they will. And when that happens,**" they said, giving me a benign look, "**sidestep it a bit as you open to receive it. Don't take it to heart, but instead simply hold it.**"

"Oh," I replied, "I see. I'm not supposed to take delivery. You're asking me to instead move into the consciousness of the container. I remember how you called this 'The power of the container to hold everything.' You taught us about this earlier."

"That's right," the Grandmothers replied. "**Be the container and do this little sidestepping movement,**" they said, demonstrating a slight feint to the side. "**Do this for a while, until you become more comfortable with yang, until you're so steady, so powerful that you no longer need to step off to the side. At some point you'll stop being disturbed by what's coming at you and will automatically open to contain its energy.**

"**Men will be your greatest challenge. This is true because for women, men are '*the other*.' Their nature isn't like yours, and this is even true for women who have learned how to '*out yang*' men. Some women have learned how to act like men, but a woman's nature cannot not fully accept what is counter to it. A woman may try to think and act like a man,**" they said, "**but try as she may, she will never *be* a man. For women, man is '*the other*.'**

"**We want you to teach women what we are showing you now and share your experiences of '*the other*,' together. As you become more comfortable with the differences between yin and yang, you'll start observing with new eyes and what may have at first looked to you like 'yang attacks' will no longer threaten you. It's the nature of yang to come on strong,**" they said, "**and yang must express its nature. Just as it's yin's nature to hold and support, it's yang's nature to move forward with force.**

"**When yang is in proper balance, it will move forward playfully and joyfully, and when it's out of balance, it will do so in destructive ways. But, each time you remember to become the container and hold yin steady, you will help bring yang back into balance.**" And when they said this, my mind immediately went to Chris, the man who worked at the men's penitentiary and spoke to us as the Gathering.

"Please step into your power," he had pleaded, "do it for yourselves and for the men who can't do it."

"Overly aggressive yang has done damage in the past and continues to do so," the Grandmothers said. **"Some people—mostly men, but a few women too—become so dominated by unbalanced yang that they commit horrendous crimes against life. But for the most part, the thrusting, aggressive energy of yang is only slightly out of balance."**

"Humm," I mused, "so in most cases yang is not *so* far out of line." "That's right," they said. **"Most of what you feel when you're around men is simply the energy of yang expressing itself. Let yang be what it is, and in the meantime,"** they said, stroking me lovingly, **"hold steady as the container that you are. You just be yourself.**

"Step into the steadiness of the container that holds whatever comes to it, and if the thrusting energy that's coming at you is dangerous, you will feel and know it. Sidestep then. You are not the target of this energy," they said, *"you are never the target of what people send to you,* **so you needn't take delivery of it. Whether the energy coming at you is a little out of balance or a lot out of balance, your response can be the same. Hold steady from your powerful position as the container,"** they said. **"Observe and accept that it is simply the energy of yang coming at you. Sidestep it when necessary, and *do not take delivery."***

"Grandmothers," I said, "I'm not sure I'm clear about this. As you spoke just now I felt the energy of attack that Alice talked about coming at me, and it felt awful.

"Your body doesn't lie, so observe this again, but this time, hold your place as the container. Hold a position of wisdom, acceptance and observation. When you do that, if what is coming at you is seeking to hurt you, you'll recognize it. And should that be the case, make that small turn away from it to deflect it. Side step. You will feel the difference in your body—the difference between the simple thrusting of yang and the distorted energy of yang attacking. You will know when to side step," they said. **"Your body will teach you."**

"Show me a little more, Grandmothers," I said. "I want to get to the point where I'm not afraid of this energy." There was a moment of silence then and after that I saw a missile of yang hurtling toward

Alice. But this time she stood in her power as 'the container,' and as she held to that position, the missile missed her and fizzled out. Her position of oneness with the container had kept her objective enough to watch it and *not* take delivery. The barbs, the gibes, the put-downs that came shooting at her were as nothing, and though they flew at her like arrows, they missed her, hit the wall, and slid down. And as she observed it all, it was as if the entire event was something impersonal (which it was), something that had nothing to do with her.

I watched then as Alice expanded until it seemed that she held everything within herself. I was so connected with her that I felt the same feeling of expansion in my own body as well. "The container that we actually are is so great," I marveled, "so connected to the Fabric of Life, that these little *things* that come flying at us are nothing. When I move into the consciousness of the container, I become huge and everything else dwindles by comparison.

"So, Grandmothers," I said, taking in a breath, "this is a different way of dealing with the aggression of yang. We don't attack 'the attacker'; we don't fight back. Instead, we observe what's happening and simply expand." I thought about this for a minute and mused, "It seems like there are two phases to this way of working. One is, if you can dance with the energy of yang that's coming at you, you do. But if the energy coming at you isn't an invitation to dance but is instead a projectile looking to destroy, you expand into oneness with the container that holds all life. And that state of expansion makes whatever is coming at you seem like a mini, mini flea on the biggest elephant that ever lived."

I giggled at my image. "Our bodies know the difference," I continued. "Our bodies will tell us when to merge into the container and let the little personality stuff just drop off. And when we don't react with fear to the runaway energy of yang, it can't feed on us. And each time it can't feed, it becomes less and less. Hummmm," I said, shaking my head. "It's simple. We don't feed it," I said, and when I glanced at the Grandmothers, they smiled in agreement.

CHAPTER EIGHT

The Sisterhood of Women Will Bind the Family of Humanity Together

"There is work for all of you now, whether you live in the New World or the Old."

The next time I journeyed to the Grandmothers I went just to be in their presence. And as I sat in their circle, reflecting on how magnificent they were, they said, **"We want to speak to you again of what we told you the last time you were in Europe. You will be going there again soon and you need to understand this."** Before I returned home from the last Gathering in Belgium, the Grandmothers told me there was a different focus to their work in Europe than in the United States. I hadn't understood what they meant at the time and after I returned home, I forgot all about it. "Grandmothers," I said, "I didn't understand what you meant when you said that. Please explain it to me."

"America and all the lands you refer to as the New World are relatively free of historical conditioning. Relatively," they emphasized and by their look, I understood that in the New World people are not *as* heavily conditioned by history, but are conditioned nonetheless.

"Wherever, over long periods of time, there have been wars, invasions, conquests, and large populations of people," they said, **"you will find layer upon layer of conditioning. In those places, psychic energy gets locked into the land. There are many heavy build-ups of old energy that infuse the earth, and these heavy build-ups affect everyone and everything. When people are contending with the vibrations of all that's gone before them, and when, on a daily basis, they are coping with layers of old energy, it can be difficult for them.**

"These areas that we are speaking of comprise much of what you call the Old World—the Middle East, Europe, most of Asia, and several other places. There are fewer layers of old energy in the lands of the New World," they said, meaning the Americas, Australia, New Zealand, and various island nations. "Whenever you have traveled between the Old World and the New, you have felt these differences," they said and looked at me for confirmation.

"Yes," I said, "I know what you mean." I'd noticed what they were talking about, and the more time I had spent learning from them, the more pronounced these differences had seemed to be. More than once the energy in certain places on earth had made me sick, and my physical reaction to these sites had puzzled and worried me. As the Grandmothers continued to eye me now, I realized how motivated I was to learn what they were sharing.

"Before Europeans came to the New World, those lands were occupied by people with a strong connection to and an understanding of the earth," they said. "Indigenous people lived in relative harmony with nature—they didn't try to dominate it. And although they engaged in warfare with each other, it was on a much smaller scale. Their world was not a paradise, but neither was it marked by the excesses of yang energy that long ago began to consume the Old World.

"Those of you whose forebears settled in the New World do not realize the blessing that was bequeathed to you by these original peoples. Because of the legacy of these original peoples, it is easier for those in the New World to connect with Mother Earth. It's easier for you to access the natural world of spirit. Unfortunately," they said, shaking their heads sadly, "most of you have not taken advantage of the generous gift the ancestors of the land left you.

"But today, as the energies of yin and yang begin to shift, we are calling you to align yourselves with the energy of the earth. We ask you not to waste any more time talking about it, but to do it. We ask you to claim your connection to Mother Earth, to stand tall, and live each moment in Beauty/Power, in Power/Beauty. Over the past few years we have shown you how to live like this, and as long as you are willing to learn what we have come to share, we will continue to teach you.

"There is work for all of you now, whether you live in the New

World or the Old. Many people in the Old World are beginning to hold the light steady now; so steady that it is penetrating the heavy layers of conditioning which have burdened the earth there. As they consistently work with the Net of Light, the points of light that these people actually *are*, are beginning to glow more and more brightly," they said, smiling. "They are becoming more beautiful, more powerful.

"When you link through the Net of Light and work together, the power of your combined light is able to break through the hardened crusts that were formed by all the wars, invasions, and cruelties that long beset the countries of the Old World. A few weeks ago in Belgium and then again in Holland you gathered to reclaim the sacred connection to the land there. The most important work you can do in the Old World," they said, "is to align with the Net of Light and magnify its power to uplift the land. As the land is lifted, so will the people be lifted, and as the people lift their consciousness, so will the land lift. The connection between the people and their land must be re-formed and fortified.

"Those of you in the New World have other tasks before you," the Grandmothers said. "You don't need to break through heavy conditioning in order to connect with the earth. You already have access to the earth, but *you need to use it!*

"Many in the New World, and especially in the United States have been drugged by a fog of materialism, a fog that's grown so thick that it's blinding you to the truth of your existence. You have lived in a numbed state for so long now that you've forgotten who you are and why you're here. Many people in your country spend all their time dreaming of *more, more and more. More!*" they cried, pantomiming this condition. *"I want more...I need more....Give me more....*

"This fog you've immersed yourselves in is dangerous!" they cried. Then they clapped their hands and shouted, "You must wake up! *Now!* If you continue in this drugged state, if you continue to worship 'the god of More,' you will miss the reason you were born."

The Grandmothers stood quietly for a moment and then they said, "You in the New World who *are* waking up have the opportunity to become a lighthouse that beams to others, providing encouragement to those who are seeking light. *This* is what we are asking you to do, and we're asking you to do it because you *can* do it!

"Stand tall now and feel your connection with the Earth. Feel your connection with the Net of Light and as you do this, express the Power/Beauty that you are. It's a simple thing we're asking of you," they said, "but you must be willing to wake up in order to do it."

"Grandmothers," I interrupted, "I want to be sure I'm clear on this. Would you explain once more this difference between the work in Europe and in America? I want to make sure I get it."

"In Europe people are drilling deep. They are plunging through layers of past conditioning in the land and in themselves," the Grandmothers said, watching to be sure I was following them. "They are reawakening the ancient power sites on that continent, awakening the feminine/masculine harmony that existed long ago in Old Europe. They are waking up the sacredness of their land and realigning themselves with it.

"They must be brave to do this work, because as they move through the psychic layers that were laid down long ago to prevent them from reaching the Source, they cannot give in to fear, but must push on. The Net of Light will be a powerful ally for them as they go forward with this work.

"In America and other parts of the New World, what you must do is somewhat different. The land is awake. It is the people who are asleep. Drugged by intense materialism, infected with an addiction to 'more,' this low-frequency energy has spread like a virus all over the world but is *deeply* entrenched in the United States.

"The task in America is to shake off this drugged state that causes you to chase endlessly after the toys of this world. To turn your focus inward, not outward," they said, eyes on me, "and allow the purity of the natural world to support you. You must be aware of the states of creeping unconsciousness that blanket your country. The Net of Light will support you in this," they assured me. "Each time you think of the Net of Light, it will keep you focused on who you are and what you are here to do.

"We will support you wherever you live. We will hold you steady and remind you of the importance of the work at hand. Don't forget," they laughed, "we work with and through you, so of course we will stand by you.

"If what we are saying rings true to you, call on us or on any form of the Divine you love. Gather together to share our messages or other messages that help you come awake. Use the process of sharing truth with one another as a discipline to help yourself stay alert. And do it to keep your attention on your communion with the Divine. We are waiting for you," the Grandmothers said. "It is time."

"Everything that lives desires to love and be loved."

Shortly after this message, our local group began to prepare for the next Gathering in Laguna Beach. Although the group would handle the practical side of the Gathering, we would need the Grandmothers' guidance for the program.

"Grandmothers," I said as I came before them, "I need you to show me the purpose of this Gathering so we can plan for it." Minutes went by and they didn't say anything, so I repeated, "I really need your guidance, Grandmothers, and I'll wait for it as long as it takes."

But this time, no sooner were the words out of my mouth than in the space before me stood a tall pole. It was the only thing present so I couldn't help but be impressed by its height. The Grandmothers were watching me intently. "You're teaching me something with this pole, aren't you?" I said and then, responding to its upright structure, I stood a little straighter myself. When they smiled knowingly, I realized I was to emulate the pole. **"If you hold to this straight posture,"** the Grandmothers' said, **"you will encourage others to also hold to it."**

"Thank you," I bowed to them, "but now please tell me now about the purpose of this Gathering. **"Our message is increasing in depth, and having a greater effect on those who work with us. We have a purpose for everyone we draw to us, and each person will flower in a different way. Each of them will bloom and bear fruit, and their fruit, their expression of our message, will be distinct from all others.**

"There is great diversity in what we are bringing to Earth. Because we encompass all life, and know each one's strengths and gifts, we can bring forth their special qualities.

"Everything that lives desires to love and be loved," they held my gaze as they spoke. **"This is true of *all*. The way you give and receive love is an expression of your individuality. Everyone who comes to our Gatherings has a unique potential for love, a potential far**

greater than they know. They carry divine love within the cell beds of their body. We stand ready to fire new thoughts within them, to activate greater health, and to open them to greater love than they can imagine.

"Many great ones who've come to earth have told you that you are divine, but none of you yet understand what that means," they smiled. "We have come to help you *experience* the truth of your divinity. And the longer you work with us, the more time you spend with us, and the more often you share our teachings with one another, the more you will recognize who you really are."

What they were telling me was beautiful and I knew how important it was, but my mind was still fixated on my question. "Grandmothers," I repeated, "What should be the purpose of this Gathering? I'm trying to get the practicalities in place before our meeting tomorrow," I said, a little embarrassed by my dogged persistence.

"Dive deep into your own greatness," they said and shot me a challenging smile. "Each of you must do this! No exceptions! You can work with us more easily when you are together than you can when you are on your own. Your communion with us is stronger when you're in community. Your feelings of connection to each other and of connection to the world are stronger when you are in communion with us. Within the words we have just spoken to you lies the purpose of this Gathering," they said at last. "You will decipher it as you go over it."

Their mood seemed to lighten then. "It's a good time for you to gather." They nodded their heads up and down. "There are many women's groups forming at this time. Women are becoming aware of the power of true sisterhood, a sisterhood that cuts across nationalities, languages, and cultures. We're happy about this," the Grandmothers said and swung their skirts from side to side. "Wherever women come together and share their experiences, there is power.

"The world needs to hear from you. The world is ready for our message now and so you must speak out. Of course there are those who do *not* want to hear from you," they shrugged. "Those who want to hold onto old patterns of dominance and separation don't want to hear from you, but those patterns are beginning to fall apart now, so you'll encounter fewer and fewer of these people.

"In recent years it has become evident that something different is needed in the world. When women work together, they foster a connected human family. *This* is something different," they said, "and this sisterhood of women will bind the family of humanity together."

"Ahhhh," I sighed as I listened. What they were saying was so true! But my feelings of relief were short lived as suddenly images of women competing with one another, jockeying for position and distrusting one another rushed into my mind. Aghast at where my mind had flown, I watched these images play out, but when the Grandmothers flicked their fingers, all those scenes vanished.

"Eh!" they said, "that's over!" and I stared at them, wondering what this meant. They laughed at me and said, "You need to help each other now. Women helping women, women listening to women, women holding and supporting one another. By behaving like that, you will help men too. When women feel supported, they also hold, support, and enfold men." And smiling happily, the Grandmothers added, "Then no one is left out.

"The movement to reclaim the family of humanity will come from women," they said. "Enjoy your new-found sisterhood and know that each time you communicate with one another as real human beings, you get a piece of yourself back. A valuable piece of yourself—one you have sorely missed. *This* is what happens at these Gatherings.

"Greet one another from your heart," they said, "and begin to relate to *all* women in this way. You'll find that it won't be difficult for you to see past the societal masks women wear. It will become easier and easier for you to make real contact with one another. To go beyond roles and expectations and communicate heart to heart, sister to sister.

"We ask the older ones of you to hold your arms open for the younger ones. The younger ones have been made brittle by the pressures of the world today, and this has left them feeling cut off from this sisterhood. So hold your arms open to your younger sisters, to your daughters, to your granddaughters. They need you.

"Hold one another and as you do that, together women of all ages will hold the men. This holding of one another will create a wonderful flow, a sharing of love. It's time," they said, beaming love at one another and at me. "It will feel to you like you're coming home!" they cried, and holding up their hands, they blessed me.

"*You are of the female line, the mothers of the earth.*"

After this journey I didn't go to them again for several weeks. I needed a break from the intensity, needed to live a somewhat 'normal' life for a while. So for two or three weeks I cooked, worked in the garden, saw a few clients, and started some sculptures. And when my 'normal time' was over and I was once again ready for learning, on we went.

"Grandmothers," I said, returning to them for the second time that day, "This morning you showed me why more women don't step forward to carry your message. You said, '**They lack belief in their own greatness.**' Now I have another question for you. You see us as we are and you also see the world as it is. So, given that what you say women are and what the world says women are is so different, how can we start *believing* in this greatness within us? And then *act* on it?" They smiled broadly when they heard this; they liked my question.

Pointing behind me, the Grandmothers motioned me to turn around and take another look at the two female figures I'd been working on. These were women from an earlier time in history. As I examined them, the Grandmothers said, "**You can't look back in history to find feminine role models.**"

"Yes, Grandmothers," I said and, as I thought it over, I realized I heartily agreed with them. As far as I could see, there were few, if any, historical role models for women to emulate. And as I continued to think about it, I noticed that off to the side of us there was a fire burning. When I turned to get a better look at it, I could feel its heat.

"Grandmothers," I said, "you're using this fire to illustrate something, aren't you? You don't waste a thing or do anything except for a good reason, so you're showing me something with this fire. Hummm," I said as I reflected on it, "I think I get it. You're letting me feel the fire of Shakti, the fire within women. Is this it?" By now the Grandmothers were looking at me with a quiet intensity, so I quickly added, "Shakti is the elemental power of life in our body and in our spirit."

"**Call on it!**" they commanded, their voices strong. "**Call it up. This fire is the life force within you. Women hold the spirit of Shakti. That's why you are the ones who carry babies, why you hold a wellspring of feeling within you, and why there are always more women than men who follow a spiritual path. You carry pure life force,**" they said. "**Shakti.**

— 104 —

"Think of this now," they said, "and give yourself permission to feel it." They paused for a few moments and then they asked me, "Where do you feel it?"

"It's right in the center of my body," I said. "It's running from my solar plexus on down." And when I said that, my body began to make a series of subtle movements, rolling slightly from side to side, from front to back, and then up and down.

"Life force," they repeated, nodding to affirm what was happening in my body. "This is where life comes from. Women are the carriers of life," they said and then they ran their eyes over me. "Do you realize what that means?"

"I.... I don't think I do, Grandmothers," I stammered. I was starting to wonder exactly where they were going with this. "You carry the fire of Shakti inside yourself," they said, "and through it you bring life into form. Without you," they bored their eyes into mine, "the world would end.

"This is a basic truth of life, a truth that has been minimized and hidden, its importance trivialized and denied. In fact, over time the denial of the power of the Feminine Principle has become institutionalized. Has anyone ever said these words to you," they asked: "'Without you, the world would end'?" I looked at them in surprise and shook my head no.

"You have been lied to, you have been dominated, and you have been controlled," the Grandmothers said, their eyes fierce. "You have been treated like property. And," they bore into me, "many women are still treated like that today. You...Are...Shakti," they drew the words out slowly and as they did, they began to rise upward until twelve massive women towered over me. "You are life force itself," they proclaimed. "This is the truth.

"You can trust the force that pulses in your veins, the force that flows through your blood and through your breath. You carry life!" they declared, "and because of who you are as a woman, you are worthy of the deepest respect. Your part in the human drama is a great one. You are *utterly* necessary.

"It's time to own the truth of yourself. The lies you have been told about the nature of woman—" they rolled their eyes. "Ridiculous! Dismiss them. Dismiss them once and for all and instead, feel the force of life within your body. Place your awareness there.

"This pulsing power came to you through your mother, through her mother, and through her mother before her. You are of the female line, the mothers of the earth." They looked me up and down then and cried, "Mothers of the earth, step forward! We are calling you.

"If you are at last ready to awaken from the *big sleep*, if you are ready to claim greatness, you must stop pretending that you aren't important, stop pretending that you aren't much. Instead, call on the fire within you. Call up the power of Shakti until you feel it. It's *real*," they said, fixing me with their eyes. "This power serves life; it is a blessing for the earth. For too long it has been told to hide itself away, diminished, and made to feel ashamed of itself, ashamed of its loving, giving beauty.

"We are calling women to power," the Grandmothers said, "calling them for the good of everything that lives. It's time to return to balance," they said, their heads nodding happily, "and we remind you that for this, women must lead."

CHAPTER NINE

Antidote to Fear

"....much of the earth still lies in a sleep state."

The Grandmothers had been right when they said I'd be going to Europe again. At the end of September my husband and I took a vacation to Southern Italy to visit a friend and explore the area. But though the food on this trip was delicious and the towns and landscapes were beautiful, while driving from area to area there, I noticed some uncomfortable feelings coming up in me. And after we'd been home for a couple of days and the weird sensations continued, I went to the Grandmothers. "These strange feelings I'm having," I said to my wise teachers, "started on our Italian trip, and I don't understand them. They don't feel good. In fact, they're scary and uncomfortable, but the odd and haunting sensations and thoughts that keep coming up seem to be somehow important. I don't understand what's going on with all this, Grandmothers," I said. "Please help me get to the lesson here."

"**This is important,**" they said. "**What you felt while you were on this vacation was a sadness, an ancient grief, and a closed-off quality *in the places* that you visited. In the people too,**" they added. "**You are still carrying this energy.**"

I shook my head, amazed by what they were telling me. "What came over me when we were there was so strong, Grandmothers," I said. "It just came out of nowhere. The frightening, almost sickening feelings that rose up were so powerful that they scared me. Whatever happened, it must be something like what you're describing."

"**There is a deadened quality in that part of the world,**" they said, "**and it's caused by a sadness lying within the earth. The land in this** region of Italy has been cut off from the Source for a long time. That's what caused this feeling in you.

"At one time this area of the world was deeply sacred, and the people there lived in communion with the Divine. They also communed with the earth," they paused, and shook their heads, "but although this is still an agricultural area, few people living there today understand their oneness with the earth. Nor do they understand their connection to Divinity.

"This region has been 'hard-capped,'" they said, and when I heard those words, a picture flashed in my mind—a dome that seemed to sit on top of Southern Italy. "That area is spiritually cut off from the Source," the Grandmothers explained. "Blocking the connection to the Source in this part of the world was something that was done purposefully. It was done a long time ago, but those in power today are continuing the process. The natural bond between the people, the land, and Divinity has been shut off for a long time.

"You will sometimes hear people in this part of the world call out 'Kore, Kore'!" the Grandmothers said. "This is part of their lexicon— their name for the ancient goddess of the earth. You know this as the story of Persephone and her mother, Ceres or Demeter. People in this region of the world continue to hold Kore in affection but they have lost their bond with her. They have also lost their bond with the earth. Disconnection from Mother Earth is common all over your planet today, but in this part of the world, lack of contact with the Source has deeply wounded the people. The discomfort you felt when you were there showed you this. That region of the world is truly suffering and most people who live there are asleep—deeply asleep."

As I listened to them speak, what came to my mind was the churches I'd seen on this trip—how dark they were and how filled with bloody statues—suffering Jesus and the saints. The dourness of the worshipers themselves, and the overall sense of longing and sadness inside the buildings. Some, like the basilica at Mt. San Angelo, had been built atop oracle sites and the power of the ancient site was still there, but so was a dark, depressed feeling. When I called on the Grandmothers in the cavern/chapel of Mt. San Angelo, I was so moved by the power in the site that I began to shake. But I also cried. The energy was profound, but heavy—very heavy.

Then I recalled another one, Santa Maria Di Leuca that sits at 'the end of the earth,' a promontory on the heel of the boot of Italy. Here once stood a temple to Minerva/Artemis and now, on the same spot, is a basilica devoted to Mary. This site has long been a pilgrimage destination that the Catholic faithful are expected to visit before they die.

On the plaza before the church stands an exceptionally high column of local stone, crowned by a statue of Mary, the Blessed Mother. The statue of brilliant white marble doesn't match the stone of the much older column on which it rests, and because of this marble missmatch, I wondered as I studied it about the statue the column had originally supported. Was it also of Mary? Minerva? Artemis?

Although there were busloads of pilgrims milling about the plaza on the day we arrived, I was able to find a place where I could sit quietly and call on the Grandmothers. I wanted to contact the presence of the Great Mother in this place, contact Her, whatever She was called. When at last I reached Her, She laughed at me. **"I don't care if you call me Minerva, Artemis, Mary, or something else. I am what I am—Mother to all."**

"Is it all right if I connect you with the Grandmothers, and the Net of Light?" I asked. **"Yes!"** She cried. Clearly She was happy for the opportunity to work through any and all forms of the Mother.

The statue of Mary at Santa Maria Di Leuca sits looking out on the sea. The wind blows and the sun shines on it, and, of all the sacred sites we visited on this trip, this is where I remember feeling truly happy. Perhaps because the site itself is not enclosed, it has a different sort of energy from those that are built over with churches or chapels. I had been puzzled by the lack of joy and lightness in the churches in this area of the world, especially because this land had once been sacred to the Mother. So after I got home, I asked the Grandmothers to explain this seeming dichotomy."

"There is a feast for the senses in this part of the world: the beauty of the land, the grace of the old cities and towns, ancient ruins, groves of olive trees, the appreciation of food, and of the language. But you were not happy on this trip because the sacred sites there have been deprived of joy. This has left the people only peripherally connected to the Divine and you felt that.

"For a long time no one has been able to hold the door to light open in this part of the world. The sacred sites there have been

closed down for so long that at this point most of them are clamped shut."

I looked up at them in shock, but the Grandmothers waved a dismissive hand at me and continued. "For eons primitive forms of patriarchy have been in control in this region of the world and these patriarchal structures continue to hold the door to light closed. This of course has affected the people there who have no inkling of who they really are. The people have been beaten down and cut off from the Source."

"Grandmothers," I said, reflecting on what they were telling me. "I tried calling on Kore in Southern Italy and again in Sicily. As soon as I found out about her, I called Her, and I was able to feel Her presence… but only a little," I admitted. "It wasn't easy to make contact. There seemed to be a sort of skin laying over everything—a skin too hard to penetrate." I shook my head as I recalled how puzzled I'd been by that.

"I worked with the Net of Light a lot on this trip, and that made it easier to feel some connection with the Divine. I specifically worked at Mt. San Angelo, at different spots around the southern coast, and in Sicily, but in most of the places on our route it felt like the ancient sites weren't alive enough to be able to support the Net. Power was buried somewhere in them, but I couldn't reach it. A couple of them responded to the Net of Light, let themselves be held by the Net, but there wasn't enough power in the sites themselves to enable them to broadcast light to others." I shook my head. "That's basically it," I said to my teachers and as I again looked up at them, I realized how confused all this had made me. "Okay," I said at last, "I give up. I've told you what it was like for me. All of this is totally beyond my understanding, but if you have something to teach me about it, please do."

"You need to understand that much of the earth today is lying in a sleep state," the Grandmothers said, "to understand that many cultures are unconscious of their connection with Divinity. This unconsciousness we speak of manifests itself in various ways at different places on earth. For instance, in your country, (the USA), it shows itself in the gross materiality of life. The push for *more*," they explained. "The same is true in China." "Oh God!" I moaned as I thought of the great numbers of people in China.

"When you travel, Sharon, you are seeking. That's what you do. On these 'vacation' trips you take, you seek a connection to love and when you find one, you look for ways to magnify it. This is all well and good, and let that continue to be your goal. But at the same time, be aware that you will not always be able to make the connection you are seeking.

"Few tourists have an inkling of the sort of travel you do—spiritually focused travel. Most people travel for sensory experiences only—for adventures. But you want more than that, and though what you felt on this trip was not especially pleasant, it was true. What you experienced was how shut down the consciousness in this part of the world is. It was painful for you," they said, "but don't worry about it any more. We will teach you now how to work with the Net of Light and lift the iron cap that lies over this part of the earth."

I perked up when I heard this, and when they saw that they had my full attention, the Grandmothers said, "Let's focus on a different subject now. Turn your mind back to the work you did in Ireland not long ago. Let the Gathering of the Grandmothers in Cork come back into focus. The work you began there—of tying the sacred sites in Ireland into the Net of Light—is still going on. So let go of Italy now and move back to the essence of what was done in Cork.

"As you focus on the great good that ensued from connecting the Irish power sites with the Net of Light, you will make that connection even stronger. Each time you think of what took place when you worked in Ireland, more light will flow into the Net of Light. This amplification of power can go on indefinitely," they said, "because there's no end to an open power site. It is connections like this one that will help lift all the hard capped areas on the earth."

As I focused again on the Gathering in Ireland, I saw waves of light rising up from the land there, rising up and flowing into the Net of Light. "There's a wellspring of power in Ireland, Grandmothers," I said, "that rushes up from the earth like…like an oil well! One gusher after another. Power, love, and beauty are shooting out of the earth there and washing over everything.

"When I compare this surging force to my feeble attempts to penetrate the hard cap on the sites in Italy, it makes me laugh. That work was exhausting while this is so joyful! It's fun to have your hand on the throttle!" I laughed. "That's how it feels and the light just keeps coming."

"**Let others know that they too can work this way,**" the Grandmothers said. "**Remind them that each time they think of the connection between open sites like those in Ireland and the Net of Light, more radiance fills the Net. Their thoughts will keep this work alive.**"

"There is no end to an open source," I repeat the Grandmothers' words. "No end. Calling on a source like this one keeps it open and when it's open, *it* does all the work," I mused as I watched light flood the Net and spill over the earth. Cascades of luminescence were now washing up against those sealed-off places I'd visited in Italy. I could see that already some of the hardness there was being worn away.

"Grandmothers," I called to them, "is there more?" "**Keep up this work,**" they said, "**but this is enough for now.**" "I will, I will," I promised.

The day after this session, I took out my travel diary and found another tidbit from our time in Italy. One afternoon while floating around in the Adriatic Sea near Gallipoli, I noticed how the pattern of sunlight on the water looked just like the Net of Light. So as I swam about, I began to work with the Net. I was singing to myself, dog paddling in the bay, when I suddenly became aware that the blocked energy around Gallipoli didn't feel as dense in the water as it did when I was standing on the land. As long as I was immersed in the water, I was able to more easily work with the Net of Light! So as I bobbed about, I began to magnify the power of the Net—humming to myself and lighting up connections between the cities, towns, and countries that fronted on the Adriatic Sea.

Then, to my surprise *the Net of Light began to web everything.* Light flooded the sea, flowed into the estuaries, rivers, basins, and streams and, following these watery pathways, made its way inland. As I marveled at how easy it was to work like this, I heard the Grandmothers say, "**Amplify the Net of Light within all the bodies of water on earth.**"

"Okay, Grandmothers," I said, "I get it. And I'll pass this learning on so others can work like this." "**Apply this discovery everywhere,**" they said. "**Each time you work from within the waters of the planet, you will easily empower the Net of Light.**" "Yes, Grandmothers," I agreed, "We'll do it."

"Go to the pure places in the land all over the earth."

The way my teachers explained what had happened in Italy made sense and although I was grateful to have this understanding, the uncomfortable feeling that had come up on our vacation was still with me. When this low energy continued to drag on, I decided to go to the Lower World and seek the help of the animal spirits. As soon as this thought crossed my mind, I became aware of a strong desire to be with Bear, a *need* to be with Bear. "Maybe," I said to myself, "it's also time to visit the earth spirits underneath the vortex in Sedona." Now that the idea of seeking help from the Lower World had come to me, I was sure the compassionate animals as well as the power source of the Red Rock country would be able to help.

"Bear, please forgive me," I said as soon as I saw him. "I haven't come to see you in a long time. I've been busy, busy, busy," I said. "I guess I thought being busy was what I was supposed to do, but I was wrong about that, and now I'm knocked flat. Getting hit like this came from out of nowhere," I explained; "it happened while I was on vacation. So now I'm coming to you asking for healing and guidance. And I also had a thought that it might be good to go to the power source under Sedona. Am I right about that?"

Bear tilted his shaggy head while he listened. Then he paused and seemed to be waiting for something, so I continued. "You may remember that I got hit by negative energy like this another time too. It was in Northern Italy that time and what happened then felt similar to what happened this time," I said. "I want to learn how to deal with negative energy like this, stuff that comes up, seemingly from out of nowhere. I'd like to really understand it. I *need* to understand it. I don't want to go through experiences like this again and again, Bear. Will you help me, please?"

He stretched a paw out then and drew me to himself. **"Listen to me,"** he said and then, **"come,"** he motioned, **"we will go to the spirits."** And before I could thank him or ask him anything more, we were there—standing inside the vortex in Sedona, inside the fiery, red rock. "Wow," I whispered under my breath. "Bear can journey here in a second! No time or space limitations for him."

As I took in the beauty of the landscape spread out before us, I became aware of a humming sound that seemed to be coming from deep within the earth and no sooner did I hear it, than I felt heat radiating outward from the rocks. "It's the generator of power!" I cried, "the generator inside the earth in this place, the one I saw before. It's blasting heat, just like a furnace and oh, God, does it feel good! The energy here is pure; not at all the way the energy felt in Italy. It was so sad there, Bear," I said as I recalled how bewildered I'd been by all that gloom and confusion. "I didn't realize it at the time, but that's what it was—so much sadness."

Bear reached for me and, pulling me close to his chest, said, **"You felt grief there. You felt the power of the cut-off. It's good to know of such things,"** he rumbled. And then, smacking me lightly with his massive paw, he said, **"but not good to carry them."**

"You're right, Bear," I gazed into his compassionate eyes, "and I've been carrying that sadness with me ever since." I stood quietly for a few moments and then shook my head, threw my shoulders back, and quickly stepped directly into the vortex, walked right into that pulsing, red rock power. And no sooner did I take that step than my sadness lifted. Tears came to my eyes and I gasped in relief. "Thank you! Thank you!" I whispered to Bear and to the spirits of the land. Waves of relief were washing over me now, and as the sadness continued to lift, one by one, I recalled the places I'd visited on that trip to Italy, the places that had continued to haunt me. Now it seemed the haunting was over.

I turned to the spirits of the land and asked them, "What can be done about that cut off of power in Southern Italy? There's so much suffering there." My question fell flat—answered by silence. No one was responding to me and so I repeated the question. I kept this up until waves of heat from the earth below my feet began to roll up and over me, making me hotter by the minute. The heat was intense and soon it claimed *all* my attention.

At last I realized that the spirits of the land *were* letting me know they'd heard me. This rise in temperature was a direct communication from the earth. "Okay," I said, "You're telling me something with this heat, but I don't know what it is." Then I thought again about what I'd experienced in Italy.

"The lack of spirit connection in that part of the world is a great tragedy," I said at last, but, growling low in his throat, Bear peered at me from under his lowered brows. **"It is a great sleep,"** he said. I looked at him with a question in my eyes, 'A great sleep'?" but he rumbled low to himself and would say no more.

The temperature dropped then and I was no longer uncomfortable. Now all was quiet and peaceful. In fact it was so quiet that I may have drifted off to sleep myself. I don't know for sure, but there was a long pause and the next thing I became aware of was seeing myself sitting with a pen in my hand, drawing. I was bent over a table making a map of the capped-off power places that I'd visited on the trip. Then I began to work with the Net of Light. I was using the map I'd drawn to connect those places with the power of Sedona. By using the map, I was able to send energy from the vortex/generator in Sedona to each place that I'd drawn.

I was absorbed in the map and was linking all the sites with the Net of Light, when the generator within the earth of Sedona began to pump power into each of them. This time there wasn't a transmission of heat, but there was a surging transmission of power. "This is good," I said to myself as I watched Southern Italy light up. "Here is something else we can do to magnify the power of the Net of Light. We can broadcast light from power sources like this one in Sedona to all the unawakened places on earth. This will break down resistance to the light and wear away any hard-capped areas."

"**Umph,**" Bear grunted and moved his big head up and down. "**Receive what the Source is giving you,**" he said, and when he said that, a hummm, hummm, humming started to run through me, its vibration so strong that I began to pulse and sway with it. "Thank you," I said to Bear and to the Red Rock country. Then I let myself fall into rhythm with that hum. I rested in its comforting vibration for a while and then there was only quiet. Quiet, and a sense of peace. After a long silence, I heard myself say, "I feel different now."

I did feel different. When that humming power started coursing through me, its rhythm somehow allowed me to let go of the last bit of the low frequency energy I'd picked up on that trip. "All of it is leaving now," I said to Bear and exhaled happily.

I took Bear's hand/paw in mine then. "Bear," I said, "it seems like we could also work like this at Mt. Shasta, in the Grand Tetons, in the Black Hills, at Joshua Tree—in so many places." I was thinking of the sacred sites I knew of in the American West, thinking of how we could connect them in light. As Bear nodded his shaggy head in agreement, I heard the holy man's voice. "**Yes,**" he said. "**Go to the pure places in the land. Let them support you, let them support the Net of Light.**"

"We will do that," I promised, and while I ruminated on what it would be like to work like this, Bear stood quietly beside me, taking everything in. He gently swayed back and forth, humming to himself, and lifting one paw, my beloved Bear blessed me.

"Keep your awareness focused in your heart."

A week after this journey I was scheduled to speak at a women's conference. The organizers were showing a film on the persecution of women in Europe during the Middle Ages and after viewing the film, different women were to speak. I was to be one of them. The film sounded important, but because of what I had just experienced with low frequency energy, it wasn't anything I was eager to see.

"Grandmothers," I said, when I went to them for guidance, "I am about to speak at a conference with a difficult topic and I don't want to pick up heavy energy there. Please help me stay in right relationship to everyone at this event. To stay clear of negativity," I said as I stepped into their Circle of Stones. "Let me be a pure vessel," I pleaded with my teachers. "I don't want to be distracted by anything. After what I've just learned from our Italian trip, I'm aware that up until now I haven't understood how to do that."

The Grandmothers chuckled at my self-evaluation. **"This is the most important thing for you,"** they said, and they drew themselves so close to me that we were stacked together like a box of crayons. We were standing in such a tight formation that I couldn't move. I felt like I was no longer my separate self but instead was part of a unit—a unit that the Grandmothers and I were now forming.

"Stay steady and don't be pulled off by negativity," they said, and I listened carefully. I was aware of their words, but more important than their words, was the way they were holding me. Being stacked together with them like this was communicating something very important and I felt it in my body. I was now as upright as they were, and with a Grandmother on each side of me, one at my front and one at my back, I had never felt so *totally* supported.

"We will lead you though the evening," they said, smiling at my response to this enforced closeness, **"but be sure to sit where you can quickly walk outside. You are correct in thinking that there will be negative energy at this event. There will be. You need to be able**

to stay objective to whatever comes up at this meeting and not get caught in it.

"Throughout the evening *keep your awareness focused in your heart. This is most important. There will be a lot of agitation at this event,*" they said, and as they said this, they showed me that the film would bring up past life memories and fears in some participants. "This is all we can tell you now, but know that we will surround you at this event. So stay close to us and stay in your heart."

The Grandmothers' advice proved to be golden. As it turned out, there was a great deal of agitation at this event, but because they had pulled me so close to them and ordered me to 'stay in your heart,' I was able to hold onto peace amidst the drama that ensued.

"You came to earth carrying a seed."

The next time I went to the Grandmothers, they shared the purpose of the upcoming California Gathering. "**The focus for this particular Gathering,**" they said, "**will be Presence and Partnership with the Divine. Many are searching,**" they said, "**searching at workshops, classes, conferences, and meetings. These events often center on topics of intellectual interest and some of the events also carry an emotional charge. But at many of them,**" they said, shaking their heads, "**something is missing.**" I was thinking about 'something is missing,' when a long-ago TV commercial popped to mind. An old woman held up what looked like a hamburger with a big bun and asked, "Where's the beef?" Laughing as they read my mind, the Grandmothers said, "***Presence* is the beef.**"

"Okay, Grandmothers," I responded, "I get it." But as I pondered 'Presence is the beef,' I happened to glance away from them for a moment and was surprised to notice that we were in the countryside. Here was a furrowed field, a seemingly endless plot of land, newly plowed. And as I studied it, I noticed that there was a woman standing in each furrow.

"**Furrows mark a place where things grow,**" the Grandmothers said. "**This is what we are showing you here. Each woman *is* a furrow so by her Presence and because of her divine connection, she holds a place of potential. In the place where she stands growth can take place. The fertile place that a woman holds allows her to feed and nurture many. At the next Gathering of the Grandmothers we will** ask each of you to awaken to the Presence within yourselves," they said. "**We will do this in order to bring *you* to fruition.**"

"Grandmothers," I shook my head, "I don't know what this means. Please be clear." "**You came to earth carrying a seed,**" they said, "**and this previously dormant seed that you've carried within you all these years will now begin to bear fruit. It's time for women to become the bountiful fields they were born to be.**

"**Our work with those whom we call to service is deep and it is personal. We invite women (and a few men too) who are ready, and when they answer our call, we take them deep. Deep into themselves and deep into life. We do not exaggerate when we say this. We're speaking here of the power of what you call the Goddess, the power of the Feminine Principle of creation. Women carry this Presence within themselves and *we will activate it*. We will arouse what has until now lain dormant within them. We will awaken women to their bounty.**" As I listened, my eyes grew bigger and bigger, and when they saw my response, they said, "**We do not work in ways that you are accustomed to.**"

"You sure don't!" I exclaimed. "You go straight for the goal, Grandmothers. You're not saleswomen. You're not pushing a product or program of some kind. You don't mess around."

"**That's right,**" they said, "**and those who are seeking the goal are the ones we call to this work. We are not here to stimulate minds or emotions. We will not waste time with that, but will instead take you to the goal. And as you move closer to this long-sought goal, you will bless many. You will become that fertile field we are speaking of—full of good, full of goodness. By giving, giving, giving, you will bring joy to others. And this will also be your joy. Boundless joy,**" they affirmed, their smiles broadening. "***This* is the purpose of our next Gathering of the Grandmothers. Say this.**"

I passed their message on and when the Gathering rolled around, we stuck to the Grandmothers' guidance. Each person who attended this event came into more power. Each of us became more fully alive, and as our time together came to a close, I looked around the room and saw that every face was lit!

"All the so-called problems in the world are fed by the energy of fear."

After the Gathering I didn't return to my wise teachers for almost a month. Grandmothers' leaders who'd traveled to California from abroad had decided to stay in our area for a while, so we local grandmothers spent a lot of time with them. We shared many meals together, and sitting around a table somewhere, we inevitably discussed the state of the world. We talked about how fear and violence were almost entirely dominating the news and we speculated on what we might do to broadcast more light on earth. After everyone left to return home, this was this last question that I took to the Grandmothers.

Greeting me with expectant looks, they stretched out their arms to me and I quickly asked, "Grandmothers, how can we broadcast more light? There's a lot of fear floating around now...fear in us, fear in the world. Fear seems to be the major block to freedom for everyone. I talked to Karen yesterday," I said, "and she told me she's terrified of the liberals while most of the grandmothers I talk to are terrified of the right wing. All over the world the right vilifies the left and the left vilifies the right. And it seems to me that every bit of this hatefulness springs from fear."

The Grandmothers stood by patiently as I talked on, until at last I became aware of the looks on their faces. "I'm sorry, Grandmothers. I got carried away. I guess the question I want to ask you is...how can we live free from fear? How can we do that?" They continued to gaze at me, their looks impassive, so I repeated, "Grandmothers, I want to know...how can we live without fear?"

Again there was silence and this time it lasted so long that I realized I must be asking the wrong question. "Okay, Grandmothers," I ventured, "how can we be strong enough that when fear shows up, it doesn't derail us?"

"Contact," they said, "**stay in touch with one another. Share and listen to one another. When you stay in contact like this *and* hold to the Net of Light, you create a force field where fear is unable to live. Fear doesn't want to be anywhere near the Net of Light. The Net of Light,**" they smiled knowingly, "**is an antidote to fear.**

"**The Net of Light holds everything in love. It is made of love so fear has no place in it. Ever!**" they emphasized. "**So each time you** take your place in the Net of Light, you automatically create an unwelcome place for fear. Staying connected to the Net of Light will protect you from fear.

"If you forget and instead of connecting inwardly like this, start looking outward, focusing your attention on the world, you will get distracted. Each time you get distracted by the world, you will find it difficult to do as we have suggested." They laughed and then, turning slightly, pointed off to the side, drawing my attention to something moving around out there.

I stared in the direction they were pointing and, off in the distance, I glimpsed an old-fashioned merry-go-round—the kind with a gold ring hanging at its center. The riders on this merry-go-round were reaching hard and jostling one another as they tried to grab the ring, and as I watched them struggle, it came to me that this is the way the world operates. We are taught to move fast, to hold on tight to whatever we have, and at the same time, to grab for the gold. And all the while we are attempting to make a grab for the ring, we must be prepared to elbow aside anybody else who's also trying to get it. "This is crazy, Grandmothers," I said.

"This bit of silliness is not life," they agreed. "This is not how life works, but this is what the mind does. Look at how *hard* everyone is trying," they said, rolling their eyes and shaking their heads at the spectacle.

"Without humanity's constant striving and all its fearful attempts to alter life's flow, life is perfect as it is. The rhythm of life is beautiful. Effortless," they said. "Life is forever spinning its patterns, and each of these patterns always goes on to foster more and more life. Always. Of course, patterns change from time to time, and as these patterns evolve, life evolves. Emotions evolve, relationships evolve, spirits evolve, and places evolve. At every moment," they said, "*everything* is evolving. It's part of the creative flow—the flux of creation. Flow creates change and change creates more flow. Life is forever in the process of becoming… something else.

"If you look back over your own life, you will see this. And now, as you enter old age you can look back and see how you were always in the process of becoming. Becoming the next thing. Becoming a wife, a mother, a teacher, a gardener, a nurturer. Becoming…more," they said. "This is the rhythm of life. There is nothing to fear in the rhythm of life.

"Every time you strive to resist what is happening at the moment, fear grabs hold of you, feeds off you, and is able to grow stronger. Change is part of the rhythm of life," the Grandmothers said. "That's why it's impossible for movements that push against the changing flow of life to do any good—ever! You've heard people say, 'Go with the flow.' Well, they're right. Go with the flow—not against the flow. It's the energy of unbalanced yang that thrusts and pushes itself *against* the flow. It is the pushing against life that magnifies fear. Pushing against always creates misery," they said and smiling patiently, the Grandmothers added, "there is nothing to push against. There's nothing wrong. Life, after all, is just being life."

They took a long pause after this and then they continued. "You ask us how to cope at this time on earth when fear is surging everywhere, and in response we ask you to turn your awareness to whatever has triggered fear in you. As you consider this question, notice the issue that presents itself. What is it that has brought fear to the foreground of your mind?

"Once this becomes clear to you, observe whether or not you can stay in harmony within yourself as the issue further reveals itself. Observe both the fear and what triggered it and see if you can stay in a good feeling place while you simply watch it all. Just observe, and if you find that you can't stay in a good feeling place, you will know that you've been sucked in by fear. Should that happen to you, should you find that fear has taken over your driver's seat," they said, "call us immediately. Call us, and call on the Net of Light.

"As soon as you call us, we will come. We will answer. Take a moment then to experience your union with us and with all those who work with the Net of Light. Together all of us will hold your presenting fear, whatever it is, in the Net of Light. Not seeking to change the fear," they said, "not even seeking to understand it, but simply holding it in the Net.

They nodded. They were signaling me to do this now, so I thought of a painful issue, one that had been causing a low level of anxiety in me. Then I called on the Grandmothers, and, closing my eyes, I took the time to feel their presence. After I sensed a firm connection with them,

I also called on those who work with the Net of Light—especially the people in Grandmothers' groups around the world.

As soon as I did that, my spine elongated so that I was sitting very tall in my chair. And within a minute the faint but sickening sense of anxiety that had been with me over the past few days faded and was gone. Gone. It was just as the Grandmothers had said. Fear could not live anywhere near the Net of Light. "Grandmothers," I said, breathing easier, "thank you for this wisdom."

"All the so-called problems in the world are fed by the energy of fear. Fear is a greedy feeder so each time fear arises it will try to make you believe that *it is the most important thing in the world.* Give me ALL your attention!" it screams. **"You *should* be afraid! You should *feed* me!"** The Grandmothers shrugged their shoulders and threw up their hands. **"That's how fear behaves. It always wants attention.**

"But you don't need to give it," they said and shook their heads. **"Start observing the issues that come to your mind when fear arises, and then call on us to take over for you. We will. As soon as you let go of an issue, we will take hold of it. Instead of pushing against fear or trying to figure it out all by yourself, think of us. Think of the Net of Light, and let us hold you."** Laughing, they said, **"Now doesn't that sound like an easier way to work?**

"Remember," they nudged me, **"as soon as you call us, we will take over. *Every time* you call on us, we will come *and we will come instantly*. We will help you with the smallest personal problems and with the largest cosmic problems imaginable. In our eyes *all problems* are equal. So whenever you catch yourself pushing against something, saying things like, 'This isn't right, This shouldn't be happening to me, That's wrong,' or the like, know that the energy of fear has taken the wheel from you."** Wagging their fingers at me, they laughed, **"Don't let fear drive.**

"Call on us. Let us take over, and then simply rest in the Net of Light. The Net of Light will hold you at the same time that it holds the problem.

"When you get caught in fear, you end up feeding the negative drama that's playing out on earth. *That's a guarantee of misery* for you and others. It is the last thing you want to do. Fear will forever try to fascinate you with its stories, but it's important to remember

that fear has been telling and retelling the same stories for thousands of years. Stories of 'us and them,' stories of the battle between 'good and evil,'" they laughed. "Just remember that underneath each one of these stories, and stretching beyond and beneath every drama on earth is the radiant Net of Light.

"Each time one of you remembers to call on us, and on the Net of Light, those dramas are diffused," they said. "One person holding steady to the Net of Light takes the power out of the voracious feeding machine of fear. So, as soon as you catch yourself holding your breath, tensing up, entertaining thoughts like 'this is scary,' know that fear has taken control. Then quickly call on us.

"The times you are living in are ripe for fear's attempts at control, but you are wise souls. Beautiful souls. Each of you has an important part to play at this time in history, so stay connected with us, stay connected with one another, and with the Net of Light. Hold to truth. And no matter what ugly mask fear may wear on any given day, don't let it fool you. Your job is to stay in the light. Each time you do that you will help us and help everyone." Wrapping me/us in their arms, the Grandmothers said, "We thank you for your true, true hearts."

CHAPTER TEN

Replace Your Stories with the Truth

"Sit Yourself Down With a Friend; Sit Yourself Down With a Stranger."

The Grandmothers were calling me again, pulling at my awareness and coming to my mind; they had something to teach. So much was happening in the world now—rioting in the Middle East, floods, tornados, fires and droughts at home. Financial meltdowns everywhere. It was pretty sobering to me.

"What do you want us to understand, Grandmothers?" I asked just before I stepped into their Stone Circle. As I edged my way between the stones that marked their places, I glanced up and saw that today they were wearing brightly patterned skirts, and when I stopped to admire them, they began to whirl together, weaving a dance in a circle.

I stood quietly and as I watched them dance, I realized how heavy I was feeling. I didn't feel like dancing. All this negative stuff I'd been hearing about in the world had stirred me up and at the same time, was weighing me down. I had taken all that drama to heart and was feeling the downward pull of all that pain—again. I just stood there, immobile, staring at the Grandmothers until at last I heard myself whisper, "Please help, Grandmothers. Give me guidance. Give us all guidance and give it *now*. Teach us what we need to learn."

They gave me a cursory look, called out, "**Listen to us!**" and then they whirled on. "What are they doing?" I muttered. Their blasé attitude was annoying me, but the Grandmothers continued whirling, dancing as if they hadn't a care in the world. "**Time is flying by**," they called out as they flew by me. "**There's little of it left**," they said, and when I heard that, I felt my heart lurch. **"Little time to prepare, little time to learn what you must,"** they elaborated, **"so listen closely."** Now I was standing stock-still, rigid with concentration.

"We were with you in Alabama," they said, coming to a stop before me, and when I heard this my eyes opened wide. A few weeks ago a friend and I had flown to Birmingham for a Gathering. But why, I wondered, were the Grandmothers talking about this now? "This isn't what I came to talk about," I muttered, but they paid no attention to me.

"We opened sacred sites in Alabama," they said, **"opened them to more light and then we brought together those who will hold that light steady. Through the work of these people,"** they emphasized, **"the Net of Light will shine brighter and hold stronger than ever. It will cradle the southern part of the United States and fully cover it. As these people in Alabama work with the Net of Light, the fearful energy that formerly held this part of your country in thrall will lift and lift. You worked hard and well with the Net of Light when you were there,"** they said, giving me a smile, **"and that work will continue.**

"Our message is spreading deeper and wider," they said, stretching their arms out for emphasis. **"Don't be concerned about how quickly or slowly our message seems to be spreading,"** they said, shaking their heads. **"Let go of all those thoughts. Let go as well of your opinions about how our work should evolve. Know that *we* are directing it.**

"*We are directing everything.* The Net of Light is anchoring and multiplying its reach throughout the earth now—just as it should. So, from this time onward," they gave me a pointed look, **"follow our guidance and do not reach for anything. Simply do what we give you to do. That's all. This is our message to you. It is our message to everyone. Follow, and let the Divine be your guide.**

"The yang-based/yin-denying ways that have controlled life on earth for so long are dying," they said. **"We know this idea is hard for you to grasp, because a yang-based world is the only one you have known, but the arrogance and selfishness of this unbalanced way of living is coming to an end now. From the time you were young, you were conditioned by the energy of yang. You were taught to ignore the energy of yin, and because of your early conditioning, it feels natural for you to assume that there is always something you *need* to 'do.'"**

Laughing at the ridiculousness of this idea, they added, **"But as this action-centered way of life comes to an end, you will recognize that we (the Grandmothers or any form of the Divine you love) will 'do' everything.**

"You can count on us. Each time you turn your attention away from the world 'out there' and instead listen within, we are able to guide you. We encourage you to do this now. You have reached retirement age after all," they said, laughing at the surprised look on my face, **"so you can let go of your addiction to being super responsible. It's okay,"** they reassured me. **"You can relax. After all, you're simply along for the ride.**

"Instead of 'working, working, working' at life, whenever possible, gather with a group of like-minded souls. Sit and listen to one another. Share time together and share your light. Hold parties, gatherings, and circles," they said, giggling as my look of surprise deepened. **"Gather around a table and share food. Talk and pray together. Embrace one another and celebrate your differences. Enjoy each other! Love one another! Let go of 'working' so hard and instead revel in your togetherness.** *You are here!* **At this momentous time in the history of your planet you are here together! How wonderful it is for you to** *share such a moment.*

"You are companions on the way, so celebrate that as you continue to follow the path. All of you are quite wonderful. We love and cherish each of you. Please love and cherish one another too, for when you do, our love is able to multiply, cover the earth, and fill all the life on your planet. It's time for you to let go of the 'hardness' and the 'efforting' of yang," they said, stroking my back with their soft hands. **"Let go of striving, let go of worry, fear, and judgment too. What joy did any of these ever bring you?"** they asked, lifting their palms skyward. **"Instead, sit yourself down with a friend; sit yourself down with a stranger. Appreciate who they are and while you're at it, be aware of how very much we appreciate you."** And flashing me a big grin, they cried, **"We do!"**

"Fear is Nothing."

A few days later, I came upon a story in the morning paper. A group of men had beaten a homeless man to death while he begged for mercy.

The whole thing had been captured on video. When I saw the head-lines, I kept reading, hoping that someone would explain the motive for this crime. But there was no 'ah ha' moment, no apparent motive—just another pointless tale of brutality.

The story haunted me, bothered me so much that I couldn't let it go. I had to talk about it, had to somehow make sense of it. "Grandmothers," I asked when at last I went to them, "how can I keep my focus on the light, keep on keeping on when I'm ambushed by stories like this one? I'm asking this question for myself as well as for everyone else," I said. "There are so many tales like this. How can those who hear about suffering like this stand steady and not collapse into pity and horror? Should I attempt to avoid the news? Should I hide from stories like these?"

"This brutal energy you read about is within you too," the Grand-mothers replied. **"It is present in everyone—either asleep at the moment, simmering at the back of your awareness, or being acted out in some way. It's always there."**

"Okay," I replied, "I get that. I've seen and felt enough ugly stuff in myself to know you're speaking the truth. But again I have to ask, what can I do when I come across something like this? These stories are in the news every day. So I'm asking. I'm asking for myself but not just for myself. I'm asking for everyone because we all have to deal with this."

"**First,**" they replied, "**don't condemn anyone for being taken over by rage as were the men in this story. Because if you condemn them, you condemn yourself and everyone else too. Human beings carry this energy within them, so no good can possibly come from con-demning. Instead, open your mind and heart to this negativity whenever it makes itself known, and once you've done that, be curi-ous about it. Observe those urges that lurk in your subconscious and in everyone's subconscious. What are these feelings telling you? Are they perhaps based in fear?**" they asked, training their eyes on mine. "**Watch for fear. Fear is the negative emotion to look for. Acts like the one you read about today** *are propelled and fed by fear.*

"**Fear is** *the* **baseline negative state,**" the Grandmothers said; "**it lies at the bottom of all misery. Not just some of the time,**" they said, shaking their heads, "**or even most of the time.** *All the time.* **So look for it. And when you find it, be curious about it. Open to it with a gentle curiosity. Simply observe it and see what it has to say for itself.**

"Fear is always looking for a place to feed," they explained. "It will feed every chance it gets, so once it comes up, keep an eye on it. Don't turn your back on fear, ignore it, or attempt to hide from it. That will never work," they said, wagging fingers at me. "Instead, as soon as you notice it, look right at it. Then sit down and have a little chat with fear. Don't judge it—just see what it has to say for itself. And after you've listened for a while, sit quietly and observe it. Watch what happens."

We'll tell you a little secret," the Grandmothers whispered. "*Fear is nothing.* Yes," they smiled at my surprise, "**you heard us right.** *Fear is nothing.* It's a parasite. It has no core, no life force of its own. It feeds on life, so when its stories don't take you in, and you don't react to them, but instead just observe it, you deny fear a place to feed. And when it has nowhere to feed, it begins to dissipate. Every time. So each time you look fear in the face, it will weaken, shrink, and finally disappear.

"Fear is the great fooler. It is able to get away with what it does by fooling everyone. It brings up scary stories, embellishes them, and makes them so dramatic that people become afraid to even look at them. They become afraid to look at fear and see it for what it is. *Fear makes people afraid of fear!*" they said, rolling their eyes. "**Now isn't that crazy?**

"Don't be afraid of fear or the feelings it calls up. Fear is *nothing, nothing.* If you sit down with it and give it steady attention, you will see this nothing. Keep on watching without reacting to the drama it seeks to evoke and eventually fear will evaporate.

"The people you read about today, those who killed this man, were themselves run by fear. They got caught up in 'a scary story' in their minds and allowed themselves to be taken over by fear. People who commit atrocities, those who murder, torture, and rape, have all been taken over by fear. Fear," they said, "if given control, will turn anyone into a monster.

"So when an instance like this one is brought to your attention, don't condemn, but rather pray for those who, for a time at least, lost sight of their soul because of fear. Affirm the lighted one that is still within them, still there underneath all the pain and mental garbage they carry. By working in this way, you will lift the victims, the perpetrators, and yourself. You will free all of you from the grasp of fear.

"*Don't stay away from stories like these,*" they said, laughing as my eyes opened wide, "**but instead use them for your own spiritual growth. A discipline of sorts. When a story like this one comes to your notice, pray for the victims and perpetrators, then check to see if this particular drama has brought up fear in you. And if it has, stop whatever you're doing and sit down with the fear, giving it your full attention. Do this until it begins to dissipate.** *Working like this is service,*" the Grandmothers promised. "**Each time you lessen fear's grip on you, you lessen fear's grip on humanity.**

"**Everything is part of a deeply connected pattern. Many times we have told you that you cannot help yourself without helping everyone and everything else and this is certainly the case here. So when fear next shows its face, go forth fearlessly and have a little chat with it. Sit down with it and then watch,**" they said. "**Do this for your own freedom and for the freedom of others. You won't be sorry.**"

"Your mother's mother's mother's mother knew..."

The next time I went to the Grandmothers I'd been thinking about a Gathering that was coming up in Europe, concerned about a misunderstanding that had occurred with the organizers there. This had never happened before so it I was surprised and wasn't sure I understood what was going on. "What?" I asked the Grandmothers, "is this about?"

"**This is the end of an era,**" they responded, "**and the beginning of a new era. In all periods of transition—like this one—there will be moments of confusion and disagreements as fears rise to the surface. Expect these things to occur, expect this in yourself, expect it in others, and don't be concerned when disharmony shows up. At times like those you're living through now, it will.**

"**So much is changing today that humans become uncomfortable, and when people get uncomfortable, they revert to the early yang-based patterns they were taught. Then judgments flare, power struggles ensue, fears, angers, a need to control others, control situations, or control feelings—all of these come up. None of them are pleasant, but during times of transition they** *will* **show themselves. So as you move through these changing times, be easy on yourself. You're at the beginning of something new,**" they said; "**you're learning new ways of being.**

"At this Gathering in Europe you will be working less in the yang modes you are accustomed to. You won't be going from point *a* to point *b* as much as you have in the past, but will instead experience the whole and your place in it. Instead of traveling toward a goal 'out there,' you will voyage deeper into yourself.

"Your mother's mother's mother's mother knew how to do this," the Grandmothers said. "Your ancestors from long ago related to the whole of life. They knew the power of the Feminine Principle, and because you carry their DNA, this wisdom, this way of being, is there within you too. Call on it. Call it up. Invite your ancestors in.

"And call on us, the Grand Mothers," they smiled conspiratorially. "Together with the twelve of us, you make thirteen. You are the thirteenth one," they laughed. "Take your place with us. You are not separate from the Divine. Over and over again you will take your place in the circle with us. Both men and women will do this.

"Sit with us. Sit and share our teachings, and as you do, all sense of separation, all thoughts of 'them vs. me,' 'I am alone,' and 'no one understands me' will dissolve into Oneness. Our teachings will protect and guide you as this work begins to live inside you. We promise that once you get a glimpse of the greathearted one you are, you'll no longer miss your old yang-based perceptions. Then you'll be free to live each day in the One Love."

"There is nothing wrong with the world."

Once again I 'just checked' to see what was in the newspaper, and got caught in the drama on the page. It was the daily mash of disasters, corruption, violence—the usual, and though I thought I'd remained calm and collected as I read, the stories that caught my attention ended up being just enough to put a kink in my equanimity.

"My beloved teachers," I said when I came before the Grandmothers, "the world seems to be filled with greed and falseness. If the governments aren't corrupt, they're inept, and as they fiddle around and line each other's pockets, the planet is being degraded. I've talked with you about this for years and you always say that fighting against things that seem wrong is an endless process, and one that won't return the earth to balance. I agree," I sighed, exasperated, "and at the same time I don't want to give up in despair. So here is that same question again:

With all that's going on now, how can I/we hold light steady? How can we do that without getting angry and overwhelmed? Please answer in a new way," I pleaded. "Say it so I can *hear* it this time. Please give me the truth. I'm ready to listen."

"**There is nothing wrong with the world,**" they replied, eyeing me benignly and when I heard this I went from disheartened to furious. "Nothing wrong with the world!" I cried, but the Grandmothers and the Holy Man continued to regard me with that same benign look so I backed off a little. I even began to question my anger. Finally I said, "Maybe there's more to this than I know."

"**Look at what matters,**" they chorused. "**Who you are in *this* moment matters, who you are in *this* moment. Life exists in *this* moment and nowhere else. Love is here in *this* moment. Beauty is here. How fully you embrace what lies before you is what matters.**" Tilting their heads, they looked hard at me and asked, "**Do these ideas that you hold so dear and do the various governmental, economic, religious, and social systems of your time really matter? Are they real? Are they eternal?**" they asked, and I felt my mind start to spin. "**Do they truly *'matter'* in *this* moment, or do they *'matter'* only in your mind?**"

I stared at them...dumbfounded. I'd never thought about this, never questioned these (to me) elemental truths. "What if they're not so elemental after all?" I asked myself, and when I asked this question, I saw the Grandmothers smile.

"**Those who seek to control the world though dishonest means don't know how to live in *this* moment,**" they explained. "**Such people are run by fear—fear of lack, fear of not being 'special' in the world—that's why they hoard, cheat and steal. They are afraid,**" they said, lifting their palms as if to say, " '**Well...what do you expect of such people?'** And when you give your energy over to fighting these people, to bemoaning your fate, to wringing your hands about the 'evils' of the world, you also become run by fear.**"

Shaking their heads, the Grandmothers continued to regard me with serious looks. "**Stay in *this* moment and do not leave it. Stay here now,**" they said, pointing emphatically to emphasize the 'here' and the 'now.' "**We are with you. We are sitting in *this* moment with you. You are not alone, and we tell you that in *this* moment there is no fear.**

"**There is nothing bad *here* and there is nothing bad *now*. *'Bad'*** is in the mind, so don't waste time condemning yourself, or others, evaluating and judging what you do not understand. Don't hurry and don't worry, but instead sit *here* and stay *here*. Stay with us. Stay out of the maelstrom that rages and blows everywhere. Blowing and raging," they said, shrugging their shoulders; "**that of course is what maelstroms do.**" And smiling, they happily shook their heads and added, "**but you needn't.**

"**Stay with us and turn your eyes to what lies before you. Isn't it life that's lying before you? Isn't beauty lying before you? Isn't love lying before you? Why would you want to leave that?**" they asked, mock horror on their faces. "**Do you really want to leave this** *now* *moment* **for the raging and blowing of the world's latest maelstrom? Is it truly** *that* **fascinating?**

"**Stay in** *this* **moment with us,**" the Grandmothers said, "**and from the reality of** *this* **moment, move forward. Let forward momentum arise from** *this* **moment. If you wait to act until you are guided, your actions will be blessed. Your actions will be blessings.**" Then, giving me a look of infinite patience, they said, "**God/Divinity/the One Love always abides in** *this moment*. **Abide with it.**"

"Yes, Grandmothers," I agreed and as they wrapped their arms around me, I said, "I will. I'll stay in this moment. And I'll let that be enough."

"You are the light within the Net!"

For years I'd heard the year 2012 referred to as the time of great change, but since we were now three-quarters through this storied year and I hadn't seen anything monumental taking place, I was starting to wonder. Things seemed to be going along pretty much 'business as usual.' The rich were getting richer while the poor were sinking further into poverty, and as far as I could tell, there was no shortage of lying and cheating anywhere on earth.

"Grandmothers," I said when I came before them, "I don't get it. Maybe I'm not sensitive enough, but I'm not seeing the big changes people predicted for this time in history. We're supposed to be entering a new era, but I don't see it. Oh, forget about the predictions," I said at last, realizing how fed up I was with all these 'stories' and with myself for paying attention to them. "Is there anything you'd like us to know, Grandmothers? I mean, at this particular time in history?"

"As this year comes to an end, so do many of the old ways that have for so long held humanity in thrall. No one is responsible for these old ways," they said, and I looked at them in dismay. What did they mean that no one was responsible? I had my list. There were plenty of people I wanted to blame for the problems in the world. I'd actually expected the Grandmothers to confirm my list, and as this thought crossed my mind, they threw back their heads and roared with laughter.

"Just as no one is responsible for the pain of the past, no one is responsible for the shift that's occurring now." I stared at them, unable to respond. "It is time," they said, giving me a level look. "Simply put...it is time.

"Whenever humanity grows tired of contraction, grows tired of a steady diet of fear and dread, and decides it's ready to live with an open heart, *no matter what*," they said, "then the heart of the human race opens. This changes *everything*, and hearts are opening now. Even though all around you, you hear the death rattle of the old ways—the convulsions of King Greed, the shrieking and moaning of those who set up systems to use people as 'things' for their own personal gain, you can be sure that a new wind has begun to blow. It will blow away contraction, control, and mean-spiritedness of every kind. Believe it!" they said, and rocked back and forth on their heels.

"Uh….uh, Grandmothers," I interjected, "what would you have us do at this time? How can we help bring about this shift you are speaking of?"

They smiled a knowing smile, shook their heads, and said, "You need do nothing. Nothing but love," they amended. "Take every opportunity to love. Be the walking prayer we've told you that you are. Living in love is your true nature so live your nature. Be who you are, and enjoy being alive. Hold to the Net of Light and observe how the Net of Light holds you. You are precious to the light, so of course the Net of Light will support you at every moment. You are the light within the Net!" they exclaimed. "So claim your birthright. It is time."

CHAPTER ELEVEN

Love is the Only Real Thing

*"We will hold you in the Net of Light
that forever holds us all."*

Near the end of November, Roger and I left for a Gathering of the Grandmothers in Australia. At the last European Gathering, we worked intensively with the ancestors, deepening our connection with the Grandmothers, deepening our understanding of this work, and most of all, deepening ourselves. So the day before the Australian Gathering was to begin, I went to the Grandmothers and asked if there was something specific we should know about *this* Gathering. "What," I asked, "is its purpose?"

No sooner were the words out of my mouth than I became aware of a large group of aboriginal people walking by me. They were carrying tools and implements with them, and as they passed by, I saw their bronze skins aglow. These were the original people of this continent.

"**We are going now,**" they said, and I looked at them in surprise, "**but before we go, we wish to give you our blessing. All is forgiven,**" they said, and I started, not sure what they meant by this. "**You are not at fault for what happened between our peoples,**" they explained and I caught my breath, but what they said next really shook me.

"**We are fading as a people. Our life as it was, is over now, so we will be moving on to another life elsewhere. Our descendents will carry on here, although they will live differently from the way we lived.**" Then they stood still, focused their attention on me and said, "**At some point this will also happen to you.**" I looked hard at them and realized that I was pressing my hand over my mouth. It had fallen open.

"**The tapestry weaves itself,**" they said, "**and we are but threads in it. We are not the weavers, yet we live and love, and the beauty of our** particular thread shines within the tapestry. There is no blame, nor is there fame or shame in anything that happens in life. We are simply threads," they said, gazing at me with untroubled looks—"you and we. We are threads, and our threads bless yours, so do not blame yourself for the things your race has done to ours, or for anything that you have personally done. Forgive yourself as we forgive you.

"Soon we will disappear into the dreamtime," they said, and when I heard this, I gasped. "Please bless us too." I nodded a wordless 'yes' to them. "In the dreamtime as well as in this so-called time, we will continue to hold you in the heart of the One Love. We will hold you in the Net of Light that forever holds us all." And saying this, they turned and walked away.

Tears ran down my face as I watched them go, and although the full meaning of their message continued to elude me, I understood enough of it. This magnificent race of people was transmuting into something else now, and would appear in another place in yet another form. And, according to them, this was not a unique occurrence, but would eventually happen to other groups as well—perhaps to every culture and race on earth. What they were attempting to communicate was enormous, but their message was too much for me to absorb. All I could feel was my heavy, heavy heart. I shook my head to clear my thoughts, and, placing my hands over my painful heart, I bowed deeply to these people as they disappeared over the horizon.

I never learned why the Grandmothers gave me this experience, but communicating with these ancient people moved me greatly, and when, on the first night of the Gathering in the mountains above Brisbane, an Aboriginal woman offered to smoke and bless us, I was honored.

This woman didn't look like my idea of an Aborigine. Like many Native American people, she too was of mixed blood, but the commitment to return to 'country' ways was strong in her. She was learning all she could about the ancient traditions of her people and was incorporating the old ways into her life.

I felt a mixture of gratitude and grief when she and her friend lit a fire and, clicking sticks together, covered us in smoke. Gratitude for the gift they were giving us, and grief for the transitory nature of this life of which we were are all part. As she herself was coming awake to her heritage, her 'people' were leaving this area of the world.

The ceremony the two women performed for us was generously and sincerely offered, and the purity of their intention to honor us and at the same time honor their mob, or tribe, was deeply touching. They had decided to carry on all the good they could take from this fast-disappearing culture, and their longing to connect with these vanishing people was palpable. In my heart I bowed to them too.

The Gathering of the Grandmothers in Australia drew people of mostly European ancestry as well as a few Aboriginal women. Together we called on the ancestors of our bloodlines and of the land, asking that peace and forgiveness reign throughout the country. We also danced, sang, passed on the Grandmothers' Empowerment, and basically had a wonderful time with one another. When our time together at last came to an end and the Australian women stood together, singing a Maori blessing song to speed Roger and me on our way to New Zealand, there wasn't a dry eye in the room.

Our New Zealand experience began in Wellington, which sits at the bottom tip of the North Island. From there we drove north to an old farmhouse where people from Europe, America, and Australia were waiting, making the Gathering in New Zealand another international event. Makere, a Maori elder who had traveled up from the South Island, performed the opening ceremony for us and then we shared the Grandmothers' message and passed on their Empowerment.

The Maori elder shared with us the teachings of the Waitaha, a seafaring people who settled in New Zealand long before the coming of the Maori. She had been one of five people who were called together several years ago by the Waitaha ancestors. This group of five had traveled together throughout the South Island and, following the ancestors' guidance, they reactivated sacred sites throughout the island. Her group had helped re-open the age-old peace trails throughout the South Pacific and in other parts of the world as well.

She was steeped in the lore of the Waitaha and gladly shared their teachings with us. This beautiful woman and the wisdom she brought with her became an integral part of the Grandmothers' work at that Gathering and, it turned out that the messages of the Waitaha and the Grandmothers were a good fit. The next year Makere joined us in California and passed these teachings on to her Grandmother sisters and brothers there as well.

"Let courage rise up within you. Nothing can daunt you."

After we returned home and I thought back on the Gatherings that had taken place in the Netherlands, in Australia, and in New Zealand, I began to wonder about them. I'd been deeply moved at each one, but now I was curious to know what had actually taken place at these meetings. We'd had a good time together, people's hearts had seemed to open, but had we done any real and lasting good? I had my own impressions of the value of these events, but I wanted to know what the Grandmothers had to say about them.

I called on the Grandmothers and entered their circle, and as soon as I asked my question, they replied, **"A great awakening took place. An awakening to power and an awakening to the family that together you form. Not one of you will ever be alone again,"** they said, **"and the people who came to these Gatherings know this. As you follow our teachings, you work together, and it is together that you will step into power. You have formed a family now, a community. And within this community everyone's strength is multiplied.**

"The Net of Light will fully support each of you," they promised. **"It will support all that you do. Because of the work you have already done, at this point the Net is able to support the earth in ways that have not been possible for thousands of years. By working together you've played a big part in this re-activation of the Net of Light."** Smiling happily, they said, **"The Net of Light loves you."**

They looked me up and down then and said, **"Let courage rise up within you. Nothing can daunt you. Fear's hold is weakening now, so each of you will be able to stand forth in full Beauty/Power. Now!"** they emphasized. **"Enjoy this time,"** the Grandmothers said, and swept their arms wide to be sure I understood that they were speaking not just to me, but to everyone. **"You've earned it. We are holding and blessing you,"** and, raising a hand, they said, **"stay the course."**

"You are in the process of becoming more than you have ever been."

Not long after this visit I began to receive emails predicting upcoming catastrophes. Batches of them. The end of 2012 was fast approaching, and with it came fear about the changes that had been predicted for this time in history. After we returned from New Zealand, there were so many of these messages stacked up, waiting for me that I got fed up. "These messages aren't elevating, nor are they giving me any useful advice," I muttered. "They just breed fear."

I'd had enough of predictions, but decided I wouldn't mind a little practical advice. So I would go to the Grandmothers, lay these warnings in their laps, and ask them for something helpful instead. "Grandmothers," I said when I came before them, "we could use something useful and uplifting about now. People are wary of this time we're living in, so if you have a helpful message for us, would you please give it?"

The Grandmothers didn't say anything at first, but just gazed at me, their faces impassive. Then they pointed to the bouquet I'd gathered in the garden earlier in the day. It was gracefully branching out in all directions, and with the yellow narcissus and orange lion's tail, it had an autumnal feel. I didn't understand why the Grandmothers were showing it to me now, but assumed it must have something to do with my question.

"**There's entirely too much worry in the air,**" they said. "**Too much fretting. Stop it!**" they commanded. "**If you are worrying about the future, stop it right now and think of us instead. Look at us!**" they cried and broke into happy laughter. Spreading their skirts wide, gaily they swung them from side to side. "**We're happy, we're always happy. We're happy because we live in love. We live in a constant state of love,**" they chortled, "**and, *when you are in your right mind*, so do you!**

"**It's the ego. That old pile of misery,**" they said, their noses wrinkling in disgust. "**It's the ego that spends its time in worry. 'What did I do wrong?' it moans. 'What's going to happen to me? What's wrong with me? What's wrong with the world? I have to take control'!**" They had thrown themselves into their play-acting, and as they continued to ham it up, they bent over, smacked one another on the back, and rocked back and forth with laughter.

When they finally straightened up and stood tall again, I could see that they were making an effort to be serious. "**We assure you that nothing is *wrong* with you or with the world,**" they said. "**No matter how things may look to you, *nothing* is wrong. We showed you these flowers today because they're happy to be themselves. They're beautiful, they're fragrant, and they're graceful. These flowers *know* that** nothing is wrong with them and they *know* nothing is wrong with the garden. They're blooming because that's what they do. It's their nature to be beautiful, fragrant, and graceful," they said, "and so they are. It's their nature to bloom.

"It's also your nature, but sometimes you get lost in the ups and downs of the world. And when you do, you forget that you too are blooming. At this very moment," they said, giving me a meaningful look, "you are in the process of becoming more than you have *ever* been. *That,*" they declared, "is blooming!"

They opened their arms to me then and said, "Turn your minds and hearts to us and let us pour love into you. We will fill you full. The power of love surrounds and envelops everything it touches, so let it touch you now. Let the flow of love carry you forward. A River of Love is rising now and as it rises, it will lift everything with it. Join in its flow. Let love in. We love you exactly the way you are," they said, "so we will gladly fill you to capacity. Just call on us.

"Let go of all the things you've been grasping at—let go of your fears and anxieties. Let them go. We will hold you in love every day and every night. It's true that love *is* all there is," they declared. "Love is the only reality.

"The 'horrors' that you see, hear, and read about are not lasting. They're only so much flotsam and jetsam that the River of Love will wash away. Will wash them all away," they repeated, nodding up and down. "Love is the only real thing, the only lasting thing."

Then they cocked their heads and peered at me over the tops of their brows. "Can you be satisfied with love?" they asked, and I looked at them in surprise. "Can you do without the daily dramas of life? Can you be satisfied with just loving and being loved? It's simple really. Love won't make you rich and love won't make you famous. No," they shook their heads, "it won't do that. Instead it will make you happy."

"You have been groomed to live in fear."

The Grandmothers had answered my request—more than answered it. I felt the ring of truth when they spoke of the relentless, sustaining power of love. Their message resonated, right down to the cell beds of my body. It therefore surprised me when a week after they gave me this message, and for no reason that I could think of, my energy and confidence began to flag, dropping down, down, down. All of a sudden I was questioning everything. Was what I was doing with the Grandmothers worth all this effort? Did this work really make a difference? Did I have it in me to keep going like this year after year?

I'd experienced these drops in energy before. I'd be sailing along, enjoying myself, full of gratitude and confidence when suddenly— *thunk*. The bottom would drop out. Whenever this strange depression had shown up in the past, the Grandmothers had known what to do about it, so as soon as I became aware of what was going on, I went to them.

"Grandmothers," I said, "I'm feeling low. It came on all of a sudden and again I'm catching myself wondering if I should continue on with this work you've given me. I'm sorry to be bringing this issue to you again," I said. "I don't know why I'm feeling like this, but I'm really tired and discouraged. Please help."

"**This is a cowardly world,**" they said, and my eyes flew open. "**The world today is run on fear. Mass mind beliefs that dominate your planet have taught you that you can do very little to make life on earth better. That one person is not important, that one person cannot make a difference.**

"**You are encouraged not to even consider this issue, to not think about it at all, but to instead go out and 'buy something' to make yourself feel better. You are taught to 'not rock the boat.' And...,**" they smiled ruefully, "**on top of that, you are supposed to be afraid for your own survival. Fear, fear, fear**" they sang. "**Over and over again you are urged to be afraid. Such teachings breed cowardice and it is a wonder that all of you have not given up by now. After all, you have been groomed to live in fear.**" I was staring at them in fascination and I could tell by their expressions that the Grandmothers weren't about to slow down.

"**You are feeling a loss of energy today because you got caught up in the busyness of the world,**" they said, pointing to me, "**and as soon as that happened, you began to look outward for guidance. You momentarily lost your sense of direction, and when you did, you looked for support to come to you from outside yourself. That will never happen,**" they said. "**The world you see before you cannot lead you. It has lost its way. Do not lose yours,**" they gave me a level look. "No, Grandmothers," I said, my eyes wide, "that's the last thing I want to do."

"You must be brave. Whenever you become overwhelmed by confusion and wonder what you are to do next, know that you've become caught in the fog of despair that hangs over the earth. Don't succumb to its gray hopelessness. If you look to the world for guidance, you will become increasingly fatigued. Eventually you will drop down into an unconscious state, and if that happens, you won't be really living any more but will only be going through the motions of life." They had my full attention now and I hung on their every word.

"The antidote to this state of confusion is to call on us or on any form of the Divine. Come to us," they said. "Come every day for a while. We will encourage and guide you.

"Do *not* look to the world for guidance," they repeated. "The world is lost. And...should you forget this and search outside yourself for inspiration, you too will become lost. The fog that hangs over the earth induces a drugged state, resulting in a loss of direction, a loss of purpose, and hope. Few are aware of this fog, and so many people actually live their lives in its stupor.

"Look to us or to any form of the Divine," the Grandmothers said again. "Come to us, call on us. There is work to do—important work, but you must be awake to do it. Call us and we will lead you."

Encircling me, they folded their arms tight against their chests and said, "At a time like this, do not try to live even one day without a connection to the Divine. A cloud of confusion lies thick upon the world and this cloud makes it difficult for you to see the truth. You need a source of support for yourself at a time like this, one that is pure, not one that's trying to control you. Call on us," the Grandmothers said, "and remember, even though you may sometimes feel like you're alone, you are *not* alone."

"Ride out the storm."

Several weeks went by before I returned to them again, but one gray and rainy day I got a feeling that they had a message for me—something everyone needed to hear. So I went. "Grandmothers," I said, "I feel something. With this change of weather there is a sense of 'do this' in me and I don't know what the 'this' is. Do you have a message for me? If so, please give it to me and I'll pass it on."

"Listen to us," they said, "**the time has come…,**" and as they spoke, I noticed that today the holy man was standing beside them. "**Yes, listen to them,**" he said and I tilted my head and fastened my eyes on them. I soon became aware of how hard I was concentrating when my head began to ache. "Please make your message clear," I said to the Grandmothers, "so clear this time that I *really* understand it. And please keep my mind quiet."

They laughed at the request for a quiet mind and drew me close. Then they gestured, pointing to something out in front of us. I looked and looked to where they were pointing, trying to see what it was, but all I could make out were some fast moving clouds in the distance. And far off on the horizon, the sun. "**Yes,**" they nodded, but didn't say anything else.

"This is pretty vague," I muttered as I continued to scan the horizon. The sky was starting to take on different colors now. The clouds were becoming orange, gray, and white, and yet through their billowing shapes I could still glimpse patches of a radiant blue sky. "**Watch,**" the Grandmothers said.

Now the clouds began to tumble, seeming to play with one another, and then I heard thunder and the crack of lightning. Suddenly Black Elk's vision of stampeding horses of many colors came to my mind and then I saw him—Black Elk. Here was the great Sioux medicine man. "At least I think it's him," I said as I squinted into the distance.

"**The time has come,**" he said, and I realized these were the exact words the Grandmothers had used. "**The time has come,**" he and the Grandmothers intoned. "**Hold steady. Hold steady and take the ride.**"

The clouds began to plunge then, to dive and race across the sky. "What a storm!" I cried. "What a wind!" Lightning lit up the heavens, crackled off to the side, and then flashed everywhere at the same time. Now the roar of the wind, the pounding of thunder, and the crackling of lightning reverberated all around. "**A great storm,**" the Grandmothers said, and all I could think of was how much I wanted to hunker down somewhere dry where I could wait it out. But here I was, in the midst of it. "**This is *the storm*,**" the Grandmothers said. "**You have no control over a storm such as this one. You must wait and watch. Wait and watch,**" they said." "Yes," I replied, my eyes locked on the sky.

"I've never seen a storm like this," I said, "not one this fierce. It's scary and awe-inspiring at the same time. Something like this is far beyond anything I know."

"**Yes,**" the Grandmothers fixed me with their eyes. "**The great storm is coming. It will create change, and change is needed. Respect it,**" they said. "**Do not try to meddle with forces such as these. You cannot change what needs to take place.**

"**Hold to the truth. Hold to the Net of Light and magnify its reach. Affirm the light for one another. This tempest must come, but never forget that underneath the roar of the storm, underneath everything on earth lies the radiant Net of Light. Remember this and stay quiet,**" they said. "**Stay within the Net of Light and ride out the storm.**"

"*The moment of giving and the moment of receiving are the same.*"

A few days after this, the Grandmothers woke me early in the morning. I'd been asking what they wanted me to share from the experience of the storm, but I hadn't expected them to wake me from a sound sleep to tell me. "**Pay careful attention now,**" they said, "**and send this message out.**" "Yes, Grandmothers," I said, awake and ready to write.

"**Think of, cast, and magnify the power of the Net of Light,**" they said. "**If you wish to be of service at this time, there is no greater act you can perform. The Net of Light reaches over, under, and throughout the earth. It covers and penetrates all bodies of water, landmasses, and beings on the planet. It holds the world.**

"**It will hold the world steady while the energies on your planet shift. It will hold the earth steady while what is no longer useful cracks off and dissolves. These are the times of change we have spoken of,**" they said. "**These times are here now, and you have a part to play in them. Do not miss this opportunity.**

"**All over the earth your sisters and brothers stand with you,**" they said. "**Many now are working with the Net of Light, and because of the love in their hearts, they are able to magnify its power and reach. Join them!**" they cried.

"**Begin by thinking of the Net of Light as a great fishing net and then walk forward and take your place on it. Somewhere where two of its strands come together is a place that will feel right to you. Sit down there and let the Net hold you.**

"**It will support you and fill you with wellbeing. Here you can truly rest, so relax in the Net and, as you do, experience that it is** your own heart that is lighting the Net of Light. No matter what pain you may have experienced in life, your heart is still pure," the Grandmothers said. "At its core, it is love, it is light, and so it is the jewel of the heart that lights the Net. Let light flow forth from your heart now into the Net of Light.

"And here is the miracle!" they cried, throwing their arms in the air. "The moment you think of sending light from your heart into the Net of Light, a great surge of light from the Net floods back into your heart. The moment of giving and the moment of receiving are the same moment!" they crowed. "Each time you think of, then cast, and magnify the power of the Net of Light *you* receive more. This is how the Divine works. There is no shortage in the divine plan," they said, casting delighted looks at me. "All is expansion, fullness, and fulfillment.

"As you think of and hold the Net of Light, you'll notice that it reaches everywhere, especially wherever there is suffering. You automatically magnify the power of the Net of Light each time you think of it. So think of it and hold it steady. Hold, hold, hold," they said.

"Amplify the power of the Net for all those who need this Divine connection. Do it for the human family—do it for people everywhere. Amplify the power of the Net of Light for the leaders of this world, reminding them of their place in the radiant Net. Hold the Net of Light steady for everyone who is seeking the Divine," they said. "We promise that the Net of Light will draw each one to her and his perfect pathway to Divinity—the pathway most fitting for them.

"Amplify the power of the Net of Light for the animal kingdom," they said, "asking that each animal receive whatever it most needs. Do the same for the plant kingdom and for the mineral kingdom. Cast and magnify the power of the Net of Light for everything that lives. Ask that everyone in all the worlds be happy," they smiled, adding, "and this, of course, includes you.

"Take your place on the Net of Light now," they directed me/us. "Do not delay. As you do this, you will not only bless the earth, you, yourself will be filled with radiance. The time is now," the Grandmothers said, giving me a fierce look. "Take your glorious place."

I sent out their message.

CHAPTER TWELVE

Why work with the Ancestors?

"When you call the ancestral spirits, let them come to you in the full strength of their youth."

The next time I journeyed to the Grandmothers, I didn't have a question in mind but went anyway because I felt them calling. No sooner did they greet me than they said, **"Ask us about the ancestors."** "Oh!" I replied, and quickly stepped into the center of their Circle. "Please teach me about the ancestors," I parroted, and as the Grandmothers stood up I saw that they were wearing full skirts with very small waists. It had been many years since they had shown themselves to me like this, as young women, and I was taken aback.

"Grandmothers?" I said, a question in my voice. **"Yes, it's us,"** they laughed, and then they placed their hands on their hips and seemed to preen a little as they twirled round and round. **"We are showing you yourself here,"** they said, as they pointed to themselves, **"and we are also showing you your ancestors."** I gave them a puzzled look. What in the world were they talking about?

"Your ancestors were young when they gave birth to your family line," they said. **"All ancestors were young when they made the decision to carry energy forward."** I must have still looked confused, because then they said, **"Bearing children. The ancestors were young when they made that decision."**

I thought over this idea of young ancestors and as I ruminated on their words, hundreds of ancestors began to crowd into the space around us and just as the Grandmothers had said, they were all youthful. **"There's a time in life for everything,"** they explained, **"and the** time for being a progenitor is early on. That's when the line is continued. So today we've brought you to this youthful period in the ancestral lines."

I took a step back to get a better look at these young ancestors, and when I did, I noticed that I was beginning to resonate with them. I was starting to feel their vigor in my own body. There was a propulsive movement emanating from the ancestors, and as it hit me, I understood that this is how it was when they were having children. When they were passing on DNA, their energy was moving like this, thrusting forward into the future.

"When you call on the ancestral spirits," the Grandmothers said, **"let them come to you in the full strength of their youth."**

"This is so different from the way I've always thought of the ancestors," I shook my head in wonder. "Before this, I'd imagined them like my older relatives—in middle or old age. But to see and feel them like this!" And there they stood—straight and confident. Rows and rows of ancestors had assembled, and the lines they formed stretched far over the horizon.

"These are the people you spring from," the Grandmothers said; **"this is your line. It's time for you to own your part in this line, to own your part in this continuous flow of vigor, vitality, youth, and strength. This power is flowing in you now.**

"At this period in history many people on earth are holding their energy back. 'Making do,' they said and they shook their heads in disappointment. **"Some of them are just barely functioning. They're coping with depression and hopelessness, and so inevitably their energy is of a low and limited quality. Your ancestors didn't lose hope,"** they said, fixing their eyes on mine to be sure I understood what they were getting at. **"If they had lost hope, they couldn't have continued your family line. You spring from hopeful, forward-looking people. Claim your heritage!"**

"People without health and strength don't procreate. This," they said, pointing to the ancestral spirits who were standing with us, **"is your heritage. No matter what you may have thought of them in the past, *this* is your heritage. Claim it!"** they said again. **"Their strength is your strength, their stalwartness, your birthright. You're not some little twig to be knocked over by the first breeze that blows through. You are a formidable force.**

"Turn around now," they directed me, "and bow to them. Honor your ancestors-especially the women of your line. Bow to them one at a time and name the ones you know. 'I bow to you in gratitude, Marie,'" they pantomimed. "'I bow to you in gratitude, Rose. I bow to you in gratitude, Carrie. I bow to you in gratitude, Antoinette. I bow to each of you.'

"Your ancestors may show themselves to you in the ways you've thought of them or they may seem to be much younger, but however they show themselves, know that what you are experiencing is your line. Notice that as you bow to them, they in turn bow to you. You are recognizing each other, and as you recognize each other, you will naturally honor one another."

I did as they directed—I bowed to each woman in my line, bent my head to her, and as I did, I felt our connection. Then I bowed also to the men in my line. This connection was real! And, as the contact between us grew stronger and stronger, my heart swelled in my chest. This went far beyond anything I'd ever imagined. I never dreamed that linking to the past like this was possible, and as the experience continued, wave after wave of feeling rose up in me. It wasn't long before tears were rolling down my face.

"Thank your ancestors for the gifts they've given you," the Grandmothers said, "gifts that have come to you down your bloodline. The fact that you are still alive at this point in time is a gift. All that you have and hold is a gift. Thank them," they said and dipped their own heads to the ancestors.

"Be aware that they in turn are thanking you—thanking you for being yourself, thanking you for stepping forward into truth, and for choosing to live this lifetime from your heart. And they are thanking you for doing all of this during these difficult, difficult times.

"Ask them to support you so that you can stand stronger still," the Grandmothers said. "Ah...," I responded, my voice breaking as the ancestors began to move in closer to me. "They're coming in around me now," I said. "They're holding me, blessing me, and they're doing it in the old-fashioned way, the classic way. They're putting their hands on my head and they're saying, 'I give you my blessing, my daughter.'" Now I was sobbing in earnest.

The Grandmothers nodded and smiled on me, nodded and smiled

on us. "From now on let the ancestors stand with you. Include them so thoroughly in your life that whenever you go into ceremony, they will automatically go with you, whenever you need help, they will be there to support you. They will do this," they said; "they are *eager* to do this.

"There are also gifts from various civilizations that run in your bloodline," they said then, and I looked at them in surprise. What were they talking about? "Some people carry the gifts of only one culture within them while others carry many. There is power in these folk connections. Bow to *this power* now," they directed, "and as you bow to it, the civilization, the folk connection that you carry within yourself, will recognize you."

I began to bow then to the cultures of my bloodline, and as I did, I felt waves of happiness rising up inside me. Warmth and goodness swelled and flooded me as I recalled my Polish ancestors and as I bowed to them and to my cultural connection with Poland, I felt a new strength pouring into me.

"Notice how you feel as the ancestors rock you now," the Grandmothers said, "experience as they move with you and dance with you." And suddenly I was dancing, spinning, and dipping with these people I had never known. I was reveling in the joy of intimate contact with this family from my past when I heard the words, 'hand fast.' Many years ago, when I was in high school, I came across this phrase and read about the power of the ancient sacrament of hand fasting, a pre-Christian marriage rite or binding ceremony.

"Oh!" I whispered, "There must be some sort of marriage taking place right now, a deep connection of some kind going on," and when I said this, the Grandmothers and the ancestors came in and embraced me. We gathered into one body then and, hugging and kissing one another, we began to cheer, stomp, and clap in celebration of our coming together, coming together beyond the confines of time. On we danced until we were flowing into such harmony with one another that we began to move as one being.

What I experienced as we danced like this went far beyond anything I could have imagined. The hand fast dance we performed was dignified, and yet as we whirled together, I also felt the wildness and freedom in it. "This is a traditional blessing," I said to myself, "and though it's nothing I've consciously known of, for some reason it's familiar.

Somewhere, at some time I must have done this before," I said, my voice cracking with feeling.

Then the ancestors came up to me and covered me with a cape. Next they placed a crown on my head. "What is this?" I asked, and when I felt the weight of the crown, I shook my head to explore whether it was my imagination or if it was really there. It was. I was amazed by what was lying there on my head and I heard myself say to no one in particular, "I'm queenly. Or kingly," I corrected myself. "I don't know which it is."

Full of wonder, I gazed around as I tried to take everything in. In the midst of it all, I stopped when I realized I didn't know what gender I was, how old I was, or even where I was. And strangest of all, I didn't care. I really didn't care. I was so immersed in what I was experiencing that the moment itself was everything to me. This adventure was so foreign, so magnificent, and unexpected that I never wanted it to end. I wanted to hold its strange beauty in my heart forever.

I gazed at the Grandmothers who gazed right back at me. I noticed that their eyes were full of tears and after that I must have fallen asleep, because it's the last thing I remember.

After this journey was over and I'd thanked the Grandmothers and the ancestors, I felt a need to take action of some kind. I needed to write, sing, or draw something to express my gratitude to my ancestors. I was so overcome with love for these long-ago relations of mine that until now I'd known nothing of that I wanted to honor them. I wanted to sing or dance for these, my people, and before I could let myself think too much about it, I got up and began to glide around the floor with my arms lifted and my palms up. And swaying, as I wove to a melody that played on in my head, I danced. I clapped my hands, I stomped my feet, and I rejoiced in my connection with these dear ones that until now I had thought were long gone from me.

I danced like this until I wore myself out and when at last I stopped and stood quietly, gazing at the Grandmothers with a slightly dopey smile on my face, they said, **"Sit down now. Write a letter of thanks to the ancestors. Write it specifically to your bloodline and culture, and at the end of the letter, thank them for continuing to move forward with you. All the work you will do with us from this moment on will include them,"** they said, their eyes on me. **"The ancestors 'have your back.' They stand with you, and all the blessings that you**

will receive in the future, the ancestors will also receive. This is as it should be," they said, and when I looked up at them, I couldn't help but notice that the Grandmothers looked very pleased.

This experience with my ancestors moved me greatly. In fact, I was so in awe of what I'd gone through that I couldn't get this journey off my mind. I hadn't known a love like this, a connection that went beyond what we think of as 'time' existed.

The Grandmothers had blown my mind wide open. Several years ago when'd they first directed me to include the ancestors in their work, I had balked at the idea. It wasn't something I'd ever imagined myself doing. Ancestral work had never interested me in the least. In fact, I'd thought of it as a primitive fixation of some kind, an unimportant, almost silly thing. "Dealing with ancestors may be something for tribal people to do," I remember thinking, "but it's nothing I have time for. After all, I'm an educated woman. Why would I want to commune with the dead?"

The very idea had seemed ridiculous—even creepy. I'd had been taught to believe that 'the dead were dead' and that was all there was to it. I had learned this as a young woman and once my mind had narrowed down around the belief, I'd been perfectly happy to keep it that way.

Because I'd known *nothing* about the importance of connecting with the ancestors, my ignorance had provided a perfect canvas for the Grandmothers. Not only was I uneducated on the subject, I was entirely unconscious of its importance. And I'm sure the Grandmothers understood my fear of this sort of contact, because they led me into ancestral work very gently. At least at first.

But after that experience with the ancestors of my bloodline, everything changed. The Grandmothers had blown my heart open and now I *loved* these progenitors of mine. I saw how closed-minded and closed-hearted I'd been about those who had preceded me, and once I understood it, I decided to do something about it. Taking out pictures of my grandmothers, grandfathers, and other family members, I made an informal altar for them, and placing flowers on it, I lit a candle for these, my ancestors.

Each day I sat before their pictures, spending time with these relatively unknown people, and when the Hawaiian forgiveness work of Ho' oponopono came to my mind, I performed this work with and for each of them. I told them how sorry I was for my ignorance and neglect of them and asked for their forgiveness. I told them how much I loved them and thanked these long-ago family members for all they'd given me.

As I began to do this work, my heart opened more, and to my great surprise, I began to appreciate and understand these family members whom I'd never known. A grandmother and a grandfather who had died long before I was born, an aunt who died in childhood, my father who died when I was very young. As I worked with them, I began to get a feeling for the people they had been and for the souls they still are. No longer did I simply mouth the words '*I love you*' to them. Now I really *did* love them, and as this transformation inside me took place, I drew close to these loved ones I'd never before known.

This work gave me back part of myself. It also deepened my understanding, not just of these long 'dead' ones from the past, but of everyone who had ever lived. The time I spent in prayer each day enabled me to feel the specific preciousness of these previously unknown lives, and through this window I was able to glimpse the preciousness and uniqueness of each life. I don't pretend to understand how all this came about, but the result of this work was humbling.

"You will heal pain that has been carried over for many generations."

The next thing on my agenda was getting ready for the upcoming Gathering of the Grandmothers in Belgium. Should I pass on this ancestral information while I was there? I'd better ask my wise teachers.

"You will come together in Belgium to heal ancient enmities and separations that grew over time between the tribes, ethnic groups, and nations on the continent," the Grandmothers responded. **"People from all over Europe will attend this Gathering and so this healing will affect not only Europe, but the whole world.**

"In the past several hundred years Europeans emigrated to many other parts of the globe," they said, **"and when they moved, they inevitably carried with them both the 'bad' as well as the 'good' qualities of their cultures. The enmities, judgments, and beliefs in separation that caused the countless wars in Europe automatically accompanied these people to the far corners of the earth."**

"Grandmothers," I mused, "I've often wondered why most of us who are drawn to this work with you tend to be of European origin. It's always puzzled me." "**It is no accident,**" they replied, and crossing their arms over their breasts, declared, "**you have work to do.**" I kept my eyes on them while I thought this over. They looked quite severe, and when I realized how very serious they were, I asked, "Are you saying that as we work with the ancestors through the Net of Light we'll be able to clean up not just the problems we're facing today, but also the damage our ancestors did in the past?"

"**You will heal pain that has been carried over for many generations,**" they replied, "**and this healing will strengthen the Net of Light. The work you will do will send waves of blessing over the earth. You will broadcast the Net of Light farther and deeper than ever before. And you will be able to do this in-depth work *because* you will be working with the ancestors.**"

I regarded them in silence, taking in the enormity of their words. Then I asked, "Please, would you be more specific about the good that will come from this work in Europe?" At this question, the Grandmothers' eyes lit up.

"**Swarms of ancestors will converge at this Gathering in the Lowlands,**" they said, "**embracing one another and being embraced. Those who were once tribal chiefs, kings, counts, presidents, and leaders of all sorts will come together for the first time in eons. Their descendents will call on them, and they will come.**"

When I heard this, the hairs on the back of my neck stood up and they nodded to let me know they understood the effect their announcement was having. Then they said, "**During their time on earth, these leaders held a sacred trust and this trust still binds them to their people. Binds them to do right by them.**

"**At this time in history, the goal of life on this planet is no longer one of separation and division—separation into individual kingdoms, countries, races, or religions. The goal today is *One People* and *One Love*. These leaders from long ago who will be called to this Gathering will help move humanity toward that goal.**

"**This change in goals for humankind is mandated,**" the Grandmothers explained, "**and so these long-ago leaders will come forward to help lead their people in a new direction. They will no longer do as they did in the past. No more will they act in opposition to one** another; now they will move towards unity. Unity is the task of the times you are living in, and all else pales before this task.

"Rivers of forgiveness will pour through the veins of every one present at this Gathering, including the ancestors. As this happens, heaviness will drop off them, leaving their old angers and grievances in the dust. These beings from long ago have *longed* for happiness," the Grandmothers said, their eyes soft, "and forgiveness brings happiness. Always! For eons the ancestors have been waiting for this shift in consciousness to occur, so when you call on them, when you open your hearts to them and request their support, you will make them *very* happy.

"Great good will come from this work in Belgium," they said, smiling into my eyes. "Schisms and wounds will heal, families will be reunited, and where once there was only grief and loss, love will blossom. The wounded will be embraced, mothers will cry no more, and the shame and blame that so many lived with will evaporate. The ancestors will call you blessed," the Grandmothers said and I gasped. "In fact you *will* be blessed; there will be rejoicing all around.

"No more looking backward. No more looking back to wars, genocides, rapine, and devastation. No more repeating history. No more distrusting one another and no more discrimination against one another. Instead," they warmed to their topic, "you will feel an appreciation for all the seeming differences between you. An appreciation for the seeming divisions between nations and races. For, as forgiveness pours into your hearts, it will fill you with admiration for all these seeming 'differences.' And finally," they said, beaming, "together you will discover the joy within your underlying brotherhood and sisterhood.

"This Gathering will heal divisions," the Grandmothers declared, "heal divisions between individuals, between nations, and heal divisions within the land itself. The land that you tend to think of as made up of separate countries and different landmasses is really only one. Do you remember the dream we gave you years ago that showed you how underneath the surface waters of the ocean all the islands and land masses are actually connected?"

Although this dream had occurred more than ten years ago, I'd never forgotten it. In it I had repeatedly dived under the waters of the ocean, descending so deep that I'd been able to see that the seeming separations of the continents, islands, and landmasses was not, in fact, real. When I dove deep enough, I saw that everything was or had been connected.

As I recalled the dream now I looked up at the Grandmothers and they nodded. **"During their lives on earth the ancestors who will appear at this Gathering related to only one area of the world,"** they explained. **"That area *was* their world. At that time it was all they knew. But when we bring the ancestors together within this NOW moment, the false divisions they once lived under and believed to be true won't apply.**

"All the kingdoms, countries, alliances, and boundaries on earth are temporary," the Grandmothers said. **"Good for a period of time only."** They looked up and when they noticed the stunned expression on my face, they added, **"All divisions on earth are man-made and as such, they last only for so long. All of them, *all of them*, are temporary.**

"A great healing will occur at this Gathering of the Grandmothers and this will reverberate throughout the past and carry forward into the future." By now I was so dazed by this information that when they said, **"We remind you that time as you think of it does not really exist,"** I shook my head in disbelief.

"There is no so-called *past, present or future*," they said. **"Only now. 'Past' and 'future' are mental concepts only—they do not actually exist. And because there is only now, when you and the ancestors take our Empowerment together, you'll be thrilled by how easy it will be for you to connect beyond the 'boundaries' of time. The timeless connection you will make will spill happiness all over the earth.**

"And from now on whenever anyone receives our Empowerment, they will receive it for themselves, for their personal ancestors, and for the ancestors of the place where they live. Earth is *one*," they reminded me. **"Life is *one*. All is *one*.**

"Forgiveness," the Grandmothers hummed as they swung their arms from side to side, pivoting on their toes. **"At this Gathering forgiveness will rain down on the earth. It will sink into the body of the Mother.**

"Today energy of all kinds is held within the earth's body," they explained. **"Both so-called 'good' and 'bad' energy are stored within the earth. We have explained this before, but when you and the ancestors receive the Empowerment together, forgiveness will penetrate right to the heart of your planet. A downpour of forgiveness will wash throughout the planet, expunging old, trapped energy that's been stored there." I stared at them, but they smiled brightly, waved their hands in a dismissive gesture, and continued.

"On a more personal note," they said, "after you've shared this group forgiveness with the ancestors, you'll find that many of your own negative habits and thought patterns will be less pronounced. You too will feel lighter. As the planet sheds the dross from the past, so will you.

"We ask you to take every opportunity to choose to forgive and let go. We ask you to choose to bless, rather than to judge, and to make this choice at every opportunity. Let the forgiveness you experience during this Empowerment Ceremony with the ancestors recur to you again and again. Each time you choose forgiveness, the benefits you derive will go on and on, spreading farther and farther. Each time you choose forgiveness, freedom will build for you and for others too. Choose!

"Because forgiveness works forward into the future, back into the past, as well as within the *now* moment, it will also give you better health," the Grandmothers said. "Each time you open to forgiveness, you will automatically release whatever you have unknowingly been holding onto. And those unconscious states you've been lugging around with you have been a drag on your energy.

"Each time you acknowledge and bless your ancestors, you bless yourself. You take a great step forward. Each time you embrace your ancestors, you break the sense of confinement that results from the grip of individual attachment. For a long time your feelings of attachment have held you in a state of false separation from everyone and everything," they said. "Hasn't that gone on long enough?"

I took a few deep breaths then, willing myself to absorb as much of what they were telling me as I could. In a minute I asked them, "Grandmothers, is there anything that might get in the way of me or anyone else doing this work? Is there anything that might prevent us from going forward with forgiveness in this way?

"The ego," they responded, "the little 'me.' The sense of 'my' and 'mine.' The ego is all that resists the movement toward truth and freedom. The ego and its colleague, fear. The non-dynamic duo," they laughed. "This pair always clings to the status quo.

"You'll recognize the presence of the ego every time you find yourself contracting in fear instead of expanding into love. And if and when you notice this, simply observe it. Don't judge yourself for your response, just watch. Observation will take the power out of fear's contraction every time. Working with the ancestors will give you new wings for our work, and you're ready to try on these new wings.

"The original energy of creation is still imbedded in the earth," the Grandmothers said. "The primal pattern, as well as the many overlays of humanity's energies, is there. The original imprint is pure, but man's input is not. Over time, human energy deposits have distorted the actual design of earth's energy, but this ancestral work will clear much of that. As you work with the ancestors, layers of contracted energy that over time were superimposed upon the earth will crack off and evaporate. When this happens, the Net of Light will shine so much brighter that its increased radiance will strengthen the earth's grid as well as the earth itself."

As they continued to explain how this worked, behind them I saw our beautiful blue planet rotating in space. It spun slowly on its axis and as I watched, I noticed how the energy grids and ley lines on the planet were beginning to anchor themselves more deeply into the earth. They seemed to be more inset now, more deeply moored. The change the Grandmothers were speaking of was already occurring.

"All so-called time periods are connected in the Net or Web of Light."

On my next journey I asked the Grandmothers to explain how working with the ancestors actually takes place. "With our limited ways of understanding, this concept is hard for us to grasp," I said. "Please explain how it's done so we can have confidence in working this way."

"Because there is no actual time," the Grandmothers began, "there is no difference between what you think of as the past, the present, and the future." This time when I heard this, I could help but think, "This may be easy for you, Grandmothers, but I've heard it over and over again and I still don't get it. *Help!*" I cried.

"*Everything* is present at this moment," they responded. "The ancestors are here with you now and they are here with you always. What you refer to as *the future* is also present. All these so-called time periods are connected in the Net or Web of Light. Your ancestors stand and have always stood behind and beside you, ready to assist you at every moment. They are eager to support you.

"Your previous selves from what you refer to as your past lives also stand with and for you, and whenever healing takes place for the *present day you*, it takes place for them too. It also takes place for those who will follow you down your family line. *Your healing affects all beings.* Many times we have told you that you cannot help yourself without helping everyone, and we meant what we said. *Everyone!*" they emphasized. "Whenever you love, forgive, and let yourself be loved, you help *everyone*.

"This concept is not difficult to grasp. "What we've just said is quite simple. The reason you struggle with it is because of your ego. It's because of the ego's desire to feel important. The ego/mind clings to familiar concepts and ideas because that's how it confirms its identity. That's how it confirms its '*rightness*.' The ego always demands to be right. Therefore, the familiar is reassuring to the ego/mind. '*I know this one*,' it says to itself. '*This is part of who I am!*'

"There is nothing difficult about the concept of no time, but the ego/mind doesn't like it. Timelessness shakes up its identity. Who after all would the ego be?" they asked, "if it had no existence *before* and won't exist *after*? Resistance to the concept of timelessness comes from the ego which is forever seeking to confirm its own importance." Then they laughed and asked, "Who, after all, coined the phrase, '*I think, therefore I am*,' if not the ego—in this case, Descartes' ego? The soul certainly wouldn't talk like that.

"To experience the truth of what we're telling you, try this experiment: Pretend for a moment that your ego has taken a vacation, gone on a trip and left you alone with your soul. Now ask this question: 'Does my soul care whether or not what I call '*time*' exists'?" They looked at me quizzically. "Well…does it?"

I did as they said, closed my eyes and thought of my ego being gone. Then I asked the question. Immediately I was struck by a sense of the ridiculous and I began to giggle. This was a ludicrous question! Laughing out loud, I clutched at my sides as waves of hilarity rolled over me.

I looked up at the Grandmothers then, and when they saw me like that, they joined in.

"Call forth the ancestors."

The Grandmothers were on a tear. For several weeks they'd taught me about the ancestors non-stop. So it came as no surprise when at last they asked me to send out a message about this work. **"What we are about to say is very important,"** the Great Council dictated, **"and only certain ones will be able to listen to what we will tell you. Only certain ones will act on it and go on to do the work we are laying out. You know who you are,"** they gestured to their invisible audience, **"and it is to you that we are speaking.**

"Whenever you come together to meditate, pray, and amplify the presence of love on earth, first call on us or any form of the Divine. Also call on the Net of Light. Then," they paused for emphasis, *"call forth the ancestors.* **Call the ancestors of your family line, the ancestors of the land where you were born and where you live now. Call the ancestors everywhere on earth. You may think of them as 'Ancestors of the light': simply think of their Higher Consciousness and invite this enlightened aspect of them to participate in the bond of love the Net of Light provides. As soon as anyone calls on the Net of Light, they will immediately feel its support, and this is as true for the ancestors as it is for you. They too will warm to the Net of Light's embrace, and because from now on they will be connected to this magnificent construct, they will be able to assist the Net in holding and lifting the earth. It is because of you that the ancestors will have this chance to take part in blessing this planet.**

"As soon as the ancestors enter into communion with the Net of Light, the pain from their many lifetimes will fade and dissipate. The past will truly then be past," the Grandmothers laughed out loud. **"Their work with the Net of Light will bless them and bless all the lives they ever touched—their children, their grandchildren, their neighbors, friends, and associates from times gone by. They will be blessed and their descendents will also be blessed. All who followed after them, all who will *ever* follow after them will be blessed. Think for a moment,"** they said, **"about what we are saying."**

"Grandmothers," I stared at them, "this is astounding. This ancestral blessing moves forward and backward in time. This means that every-thing my grandparents passed on to my parents and my parents in turn passed on to me will be purified. Instantly," I said, the enormity of this act dawning on me. "No more 'sins of the fathers visited upon the sons.' No more carrying on of family karma."

"Yes," they nodded. **"We are speaking here of true power."** They smiled, shook their heads slowly, and repeated, **"There is no time. Time is only a mental concept. A man-made concept, not an actu-ality. Time does not exist. Now is forever! And so whenever you enter into *the now* and include the ancestors in that moment, *all* are touched. Everyone receives the taste of love—NOW!**

"The power of this blessing will wrap the earth in a blanket of forgiveness. Heaviness of every kind will lift. Ancient enmities will collapse, tribal hatreds will disperse. Racism, sexism, and prejudice will no longer have a place to call home. And the term, 'stranger,'" they smiled, **"will become obsolete."** I sobbed as I listened to them and after I did that for a while, I began to laugh. "Grandmothers," I said, "how wonderful you are. How *completely* wonderful you are."

"Yes," they said, seeming to agree with me, **"and *you too* are won-derful. This that we are asking of you is wonderful work and all will be struck by the wonder of it. What we are asking you to do is sim-ple, but because humanity has for so long believed in the myth of time, no one has yet come forward to do this healing with the ances-tors."** For a moment they appeared to be lost in thought and then sud-denly they said, **"You are right. It IS wonderful!"** and boring their eyes into mine, they cried, **"Do it!"**

"The longing of the ancestors to share their love and wisdom has reached massive proportions."

It had been a long time since I'd received this much information on something so utterly new to me. This ancestral material continued to fascinate me, and it just kept coming.

One day it dawned on me that there must be something about the times we are living in that was calling this work forth. I had never been the least bit interested in ancestors before—mine or anyone else's—but now the Grandmothers were giving an entire course on the subject. So the next time I went to them, I asked, "Is there something about the times we're living in that makes it important for us to learn about the ancestors? Why now, Grandmothers?"

They smiled at the question and quickly wrapped their wings and cloaks around me. It felt so wonderful to be enfolded by these precious women and for some reason it made me cry. As the Grandmothers rocked and comforted me, I realized how meaningful everything they were teaching me was and how grateful I was to be learning something that had been so entirely unknown. My teachers were introducing me to something so important, and each time I journeyed to them, they taught me more.

"The time for this ancestral work is here," the Grandmothers explained. **"Nothing happens before its time. Are *you* ready for *it*?"** they asked then, their fierce eyes burning into mine and mutely I nodded, 'yes.'

"There is a great longing coming now from those who have gone before you. An upwelling of longing and grief is now rising from all the lands on earth." I began to sob when they said this because I felt the grief they were speaking of. I 'knew' it somehow and as I cried, I realized that the longing of the ancestors and the longing in the land mirrored my own. I too had lived my life aching for something more.

The Grandmothers observed me and nodded in understanding. **"Energy must reach a certain pitch before change can take place,"** they explained. **"Before there can be a switch over, a certain build-up is necessary."**

Then they showed me what looked like a teeter-totter with one end planted on the ground, the other up in the air. "Oh! I see what you mean," I said. **"There has to be enough weight moving from end to end for this shift to occur,"** they said. **"We have been waiting for this mass to build, and now it is ready.**

"Longing holds the power to effect change," they explained. **"You've been told that when a person wants God as much as a drowning man wants air, that person will reach God. Longing for the Divine will lead one to God every time. And in this case, the longing of the ancestors to share their love and wisdom has reached massive proportions. They are tired of seeing their descendents suffer and the suffering of Mother Earth sickens them. The ancestors stand ready to work with us and work with you to make this shift from ignorance to wisdom, from darkness to light.**

"The ancestors can no longer abide the myth of the separation of death. For eons this myth has created so much misery for humanity and the pity of it is, the myth is false," the Grandmothers said. "*There is no death.* You don't yet understand this, but the ancestors know the truth and they wish to help free you. They want to help remove the prison of ignorance that presently surrounds you."

I was leaning forward, focusing all my attention on them, when I began to catch glimpses of various ancestors standing behind the Grandmothers. Some of them were in human form while some were huge, non-specific figures. Some of them reminded me a little of animals, and some were semi-formless, just a vague presence of energy. Each of the ancestors, however, carried the undeniable presence of love.

"Oh, beloved ancestors," I cried as I bowed to them, "thank you for coming. Thank you for your great love. We need you so much. There's a fear of death hanging over the earth now," I said, "so much fear that it's pushing against the forward momentum that's working to carry us toward the light. Fear is blocking the light. It's paralyzing humanity.

"Our energy has become static," I said. "Instead of expanding into love, we're contracting into fear and drawing fear in on ourselves. Today it's hard for us to freely act and so most of what we do is react. We're always reacting to something.

"In spite of this, there are lots of us who would like to expand," I said, "would like to love more and experience more, but it's difficult to do that because we're so closed down. We're wound so tightly inward that we can't free up our energy and let it flow. It may sound simple, but it's hard for us to just let go and love."

As I heard myself speaking these words, I realized I wasn't talking only about individuals. I was also talking about nations, races, and whole cultures. "We're stuck," I said at last. "We're stuck in fear."

The ancestors had remained quiet and now they nodded their understanding. **"This is what has drawn us to you. You need not suffer like this,"** they shook their heads in compassion. **"You are not alone. There is no death, no separation from anyone or anything. You misunderstand, and you have misunderstood for a long, long time. This fear of death and separation that you carry around with you is THE elemental fear,"** they said. **"It is what lies behind all your *lesser* fears. This old pattern of fear is simply not true, and as soon as you call us** and invite us to work with you, this age-old fear of death and separation will melt away. We are here to help you.

"Whenever you come together and work with the Net of Light, remember to invite us to also work with you. We cannot come to you unless you invite us, but we want very much to help. We know the truth of life and of so-called death," they smiled, "so call on us. You needn't be afraid of us. We are now as we ever were except that we have passed through the veil of death and know how insubstantial it is. It's funny, really," they said, and as I listened to them I noticed that I was beginning to feel lighter in my heart. Those heavy feelings were leaving.

"Ancestors," I said, "I really want to learn what you want to teach us. I want to absorb it and move beyond fear. I'm tired of being stuck and confused. I want this freedom you're talking about. I want it for myself, and with your help and the help of the Grandmothers, I promise to spread your message to everyone who's willing to hear it."

They really smiled then. Standing shoulder to shoulder with the Grandmothers, they held hands, and lifting their arms, the Grandmothers and the ancestors began to dance. Forming a circle with me in the center of it, they waltzed in toward me and then out away from me. As they come toward me, I could feel them filling me with love and courage and as they danced away, I felt them pulling away fear. As layers of old energy left me and new energy entered in, I remembered that the Grandmothers had performed this dance shortly after they first appeared. It had felt wonderful then and it felt wonderful now. "Ahhhh!!!" I exhaled and I thought of opening my heart to receive even more of what they were so generously giving.

After this in-and-out dance had gone on for several minutes, I got up and then I began to whirl around in the center of their circle. I did this for a quite a while and when I began to slow down, I flopped down on the ground at their feet. "I'm so tired," I whispered to them as I lay there, "so tired. I had no idea I was this worn out. Thank God," I whimpered as I lay there, unmoving. "Thank God for your help."

I lay flat out like that for a long time. I had no energy left and had lost the ability to move, even the desire to move. As I lay there, just resting, the Grandmothers and the ancestors continued their dance. Filling me with love, taking away fear, and all I could do as they wove in and out around me was to whisper, "Thank you." Over and over and over again—"thank you, thank you."

I rested for a good, long while, and when I finally came to myself, I sat up slowly and then bowed to the ancestors and to the Grandmothers. My energy had returned.

"I can't lie here all day," I said to myself at last. "I've got a lot of stuff to do." And, considering what had just taken place, this statement sounded humorous, even to my ears. I shook my head, laughing at myself, and the Grandmothers put their arms around me and rocked me back and forth. Then they and the ancestors waved me on my way, calling out good-bye.

When I returned to ordinary reality I let myself lie quietly in my room a few minutes, giving my energy time to settle in, and when I felt ready, I walked down the stairs to the kitchen where I fixed myself some lunch. After that, I worked in the garden for a while. Then I began to straighten up the house, dusting and sweeping the daily accumulation of dog hair and as I was cleaning the bathroom mirror, my eye caught my own reflection looking back at me. I stood still for a moment and stared at myself. "There," I said as I looked in the mirror, "is that near and dear stranger."

Pausing while I peered deep into her eyes, I said to her, "It never dawned on me that working with the ancestors would melt away my fear of death." And as I spoke those words, I couldn't help but notice the stunned look on my face. I never *had* imagined that.

I sat down on the edge of the tub then and thought about the progression of this work, thought about how, bit-by-bit, the Grandmothers had led me into ever-deeper contact with the ancestors. I was mulling this over in my mind when I heard the Grandmothers say, **"Everything is laid out. There is a pattern and a perfect time for each occurrence. Timing is always impeccable,"** they said, **"and our time is now. This is the time for our work to flower."**

"...the ancestors will call you blessed and you will be blessed."

As we began to prepare for the next California Gathering, I started noticing how much the Grandmothers' message had already flowered in us. We were really working as a team now, a team rich in leadership and full of harmony. The Laguna Beach group had completely taken over the tasks for the Gathering and the way we were working together showed how thoroughly we had ingested the Grandmothers' message. As we prepared for the arrival of those who would travel to California to take part in this eighth Gathering of the Grandmothers, everything was flowing smoothly. This time we would do deep ancestral work—to heal ourselves, heal our family lines, and heal our beloved planet.

Working from within the power and protection of the Net of Light, we began by breaking into groups of three to send healing as far back down the ancestral lines as possible. As we progressed, the Net of Light embraced, lifted, and healed the pain we had carried for longer than we could remember. No sooner did pain surface than the Net lifted it, healing suffering that had dogged our families for many generations. A lot of crying and embracing went on as together we sang and danced with our ancestors. And, because people from all parts of the world had gathered for this event, the healing that flowed from this retreat spread peace all over the earth. Two months after this there would be a Gathering in Switzerland and another one in the Netherlands.

Because the Gathering in Switzerland was for people new to the Grandmothers' message, we wouldn't do in-depth ancestral work with them. But in the Netherlands it was a different story. The Grandmothers had assured us that great healing would pour forth from this particular Gathering, so when women and men from across Europe, Canada, and the United States showed up for the Dutch Gathering, we were thrilled. With so many different nationalities represented, we anticipated that the depth and breadth of the work we would be able to do might well exceed our expectations. Together we would firmly anchor the Net of Light and this anchoring would protect us as we progressed. From within the safety of this powerful network of support we would be able to amplify the reach of love across time and space.

Everything was unfolding beautifully until I launched into an explanation of how we would actually perform the ancestral work. No sooner did I introduce the subject than the room was filled with anxious faces. Hands flew up everywhere and there were so many questions that it was impossible to address them all. In an instant we had gone from loving peaceful energy to anxiety and disquiet. What was going on?

Then I began to feel the anxiety and fear that were sweeping through the room. There was an inner quaking in my body too and as I became aware of it, I realized it had to be fear. What else would be causing this upheaval? Quickly I asked the participants: "Does anyone notice that fear is arising now?" and a raft of hands shot up.

"This is why this ancestral work has not been done before," I explained. "This sort of work brings up fear—lots of it. Fear of death and fear of the unknown. That's why people have hedged away from what we are about to embrace, why this work hasn't been done before."

While I was speaking, I noticed a young woman standing in the middle of the room who appeared to be extremely agitated. Pacing back and forth, she kept saying, "I must speak, I must speak." Her lovely face was so ravaged by pain that she looked much older than her years, and though I had no idea of what might come out of her mouth, I could see that she did indeed have to speak. So I took the microphone to her.

As I stood beside her and held the mike, I felt her body trembling. She struggled to calm herself and at last she got the words out. "I am from Germany," she said, "and I have felt separated all my life. I've felt separated and alone myself and I've felt it in other people too. So many people are living like this. It's terrible," she wailed. "There is no closeness and there is no love. All is separation!" Then she sobbed, "The pain of this separation is more than I can bear!"

She stood beside me shaking and sobbing, and I watched as the people in the room moved to the edge of their chairs and leaned toward this woman. Speaking with their eyes, they were willing her to let go of the terrible pain she had carried for so long. I was still there beside her, holding her, and praying that her suffering would cease, when, from the back of the room, came the most beautiful sound.

"Oh, how we love you, Oh how we love you," a voice sang. This is what the Grandmothers sing to us when we receive their Empowerment, and now the whole room joined in with the singer. Hands reached out to the young woman while all eyes remained fastened on her and as we continued the song, we watched her face soften. She was absorbing our loving embrace. We could see it! She was starting to let go of the pain she had carried all her life. The Net of Light/Net of Love was holding her.

In less than a minute everything changed and as we watched her soften, most of us cried. In the few moments that had elapsed since she had begun to speak, we had become the One Heart the Grandmothers tell us that we are. We had *become* the Net of Light.

I don't know who began the song that brought healing to this suffering woman. I'll probably never know, but, along with lifting her up, the singer brought a sense of communion to us all and for this, I am forever grateful. I thank the singer for giving voice to this great love and thank everyone who joined in with the song. As over and over we sang, 'Oh, how we love you,' we magnified the power of the Net of Light within ourselves. And it was our Oneness, our presence in the great love that enabled this young woman to feel the sacred connection within her own self.

The instant the people in that room saw her pain, they responded, and because their hearts were so open, the Divine was able to manifest through each of them. Together we experienced a holy moment. From that point on, fear was gone from the Dutch Gathering. Now there were no more anxious questions, no more hesitations, and no more fearful looks. At last we were able to plunge into the ancestral work we'd come together to do.

So we dove deep, welcomed our ancestors, and were welcomed by them. We felt the presence of timeless love in action—witnessed as love and forgiveness moved down the ancestral lines into the past and forward into the future. We forgave and we were forgiven and after we'd done that, we were rewarded with unimaginable healing—for ourselves, for each other, and for everything that lives. We were stunned by the beauty and goodness that filled the room.

Several months before this Gathering was to take place, the Grandmothers had told us, **"When you do this work, the ancestors will call you blessed. And you will be blessed."** Now we understood what they meant.

Note on performing the Grandmothers' ancestral work:

When we invite the ancestors to the Net of Light, we call on their higher consciousness. Essentially we are calling on the Ancestors of the Light—those who, like us, love all and wish to serve. We do not call on the personalities of the ancestors or call up the stories of their lives. In fact, we purposefully stay away from stories, because although every life is filled with them, stories are not who we are. When we work with anyone, we call on the being of that one, so when we call on those who have gone before us, we call on the being that they are and have always been. The *being* that each of us is, is eternal, unchanging, and one with the Divine. This is the one we work with.

Dissolving the supposed barriers between 'life' and 'death' is inevitably part of ancestral work. It doesn't take long to see that 'life' and 'death' are actually one, each an aspect of the flow, not two separate states.

Each time we connect with the ancestors, we ground ourselves in our abiding connection with the Net of Light that loves and supports life throughout time and space. It is from this steady place, the template of the Net of Light, that we work. So if you also wish to do this work, we urge you to first ground yourself in the powerful presence of the Net of Light. The Net provides a lighted highway to other realms, at the same time that it holds and protects us within its matrix of love.

The Ancestral Declaration
by the Great Council of the Grandmothers

I call upon the Net of Light and affirm my union with the Divine. I honor my loving connection with those living today, those who lived in other times, and those yet to be born. Love is not limited by the calendar or by the clock. Each of us is an eternal being, part of the One Love. Recalling this truth, I bow my head in gratitude, saluting the Love within my higher consciousness and within the higher consciousness of everyone else. I invite the ancestors of my family line and the ancestors of the land where I live to join me in this blessing work. I welcome all who love and serve the light to connect within the Net of Light.

As we gather together, I ask forgiveness for my past ignorance and small mindedness; I no longer wish to judge and criticize others; nor do I wish to judge and criticize myself. I also gladly forgive anyone who ever judged or criticized me. I am able to do this with ease each time I remember that it is the breath of the One Love that breathes through me, and the beat of the One Heart that pumps life through me. My immortal self exists outside the limitations of action and beyond the circumstances of time and place. So, as I turn to this presence within me, all pain from the past as well as any fear of the future falls away. All is forgiven.

With my heart open wide, I offer blessings to all beings everywhere. And as we joyously embrace one another, together we sing:

May everyone in all the worlds be happy.
May everyone in all the worlds be happy.
May everyone in all the worlds be happy.

CHAPTER THIRTEEN

Women Across the World Speak on the Net of Light

Ruth Polak, Holland

"I work as a psychotherapist and healer. My age is 79, so I am a grandmother myself. I use the Net of Light every evening before I go to sleep to support our Mother Earth. I also lead a meditation group and we visualize the Net of Light when we are together. I love to see the earth brighten up with the Net. It is a joy for me to feel that there is something I can give to the Earth to help her stay stable in these times."

Kate Hedlund, California, U.S.

"I experience the Net of Light on a physical level when I do my meditative and Qi gong practices, particularly in the middle of the night. During these sessions it feels as though I am embedded in a viscous grid, where the air has taken on the density of water. Rather than moving through this grid, which is both inside and outside my body, there's a sensation that I am being moved by it. At these moments, my mind is quiet, and I am enveloped in a sense of well-being and peace."

Caroline van Daal, the Netherlands

"I started reading the Grandmothers' books and have been working with them ever since. It is like coming home. I have received amazing signs of their presence in my life, and I have felt very close, receiving many messages. When I received the last message about the Net of Light, with a picture of the Net (which helped a great deal in visualizing it), about linking the Net of Light to the earth I realized that the Net of Light is everywhere. But in some places it lies dormant and needs to wake up again. I read the instructions on how to do that quickly and then went off to a vacation in Denmark.

"Standing on the beach in Denmark, hearing the waves, feeling the land, I felt compelled to call on the Net of Light to be re-awakened in that place. I made my own prayer, to re- awaken the Net, and asked the Earth there to remember her power, and her light, and thanked her for carrying us and giving us so much and loving us so much. I felt a deep energy and then I left the beach.

"That night, I returned for a short evening walk in the dark with my husband and our dog. While walking, something caught my attention: lights everywhere on the sand and in the waves! Whenever a wave would crash, there would be lights like stars in the water, and then the sand and stones on the beach would light up as stars as well. Wherever we walked, we left a sparkling trail of light. It was amazing! A true miracle! The evenings before and the evenings after there was nothing like that to be seen, just that one evening. I felt the earth was responding to linking with the Net of Light, and was literally SHOWING us the Net of Light. SHOWING us that we leave a trail of light when we are connected to the Divine and walk our paths fearlessly, with our hearts wide open, holding whatever lies before us.

"We stood and walked and oohed and aahed for a long time that night, feeling very grateful to be so connected and shown such a wonder of life. Thank you for bringing this teaching to the world, and leaving your trail of light. Love and peace from across the ocean."

Janet, Alaska, U.S.

"Recently, during a lunar eclipse, when a group of us connected with the Net of Light (Life), the Tibetan chime in my home began to ring!"

Su Guest, Stafford, UK

"The first time I connected with the Net of Light was in Holland in 2011 at the Gathering of the Grandmothers. It felt vibrant and very comforting. I realized then that I had been working with a similar 'net' for many years, taught to me at a meditation workshop in Asia back in 2001. As time goes on, the Net feels much more fluid and now I sense it more as a moving, changing construction. I work with it every day, and call upon it to hold me in times of need. It feels like a huge lighted security blanket!

I was once at the gym on a quiet afternoon, walking on the treadmill. Hardly anyone was there, just a handful of folks spaced out on various pieces of equipment. I began to visualize the Net and wrapped it around me. I then sensed just how 'yang' the gym was, with all its noise, TV screens, and disconnection amongst people driven by their goals, not giving eye contact to one another, all just chasing time. So, I cast the Net of Light out around the gym, and within five minutes, I had a circle of people around me, chatting, stretching, and exercising on the treadmills next to me. It was quite amazing! I left them to it after a short while, and walked away smiling in my heart...."

Martha Apaza, California, U.S.

"Exactly two years ago my marriage was in a precarious state and our son, a gifted six year old, was also having a hard time. I contacted Penni Thorpe whom I know and respect and she started telling me about the Grandmothers. It really got my attention and I opened my heart to them.

"Every night before going to sleep I would talk to them and ask for help. One day while taking a shower I felt a comforting, warm sensation and while my eyes were closed, I felt a bright light showering me with goodness. Later on while seeking guidance, I heard a clear message, "Everything is how and where it is supposed to be."

I am learning to surrender. Our family is now thriving; we are very fortunate. I've had the honor of relaying some of the information from the Grandmothers to both friends and strangers in need. The beauty of it all is that the Net of Light not only helped me, but has started me on a path to making a difference for others."

Molly Moondakini, Maine, U.S.

"What comes up time and again with the Net of Light is a numinous presence. The Grandmothers are steadfast, supportive, and very much present in the collective. They will meet you with open arms in journeywork, dreamwork, meditation, hiking, painting, even while you're waiting in line at the grocers! The Net of Light is there. It has been cast and will continue to be there for you always, even after you leave this plane of consciousness.

"The biggest lesson I have learned from the Grandmothers is that they stand behind every sentient being, even individuals with whom we feel dissonance or anxiety. It is as if, through our everyday encounters with strangers, family, or friends, the Grandmothers are introducing their extended family to one another. Once we acknowledge that we are all their grandchildren, we will realize that we are all on much stronger common ground than we ever thought we were. The community that comes about because of this awareness then goes on to strengthen the Net of Light."

Anne Calweart, Antwerp, Belgium

"I always say to the Golden Net of Light,
Dear precious, electrifying life,
I am here
I am present
Ready. Here and now.

"I see the Net of Light everywhere, like a golden rain that is falling and going deep into everything that exists. When I think of it, I feel lighter. It's magic."

Farion Pearce, California, U.S.

"I love starting my day with the Net of Light meditation. It reminds me that I am Love; I am Light; and inextricably a part of Everything. In this recognition and experience of being one with our source, I also experience the blessing of being able to help the world and everything in it at the most core level. Taking that awareness into my day, I am supported in acting from that realization."

Karin Alliet, Belgium

"About three years ago I read your first book and for me, the buzzard/eagle seemed to be the bird that represented the Grandmothers. I live in a little house and a few days after I read the book, there was a young buzzard sitting on a wall in the garden, looking at me. It felt like he was saying hello from the Grandmothers. Since that time I've felt a special connection with buzzards and often three of them circle above my house and call me with their special singing sound. Later I went to France and on my way back home, buzzards accompanied me all the way. This was very moving to me and gave me more confidence in my contact with the unseen world."

Nancy Pfeiler, Oregon, U.S.

"I have been meditating with the Net of Light for the last two days and find I am being called to specific places to work. I was called to a river near here and as I worked there with the Net of Light, I watched the connecting light flow to the ocean. I was then called to work with the Net of Light in Minneapolis, Minnesota, throughout the Middle East, particularly in Turkey, and then in Salem, Oregon, where I live. I am certain that working through the Net to connect all these places in light makes a huge difference. Thank you for letting me help."

Miriam Levenson, Belgium

"The Grandmothers recently showed me a new use for the Net of Light. I am empathetic with people who are suffering, which often leads me to feel drained and (sooner or later) resentful. Despite wanting to help as much as possible, I know I can't help everyone, nor can I resolve the cause of their suffering. This chronic, seemingly hopeless state of affairs was getting me down. The only way I could find to disconnect was to become too harsh and strict and even break contact with certain people. I knew I needed to find a way to disconnect from others' suffering in a loving way, while still remaining in a caring relationship with them.

"I went to the Grandmothers in meditation and asked their help. They showed me how I lose energy when I *get hooked* into a person close to me who is suffering, but whose suffering will not be resolved quickly. Then the Grandmothers erected the Net of Light between me and this person—like a strong wall of light. They told me to focus on the Net of Light instead of on the person or their suffering. By focusing on the Net of Light, I would be doing three positive things: I would keep my energy where it belongs (with me); I would strengthen the Net of Light, which will help ease all peoples' suffering, including my own; and the Net of Light would also shine on that specific person, softening her pain and making her life more bearable. All of this would happen without my direct, controlling intervention.

"I immediately replaced my previous, frustrated, and negative thoughts about the situation with that visualization. Within a day I had stopped feeling depressed and angry. After three days, my resentment and frustration were completely gone. The feeling of having to defend myself against this person or her suffering disappeared; I didn't need to walk away nor did I have to take any specific action. I was even able to be in loving contact with her, without feeling judgment of her situation or a desire to rescue her. This was a major breakthrough in a long-standing pattern of relating to others."

Sister Rosemarie, no address

"The sunbeams on Ocean Mother's breast
Form sparkling jewels as I meditate
I am lost in the immensity of Light
Of Love so deep and vast
Waves of blissful harmony and song
Are chords of care and healing
Joining the song of whales and dolphins
Resonating the heartbeat deep below
Earth Mother's flaming core
We are spinning the dance of life
Amid galaxies too myriad to count
Stars join the Net as diamonds
I am held and comforted with preciousness
Beyond all telling...beyond all telling
As my soul searches suffering of ebola,
Typhoons, wars, and humanity's cruelty,
This mysterious presence of Net of Light
Gathers us into One with a Mother's caress
'All shall be well...all things shall be well'
Sings light upon light upon light infinitely"

Catharina Schilperoort, The Hague, Holland

"For many years every week I have taken the Net of Light to a men's prison. Always they look forward to it and if we start to talk before the meditation, they ask me to do the meditation first. Some of them ask me to come for that meditation every day."

Stephanie Lavelanet, Missouri, U.S.

"What you call the Net of Light, or Cosmic Web, in my opinion, is the Energy body, or Dynamic force of the Universe. I felt this a very long time ago and realized my connection with the whole when I was still pretty young. I had a direct experience with the Net of Light when I was about fourteen.

"I was on vacation in Vigo in the Spanish Province they call Las Asturias. My Spanish friends brought me to the beach and while playing in the water, I clearly saw that it was made of particles of Light. This happened to me after reading *The Harpsichord of Saint Francis*, where I was also able to see the aura of everything. I saw the light in the water, and the trees were surrounded with a mist made of Light. This lasted for a whole week, and I understood what the mystics or Native Americans talk about as worlds between worlds. Yes, everything is interconnected. I saw the Net of Light like a web, a transmitter of the power of Life."

Ruby Harvey, Sierra Nevada Mountains, California, U.S.

I have been conscious of the Net of Light beginning in 1999 through the practice of chi-gong. We are a part of the Net but until we are aware of it, we are not plugged in fully. Once we are fully plugged in, waking up allows us to practice awareness and being in the now. Then everything we do, we do for all of us—our mother earth, father sky, and all of us in and on the earth and in the sky. With this knowing, our hearts open and become instruments of spirit for the wellbeing of us all. Finding your page is a delight as then you can feel the energy of all of us working together.

Ragyi, Thailand

"I asked the Grandmothers to show me how the Net of Light works through me and then I realized that I had been working with it for a long time before I knew the Grandmothers. I sit cross-legged on the ground, Namaste, and when I close my eyes, energy comes up through my heart and from there, love spreads.

"There's a tingling feeling at the top of my head and when I feel that, I raise my arms and open them and send light/love out. I respect and recognize the holiness that is moving through me. After that, I'm full of gratitude and place my hands in Namaste/prayer over my heart and often bend forward to the ground.

"I love to do this so much and do it for people, places, the earth, a tree or an animal. I just love this and when I am in a public place, I do it without the gestures."

Judy Ponio, Arizona, U.S.

"It has been a few years now that I've been connected with the Net of Light. Before that I was searching for (not sure what) and wandered aimlessly through my life, hoping for wholeness. The moment I became a '*grandmother*,' I changed. I became more committed to healing the earth, as well as on connecting with my consciousness as we drummed and focused on the Net of Light. The Net connects people in a profound way and helps heal inner conflict—whether you want it or not!

"My experience at the Grandmothers' retreat in California was such a profound time for me. Scared, confused, and feeling like 'I do not belong' was my first thought. Never, and I mean never did I feel like a school kid who gets disrespected by playmates when I was at this retreat. Never before did I feel so soulfully loved. And all because of a Net of Light that caught me while I was spinning through life. My journey of spirit health has moved forward since the first moment I began '*grandmothering*' the earth."

Anna Kente, The Netherlands

"My experience with the Net of Light changed over the years; it grew with me. Now when I work with the Net of Light, I ask that all persons come home to themselves. In September, a group of us women got together and shared our concern for our troubled world—war, and people on the run for their lives, here- there- everywhere. Ebola, and the fears it brings up of a sort of plague, or leprosy... We decided to do a meditation then around the wish that everybody and everything would be able to come HOME to themselves. When I did this, I combined the image I have of the Net of Light with a sense of coming home—for the greatest good of all.

"I still feel the most complete when I cast the Net of Light over the sea. Casting it in and over the sea makes me feel complete because of the water cycle. And somewhere in the ancient movement of casting a net is home for me. Though I am not a hunter, I am a protector, I am a 'watcher on the wall'!"

Jean Oulette & Gloria Edgar, Saskatchewan and Manitoba, Canada

"We each started our journey on our own, having resonated so deeply with the Grandmothers' messages, and we had exceptionally high hopes that a group would begin to form around us in no time at all. We live in separate provinces in Canada and were both experiencing the loss of family and friends in our lives. We felt very alone. It seemed each day was a struggle to deal with feelings of abandonment, fear, wounds, guilt, shame, blame - you name it, and so the comfort a group might have provided would truly have been heaven on earth. Alas - it was not to be - no group then and not even now.

"The Grandmothers had a very different plan in mind for us. They were on a mission to show us just how strong we both were—all on our own. With no fellow human beings to turn to when we experienced fears of solitude and doubts about our lives and ourselves we were given no choice but to reach out to the Net of Light and the Grandmothers. We feel it was the Net that held us together during those times and we are proud to say that today we are strong, full of joy, and looking forward to the future, no matter what it holds, because we know in our hearts that we will be able to handle it with love. We have learned that no matter what your problem is, *wrap it in the Net* (love) and all will be well."

Stephanie Mainberger, Zurich, Switzerland

"Since receiving the Grandmothers' Empowerment, I cannot feel lonely anymore. If I do feel alone, immediately I recall that I can call the Grandmothers, be it the archetype within myself or the members of Grandmothers Speak that I know. I imagine they are with me and the lonesome feeling can no longer linger upon my soul. When I know that someone is desperate, besides praying for them, I can ask the Grandmothers to go there and help, sustain, and console them.

"When I read awful news in the newspapers, magazines, or see it on TV, I recall the Net of Light and concentrate on it over that specific place (like Syria) and I hold that image. Thus, I'm 'doing' something to heal the world and I hope it helps.

"I am a housewife—no special talents, no specific great tasks—but I try to remember to hold a situation, just listening to what my husband, children, grandchildren, or friends tell me. Often I just listen and hold while they pour out their feelings and thoughts. Even though I cannot do much about the situation, I can hold them. Much has changed within myself and I am extremely grateful to have had the opportunity of receiving the Grandmothers' Empowerment."

Barbara Moore, North Carolina, U.S.

"The most recent experiences I had with the Net of Light involved two pregnancies.

One mother is my 'tribal sister.' You know—in the 1970s when you had a tribe of people who were like family? Well, when we met I was sixteen and she, my tribal sister, was three. She is now forty-four, got married four years ago for the first time, and wanted to have a child. Her heart longed for this. Earlier in her life she had her tubes tied so she had the surgery that successfully reversed this and nine months ago she got pregnant.

"A short time into her pregnancy, she called and asked for spiritual help as her doctor said her cervix was already opening and thinning. As soon as she asked for help the image of the Net of Light flashed in my mind's eye, and I began to describe it to her. We went to work together, weaving the Net of Light into her cervix to hold, hold, hold her child. For months we worked long distance, me on the east coast, and she on the west coast.

"We worked together, weaving and holding. We saw her infused with Net of Light and that settled her body down into gravity, calming her, and she was able to rest. Her doctor told her she had to be on bed rest, and let me say that sitting still or lying down was not her way! The Grandmothers helped her over and over throughout the many months as her son grew inside her body, surrounded by and floating in the Net of Light. He was born last week. There were some complications and we continued casting the Net for him and his mother to provide them both with comfort, ease and healing. And I just got the word—they are home now. Mother and son both doing well!

"The second mother is the daughter of a close friend. She was in labor for forty-eight hours with complications. My friend, who was in the delivery room with her daughter, texted me, saying they were exhausted and scared. Once again, the Net of Light came to my mind's eye. I texted a picture of the Net of Light to her and suggested that she 'place' it in her cervix. The mother was able to do this and brought the Net of Light to life within herself. My friend said she was so grateful as after that she felt more peace in the delivery room and her daughter was able to center herself. The baby is safely in the world now.

"Both of these children feel precious to me and I am grateful to the Grandmothers for allowing me to be an instrument in this way. I have never been physically present at a birth, yet now I truly feel connected to the womb of life."

Heather Small, address unknown

"If there's one way everyone can know the Net of Light is real, it is to get to know in their own bodies what is known among body workers as the *fascial web*. Fascia is connective tissue within our bodies, connecting everything to everything else. It is one continuous unit throughout our physical structure, holding in place everything from our organs, to our bones, to our vessels of fluid. It supports everything!

"I am an energy healer, which is how I encountered information on this marvelous structure. I experience it in two ways—one is through the physical feeling of touching and stretching it. The other way I experience it is through the energy it carries throughout the body. The way I *see* it when I work with someone is more like the way photos of the *Cosmic Web* look, sparkling with life and vitality.

"It's real, and every single one of us has it inside us. It can be felt, whether in the physical, or in the broader, energetic sense. The web is not limited to any one kind of perception. It exists on *all* levels and it's everywhere—in our bodies and in the cosmos.

"I was seeking God for so long and the Grandmothers were my point of direct, unmistakable connection—the first way of receiving Divine guidance for myself that I could believe in. They found so many ways to get to me and have opened my understanding and perception more and more. It just keeps going. I am so pleased, so pleased, to be part of their work. It brings me such joy to re-affirm the sacredness of every spot of Earth, of every being, that I touch, wherever I go. Working with the Net of Light is an effortless, universal way to extend their love."

Linnea Haley, California, U. S.

"I am the inner Net of Light that gives back to the outer Net of Light from which I receive."

Marianne Iten Thurig, Switzerland

"I had never heard of the Grandmothers' message but deep in my heart, I sensed a connection with people, whether I knew them or whether they were strangers to me. I felt this connection even when there were unsolvable difficulties between us and I desired to express this feeling of connection on a large silk cloth.

"The connection revealed itself as a mesh that existed endlessly throughout time and space. Woven within it were goddesses and idols that I recognized from my studies in women's history and superimposed upon this Net of Light were large blue dancers with caressing hands.

"As I began to work on the silk, I realized that it is the feminine qualities that make these connections possible and I became aware that I, myself, need these feminine qualities and abilities if I am to effect change in the world. I worked on this piece for months and as my joy in it increased, a girlfriend, upon seeing the work, invited me to 'A Call to Power' meeting.

"I was hugely surprised as Ulrike Stedniz, the German translator of the Grandmothers' messages, read out the most recently received teachings! She said aloud what I had believed were my own private thoughts! Now everything made sense and I had a feeling of being at home. Gratitude, inspiration and joy have lived with me since then.

"A few months later I met Sharon McErlane during a Gathering of the Grandmothers in Switzerland. She requested that my silk painting hang behind her so she could refer to the Net of Light portrayed there. Our meeting and that wonder-filled day stayed with me, and I asked the Grandmothers what did this all mean in connection with my work on silk? They answered, saying that the silk painting belonged to Sharon. It was my privilege to then send it on to her.

"My work on silk continues to develop, involving friends in my creations. Together we bring into existence feminine strengthening and connecting scarves of light. My heart-felt gratitude goes to the Grandmothers."

Diana Boyce, North Carolina, U.S.

"I've had some serious health challenges lately and for the first time in my life found myself asking anyone and everyone for prayers. I asked my Grandmothers' group friends to send me light and love and asked my church-going friends to pray for me. My name was on several prayer lists and at many meetings of my Grandmothers' group, they worked with the Net of Light for me.

"I had never asked for so many prayers in my life... so one night when I was meditating with the Net of Light, I asked the Grandmothers, Why am I asking for so many prayers? Am I doing this out of fear? I didn't want to be afraid and I didn't feel especially afraid. But why then such a desire?

"The Grandmothers told me that though my faith was strong, the Net of Light and all these prayers I was asking for would do great good. There are many, they said, who are afraid and for many different reasons. Through spending time with the Net of Light and praying, *all of these people* would open to receiving love and light. *Every one of them* would have the opportunity to heal. They told me that I was cared for with or without the prayers of others, but by asking for all these prayers, I was helping make it possible for great good to occur for many. I was helping open the way for them to also receive."

Heidi Nystrom, Finland

"An amazing thing happened last week. We visited Bulgaria to play golf by the Black Sea and two days before coming back home, we woke up and noticed a big black worm or snake-like thing on our floor. I asked for the message of this black thing and soon understood that it was not a message of love. Something about it was disturbing.

"During the whole five hours on the golf course that day I prayed and talked to all the powers of love and light, working with the Net of Light and asking light to come in and forgive the past. That night I dreamed of a huge being that looked like one of the ancient sons of God. I asked for him to be brought to light and for all the souls that had ever worked for or with him to do the same. They all responded to this prayer of forgiveness and there were as many of them present as my eyes could see. Then I asked them to forgive, to be forgiven, and to forgive themselves. When I asked this, the huge being fell into pieces and I asked that all these souls be freed and that there be peace between them all.

"The next morning the sky was cloudy but the sun shone though holes in the clouds over both the land and the sea. As I walked and played golf I kept asking for more love and light and for the Net of Light to be strong. Then I heard the words: *the Net of Light is being built.* After our game of golf was over and we were sitting outside to have something to eat, suddenly we looked up and there was an eagle circling above us."

Anonymous, somewhere in Europe

"The first time I connected with the Net of Light I just had to cry, without any sound, crying happily, tears streaming over my face. It felt good, like being healed. Later on you asked us to think of the sacred places in Ireland that were pouring light into the Net of Light. And as I thought of that, the Net became stronger and stronger, and I felt that too.

"Every month I looked forward to the messages from the Grand-mothers and many times I had the idea that their messages were meant for me; exactly right in my situation. I really lived with the Grand-mothers then, blessing the people on the tram and the train and in the streets.

"I am now a minister in the Protestant Church. I am happy in this job and the funny thing is, that there are many grandmothers in my church. But the sad thing is, that now I can use only the words and images of the Christian tradition. I would love to tell all these grandmothers in church about the Grandmothers, but they wouldn't understand.

"Still, I connect to the Net of Light often, throwing the Net over the countries, over nature, and people. And I still bless the people in the streets and I share blessings in that way with my colleagues and other Christians in church."

Claudie Penn, England

"I'm a business coach and facilitator, and for the last ten years a lot of my work has been focused on women's empowerment, running leadership programs for women, and coaching women emerging into management roles. It's a real passion of mine. In December 2013 I had re-launched my business and was exhausted so I decided to spend a few weeks at home meditating, writing, and reflecting. At this point the Net of Light began to appear in my dreams and meditations, and I began writing about it in my journal. I'm not sure exactly when it happened, but I suddenly had this constant vision of a net, almost like a fishing net connecting and holding everything and everyone in the world and creating a real sense of safety and calm inside me.

"After a few days I was sitting at a bus stop thinking about this net so I took out my smart phone and googled 'Net of Light,' and the first thing to come up was the Grandmothers website. When I started reading it, I nearly fell off the bench. It was exactly relevant to my life and the yearning I'd been feeling for meaning and a connection to the Divine as a woman. I ordered both books immediately and it's already been massively life changing for me. I saw that the Gathering of the Grandmothers in California was in March and decided I really wanted to go, even though I wasn't connected with any Grandmothers' groups, hadn't received the empowerment, etc. It just felt important. Funnily enough when I decided I wanted to go I had no idea how I would afford it, so I decided that if I got some new work, then I would go. The week after that, I suddenly had four major contracts appear with more money than I've made in the last couple of years so I decided that was a bit of a sign!!"

Sally Schoof, California, U.S.

"The Net of Light is my friend. When I call on it, I am empowered and filled completely with love, hope, and the energy to do the work that is so necessary to do. Whenever I need a place to go, I head to my spot on the Net of Light because there I feel safe and connected to the Grandmothers and Mother Earth. This is necessary work we are doing, and being a part of it helps me feel connected to other like people. The Grandmothers are helping me to heal the world and for this I am very grateful."

Anonymous, Northern Europe

"A few years ago, there was a group of men who came to one of our Gatherings of the Grandmothers. During our ceremony they stood together, spoke to the women there, and bowed to them. I was moved by that gesture and cried. You asked the crying women to tell their story and I didn›t answer then, but I will now.

"My grandmother, along with her five children, was interned in a Japanese concentration camp in Indonesia during World War II. The youngest was only a baby. They had to leave their house and belongings and my grandfather was sent to the camp for the men while my grandmother and the children were sent to one of the camps for women and children. My grandmother, father, uncles, and aunts had to live there in a very small room together with two other families and lots of rats. There was hardly any food, but many diseases. My Father, who was very young, was ill for half a year and he hardly survived. But they did survive, all seven, thanks to God.

"Every day, so the story goes, the women and children had to turn up at appeal and

bow to the Japanese soldiers for an hour in the heat of the day. A lot of dirty, hungry, sick, and thirsty women and children bowing in the heat of the day to a few armed soldiers. That is a painful image that I carry with me. My father never really came out of this period and suffered from traumatic stress syndrome all his life. That was difficult for him and for us—for his wife and his children.

"So when the men at our Grandmothers' ceremony bowed to us, it took me by surprise.

It was as if the world had turned around: a few vulnerable men bowing to a large group of women in respect and appreciation. It made me really cry. It is a healing picture that I carry in my head that I will never forget.

"This war-story and the role of my grandfather, who was a professor of theology, caused a great deal of suffering in my family. My grandfather did not have enough appreciation for his fantastic wife, my grandmother. He took her and all that she did for granted. He was a great man, but he did not give much thought to his wife and children—certainly he did not consider all that they had been through. Women, in his opinion, were not supposed to study. Their place was at home. But my aunts (later on in their lives), my nieces, and I did study, thanks to the big changes in society.

"Connecting to the Net of Light helps me to forgive my father and grandfather as well as to forgive the Japanese. It is comforting for me to be able to help heal the pain and frustration in my family by connecting to the Net of Light. It is also comforting to work with my ancestors through the Net of Light. The idea that this action of connecting will heal generations before and after me is a real comfort!

"The world seems to be on fire today with war and tragedy but in spite of all the suffering in the world, I thank the Grandmothers and the Net of Light for the LOVE that we can spread."

Terry Du Beau, Montana, U.S.

"When I hear news of a hurricane, accident, fire, or other calamity in the world that involves the planet, people, plants, or animals, I SEE myself casting the Net of Light to that place almost like a fisherwoman casting a net off the side of her boat. The Net has lights in it at all the intersecting webs. WE ARE THOSE LIGHTS! And we cast our energy and prayers to those places that need our love and support because we are one! Visualizing the Net of Light like this helps me place my energy more directly into the scene I have witnessed or heard about!"

Aisha North, address unknown

"There is a new grid of energetic filaments criss-crossing the globe that can be likened to acupuncture points, set into energetic pathways at junctures that serve not only to anchor these energies, but also to magnify them.

"What we are talking about is the brand new energetic system of pathways that many of you have been instrumental in setting up. As you all connected you anchored a vast number of these grid points, manifested through the interaction between your physical bodies and these incoming energies, bringing this whole net of pathways into being. Now, it is up and running, albeit not at its fullest potential yet. A certain period for adjustment is needed as this is a new energetic environment not just for you, but for this whole planet.

"This vast Net not only covers your globe, it is also deeply embedded within the structure of this planet, all the way down to the very core. It can be likened to a continuous field of energy that not only surrounds you, but is embedded within every particle of your being, connecting you all in a very new way. This all-encompassing field will interact with everything you see around you, and everything that is still unseen, and cannot be likened to anything that has ever been put into place around this part of Creation defined as Planet Earth. It will enfold you all as if in a womb of energetic fabric to heighten the frequency of everything it interacts with. A huge shift will lift the entire planet to a new octave, and as this happens, you will be lifted along with it and start to vibrate at an ever-increasing frequential tune."

Peggy Huddleston, Alabama, U.S.

"In the four years since the Grandmothers came into my life, I've learned that their timing is perfect. And their perfect-fit gift to me came on a trip home from a Grandmothers' Gathering in Lithuania in 2012. Flying from Vilnius into Copenhagen at dusk, I saw a network of light that no one else seemed to notice, but one I recognized. I had been gifted with seeing the Net of Light! Already blown away by this experience, a few hours later when we were flying over Greenland, I felt an overwhelming gratitude and love for the Divine and when I looked out the window, I saw two coastal islands coming together to form a perfect heart. Then the entire landscape turned an exquisite shade of pink and I cried, overwhelmed with happiness for being shown something so beautiful and miraculous. '**We knew you'd love it,**' the Grandmothers said."

Anne, Holland

"I use the Net when I am biking, when I am walking; I work with the Net of Light in my cells, and the experience now is that *I am the Net of Light.* There are no boundaries anymore. There is only the experience of the Light, the connection of the Net of Light.

"I use the Net of Light for pain or little traumas. It is helping me! I also use it to make things better in the world because there is only One, but in that One, there are many sick parts. The Yang parts in the world are out of control now, and by using the Net of Light, I help place seeds of light in the parts that are out of control. When we do this, we bring back the balance of yin and yang on Earth that is so much needed. I am confident that we will all become aware, in our own time, and become only LIGHT.

"When the Grandmothers call me, I go to their Gatherings in Holland and Belgium. Once in a while I attend a Grandmothers' study circle but mostly I work alone. But we are all One so I am never alone! I use the books for studying and go deeper and deeper into what the Grandmothers teach. When I want to know what the Grandmothers want to tell me, I listen to my heart and hear it speaking the truth. But when I want to have a quick answer, I open the book and see what the text has to say. It is always the right solution and answer.

"So, from my heart I pray, 'May all the people in all the worlds be happy.'"

CHAPTER FOURTEEN:
THE GRANDMOTHERS' WORKBOOK

"These are tools for furthering individual empowerment."

'Knowing about' something, even 'knowing' it, is not the same thing as living it. The Grandmothers' meditations are therefore designed to give a visceral understanding of the truths they have come to impart. These meditations have been gathered together here so the reader can easily access them.

These teachings contain layers of meaning and are **"tools for furthering individual empowerment."** Whether or not you have chosen to receive the Grandmothers' Empowerment, these tools will help you put their work into practice. They say, **"These meditations anchor our teachings, allowing our lessons to go deeply into the viscera of your body/mind and be held there. Then they can become your own truth. When you have owned and taken in these truths, they will no longer be just thoughts that pass through your mind, but will be deeply known."**

The Grandmothers' meditations create change. Not just intellectual exercises, they are opportunities to experience another way of being. This part of the book is a workbook for those who seek an active part in this work. Some meditations are simple, while others are more complex, but all of them are designed to help you heal, balance and expand your awareness and consciousness. As this happens, you will, by your very being, bless all life on earth. You can, if you like, record these meditations so you can listen directly to the power in the Grandmothers' words.

PRELIMINARY RELAXATION EXERCISE

If you are unfamiliar with meditating, this simple method will bring you to a point of relaxation, enabling you to work with the Grandmothers. Use it as needed to precede the following meditations.

To begin, find a place where you can be alone, take a seat and once you have, think of why you are doing this. What is it you want from this experience? You may be curious about these so-called Grandmothers, or you may want to open yourself to the presence of the Divine. Be clear about what you are seeking as you approach this work. Your clarity honors them and you. *This is your intention.*

Once you have taken your seat, let your body assume an open position. Uncross your hands and feet, unless you are sitting cross-legged on the floor, and take a moment to notice how perfectly the chair or the floor supports you. They hold us at every moment, though we are seldom aware of it. Feel your contact with the chair or floor and notice how comfortable or uncomfortable you are.

How is your body occupying space? Where is its weight placed? Notice your entire body. Are your feet heavy on the floor? Do you feel your feet? Take the time you need to settle in and observe your total self with a somewhat disinterested air, like taking inventory. Is your heart beating fast or slowly? Is the rhythm of your breath regular or irregular? *Just notice.*

Take in a slow, deep breath and as you exhale, think of letting go of the old (old thoughts, old attitudes, old air) and when you inhale, think of taking in the new. Close your eyes and do this three or four times, feeling your breath moving in and out with a deep, slow rhythm. *Letting go of the old, opening to the new.*

Observe your heart beating and notice its rhythm. Is it slowing down? Speeding up? What is the temperature of your body? Your heart may beat fast or steadily. Your body may feel warm or cool. You may be tense or relaxed as you begin, but don't try to change anything about yourself. Don't force yourself to 'try' to relax. Simply observe without judging yourself. *Observe and take your time.*

Notice where your body feels tight and where it feels softer, if you are holding your breath or breathing fast or slowly. No judgment. No hurry. *Just keep observing* without evaluating yourself and when you are ready you can let the Grandmothers know you'd like to begin.

MEDITATION ON THE NET OF LIGHT

We begin with a meditation on the Net of Light. The Grandmothers ask us to do this meditation often in order to extend the grace of this lighted support system to everyone and everything on Earth.

"Begin to work with the Net of Light," they say, "by thinking of a vast lighted fishing net spread over the earth and stretching into the distance, as far as your eyes can see. This is the great Net of Light that will support the earth and all life on this planet during the times of change that have come. The Net of Light covers the earth from above, from below, and permeates the earth like a great grid. It penetrates, holds, and touches everything. This is the Net of Light that will hold the earth while the energies of yin and yang shift. And they *will* shift," the Grandmothers say; "the change has already begun.

"Walk forward and take your place on the Net of Light. Somewhere where two of the strands come together forming an 'x' or a 't' is a place that will feel just right for you. Walk forward and take your place there. Here you can rest and allow the Net of Light to hold and support you while at the same time you support it.

"We have many times said that the Net of Light is lit by the jewel of the heart. This is true. Experience now as the radiant jewel of your own heart begins to open and broadcast its light along the strands of the Net. Every person who works with the Net of Light is linked in light with others who also work with it. Experience your union now with people all over the globe who are connected by the Net of Light. Some call it a Web of Light, a lighted grid, the Cosmic Web, or Indra's net, but whatever they call it, it is the same construct.

"Call on the Net and find your place on it and think of receiving and sending light throughout this vast network. As soon as you think this thought, your energy will follow it, and you will feel the Net of Light working in and through you.

"Experience your union with us and with all those who work with us. There are thousands of you all over the earth. Experience your union with the sacred and holy places on this planet and all the sacred and holy beings—the great saints, sages, and avatars who gladly give their lives in service—who have come at this time to avert the catastrophe that looms over the earth. Experience your union with those of good heart who seek the highest good for all life. Know and feel the power of this union and let your body experience this force of and for good.

"Once you have strongly felt this power, begin to cast the Net of Light to those who don't know about it. Cast wherever there is suffering—to human beings, to animals, to conditions of every kind, to all forms of life, and to Mother Earth herself. Magnify the presence of the Net of Light for people who are longing to serve, but haven't yet found a way to access the Divine. As you cast the Net of Light, many who have, until this moment been asleep to the fundamental connection that we all share, will begin to awaken and feel the spark of Divinity coming to life within them. Ask the radiant Net of Light to hold all life in its embrace and know that each time you work like this, you are adding to the reach and power of the great Net.

"Cast the Net to all women and men everywhere. Cast to the leaders of this world to remind them that they are a precious part of the Net of Light that holds and supports life. Cast to the animal kingdom, asking that every animal receive what it most needs. Cast to the plant kingdom and to the mineral kingdom as well. Cast to everything that lives, and when you have done that, ask that everyone in all the worlds be happy.

"This is how to work with the Net of Light. There is no greater service you can perform. We ask you to give from your heart and work with the Net of Light every day. Do it for yourself, and for the sake of everything that lives. We bless you."

Meditation on living as the Container that You Are

Perhaps one of the strongest and most telling qualities of yin energy is its ability to hold, accept and nurture whatever presents itself. When we don't push against something, don't exclude or judge anything or anyone, but instead bring whatever comes onto our lap and hold it there so it can settle into itself and find its place, we allow yin to work through us. Not dramatizing the challenge of the moment, but simply being *with* the moment. This quality of nurturing acceptance belongs to the Mother, and we ourselves can open like this to the Feminine Principle and deal with people, ideas, and situations—in short, with everything—in this way. Accepting, accepting. Initially this may seem a strange idea to you—a foreign one, but that's only because this concept has been missing from our world for a long time.

A position of openness and acceptance creates a force field of harmony. There is an undeniable greatness in what the Grandmothers call the *Container*. "She who holds" accepts what is, and this acceptance allows everyone and everything to relax and be who and what they are. Held by and at one with the Container, we become 'real.' And because this is so, this meditation creates a foundation for harmonious relationships. It harmonizes women and men, seeming opposites, yin and yang.

"**It's time to experience the container that you are,**" the Grandmothers say. "**You are the container that holds love, that holds life, and supports everything that lives. Your capacity is enormous. Become aware of yourself.**"

To experience yourself as this Container they speak of, begin by moving into a state of relaxation, sitting with your arms and legs uncrossed and your spine straight. Place your hands palms up on your lap and notice what it's like for you to sit in such an open posture. How does your body feel as you sit this way? How do you feel? As you do this, don't judge yourself or try to change anything about yourself—just notice. As you sit, you will find yourself dropping into a deeply receptive state, the position of the Container. Open and receptive to whatever comes. This position evokes the presence of the Great Mother—She who accepts all life and holds everything. As you sit this way, you may become aware She is with you, holding you, and at the same moment, She is sitting inside you. Take a few minutes to enjoy your powerful connection with the Great Mother by being open, receptive.

As you sit, you may also become aware of the chair underneath you and the support you are being given by both the chair and the floor. At this very moment you are in your right place.

Now take a moment to invite whatever comes onto the screen of your mind. Let it come up as it will, and when something appears, quietly hold it there. Simply hold whatever shows itself. Don't move toward it, and don't move away from it. Let it come to you and be with you for as long as it wants, and when it gets up and leaves, accept and hold whatever comes next.

You will find you're able do this because you are a container and this is what a container does. It holds. A container is not the least affected by what fills it. If you pour water into a pot, the pot is unchanged. If you pour milk into it, it is still unchanged. Become aware of how it feels to simply hold like this—just for this moment, unaffected by whatever comes to your mind. No judgment, no evaluation, and if judgment should appear, well, hold judgment in this nonjudgmental way too.

The Grandmothers are performing this action with you—holding you and holding with you so you can learn what it's like to be the container that you actually are. **"In the vastness of your being, you can do this,"** they say. **"You are great enough to hold everything."** You may become aware of the truth in their words: that *just for now you can accept and hold everything.*

A succession of people, problems, and stories may parade through your mind. Let them. You can simply sit there, and knowing that the Grandmothers are present with you and are holding you, you can relax and watch the parade. You may discover it's a lot like being at the movies. Scenes come and go, rise up and fall away, and should a scene stay on for a while, hoping perhaps to become the main feature, let it. Simply hold and observe. **"Hold, hold, hold,"** the Grandmothers say, for as long as is needed and while you're holding, be aware of your body and notice how you're feeling. What is it like to be a container?

"As you go through life, stay within the awareness of the container that you are and hold whatever comes to you. Hold it as a basin holds water or as a planter holds earth. Water does not change the shape or color of a basin. Earth does not alter the size or shape of a pot. A container is. It simply holds. *You* hold. You can encompass all this because *it is your nature to be the container. This* is Yin." Feel it.

WORKING WITH THE CIRCLE OF STONES

I asked the Grandmothers for a simple, safe, and easy way to work with them, and they gave us the Circle of Stones. The Grandmothers sat themselves down on the ground and formed a circle with a large, smooth stone facing each one of them. **"This circle is a sacred space, an opening to the great below and the great above,"** they said. **"Unless it's something you enjoy doing, you need no longer journey in the old way. Instead, you can let *us* call the spirits to you.**

"This way will be easier because you won't have to perform the work alone, but can journey to different levels of non-ordinary reality under our guidance and protection. We will be there to show the way and help you get to where you want to go." Here is a simple way of working, one you can use yourself in order to communicate with the Great Council of the Grandmothers.

To experience what it's like to journey with the Grandmothers, think of them sitting directly before you, in formation with the Circle of Stones described above. Then enter their circle and walk forward until you are standing in their midst. "Feel your place in this circle," the Grandmothers say, "and remember that all forms of the Divine are with us as we work together. You are an integral part of this circle, and the fact that you are *part* of this circle, and not separate from it, is important. You are one with us, one with the Divine, and this is true for everyone who chooses to work with us. Also, once you step into this circle, you will become the focus of the entire circle. Your questions will be answered here.

"Ask only one question each time you step into the circle and everything you hear, see, and experience after your question will be in response to it. Pay attention to what happens after you ask, and do not stray from your question."

You can journey to the Grandmothers with the monotonous beat of a drum, to the swish/swish of your windshield wipers, or to any repetitive sound as background music. You can also do it silently. Somewhere between ten and thirty minutes will give you enough time for a journey.

Ask the Grandmothers about something you have already put some energy into and don't ask them a 'yes' or 'no' question, as this won't give you much information. Ask the Grandmothers something you *really* want to know and take the time to hone your question. I suggest you begin your journey in humility, asking something that will help others in addition to yourself. The Divine *is* compassion and therefore operates on compassion. So if your question has to do with being of service in the world, it is much more likely to be answered.

You will be able to enter both the Upper and the Lower World from the Circle of Stones but since journeying isn't the subject of this book, we won't go into what working in these worlds is like. The Circle of Stones is designed to make journeying simpler, safer, and easier and, as I mentioned, everything in non-ordinary reality can be explored by starting from the center of this circle.

After you have formulated your question, greet the Grandmothers and then humbly and sincerely ask your question. Once you've done that, notice what comes to you. What do you see? Hear? Touch? Feel? Think? Smell? Taste? The Grandmothers may tell you something, show you something, or allow you to experience something. These journeys to and with the Grandmothers can be emotional and surprising, as the Grandmothers know how to circumvent the limitations of your mind and go directly to your heart. They know what it will take to bring you to an understanding of the question you have asked, and that is what they will give you.

Once you've asked, open your mind wide and *observe*. Be curious about the process and while you're noticing whatever it is you're noticing, remind yourself not to judge your experience, the Grandmothers, or yourself. *Just observe*. The Grandmothers are consummate teachers and know what they are doing so let the good student you are turn your awareness to whatever comes to you. You may find it helpful to speak your journey into a recorder so you won't have to try to remember everything that happens. Also, if you record it, you can go back later and listen to what transpires during your adventure.

When you make the decision to step into the Grandmothers' Circle, you enter the realm of non-ordinary reality and when you step out of their Circle, you make the decision to return to ordinary reality. So, after your journey is over, thank the Grandmothers and then respectfully step out of the Circle of Stones.

When we journey to and with the Grandmothers, we do so to learn how to be of greater service in the world. Working with the Grandmothers is not meant as an escape from the pain of life but as a means of being of service *in* and *for* the world. To be effective in the world, you must keep your feet on the ground so I suggest you journey to the Grandmothers no more than two or three times each week.

HEALING THE ANCESTRAL LINES

Ancestral work magnifies the power of all that we do with the Grandmothers. We invite the ancestors to join us each time we work with the Net of Light and, as we've worked with them, we've learned that because there is no actual 'time', whatever is helpful to us, is also helpful to the ancestors. Whatever heals us, can heal them. When we pass the Grandmothers' Empowerment on to others, we also offer it to their ancestors, who, in turn, may pass it further down the ancestral lines. Thus, not only is life in the present moment healed, the whole of life is healed.

Here is a potent piece of work that you can do, to heal your own ancestral lines. Working in groups of three, one at a time, you will play three separate parts. Decide which person will be the *receiver* first and this person will face away from the other two, hands crossed over her heart to remind herself to center the work there. The other two, who will be the *ancestral representatives* of her maternal and paternal lines, will stand, her maternal representative behind her left shoulder, her paternal representative behind her right shoulder.

Together, all close their eyes and feel, picture, or imagine the Net of Light. Call on the Grandmothers who will then link you with the higher consciousness of the Ancestors of Light. The Ancestors of Light are those who have gone before you who wish to be of service at this time. Like you, these beings from times gone by are working for the highest good of all.

When you've made a good connection with the Net of Light, the Grandmothers, and the Ancestors of Light, the *receiver* asks the Grandmothers to show her or guide her to a wound that's been carried for a long time—something that may be from her own life or may have been carried by someone else in her ancestral lines. Whether or not she is able to get in touch with this wound at the moment, because she is asking to make contact with it, the proper energy will be sent to this wounded place to bring light and healing.

The *receiver* then turns and faces the other two and all three Namaste with hands in a prayer position at heart level (I salute the Divinity within you) to each other. When she feels ready, with hands still in the Namaste mudra, the *receiver* speaks the classic Hawaiian Ho'oponopono prayer to the other two, one at a time, saying, *"I'm sorry, please forgive me, thank you, I love you."* The maternal and paternal representatives make no reply as she speaks to them, but hands over their hearts, they simply receive.

The *receiver* next thinks of the blessings she has received in this life-time and offers a statement of prayer, of thankfulness, and blessings to the *ancestral representatives*. She may mention some of the gifts she was given at birth (for example, "Thank you for my intelligence, for my strong constitution," etc.) She may speak these blessings out loud or silently, but it is more powerful to speak them out loud. While the *ancestral representatives* receive the forgiveness and the acknowledgment of the blessings and gifts from the *receiver*, their hands remain crossed over their hearts so they can receive and ground the work there.

The *receiver* then turns around and faces away from the *ancestral representatives*. The representative of the maternal line touches the back of the *receiver's* left shoulder and the paternal representative, the back of her right shoulder. As they stand in this position all three of them call on the Net of Light to send forgiveness as far back as possible down the ancestral lines. The *ancestral representatives* then both quietly speak words of love, encouragement, solidarity and strength to the *receiver* (for example, "I am proud of you. I like who you've become..." etc.)

Holding hands with one another while their other hand remains on the *receiver's* shoulder, the *ancestral representatives* together speak the Ho'oponopono to her. "We're sorry, please forgive us, thank you, we love you."

After that, the *ancestral representatives* remove their hands from the shoulders of the *receiver*. She then turns around to face them again, and all bow with a Namaste. All of them take a minute or two of silence and then quietly share with one another what they each felt or experienced. The work then proceeds with the other two taking the position as the receiver.

You will find many more Grandmothers' meditations at the back of their other two books, *A Call to Power: the Grandmothers Speak* and *Our Love is Our Power*.

AFTERWORD

*"You were born to love—
to love and lift your planet."*

I had now reached what seemed to be the end of this book. It felt like I'd
said all I needed to say and I hadn't received new messages from the
Grandmothers in quite some time. But just as I was about to wrap it up,
this message came. It came for me and it came for you, dear reader. So
here is the Grandmothers' *last word*—at least for now.

"You need a nudge to move you to dive deeper within yourself,"
the Grandmothers said, eyeing me over the tops of their noses, **"to tap
you into the core of your being. We see you and we notice that the
world is distracting you. This continuous distraction will lead you
nowhere. You will go round in circles if you keep paying attention
to the world and will become lost. We believe in you,"** they said. **"We
believe in you because we see what and who you are and so we have
come to prod you to turn your awareness, not outward to the world,
but inward. Step into your heart now, and call on us. We will never
fail you.**

"You are a great being," they said, **"and your taking birth at this
time was not an accident. There is important work awaiting you.
You are needed to pass on our Empowerment into the energy of
yin—to pass it to women and men, to young and old, to pass it to
every race, faith, and religion on earth. Pass it on!"** they cried.

**"Work with the radiant Net of Light each day and teach others
how to work with it too. Working with the Net is effortless,"** the
Grandmothers declared. **"It is the Net of Light that is holding your
planet steady now, holding it steady in spite of the upheavals and
tragedies that are occurring each day. Don't get sucked in by these**

daily dramas," they said, "but instead hold, hold, hold the Net of Light and observe as it holds you.

"Each time you connect to the radiant Net, you become stronger, and when you do, *it* too becomes stronger. Stronger, farther reaching, and more brilliantly lit," they said. "Your heart provides the wattage for the Net of Light and in turn it provides peace, strength, and fulfillment for you. And each time you connect with it, the Net of Light provides these blessings not only for you, but for everything that lives.

"This is selfless work we are calling you to and you were born for it. Why do you think you incarnated at this time in history? This is why," the Grandmothers' said. "You were born to love—to love and lift your planet. If you want to fulfill your destiny, call on us or on any form of the Divine you love and then step forward into this blessed work. Pass on our message of the return of the energy of yin and then hold, hold, hold the Net of Light. We ask you to do this for yourself and for everything that lives.

"This work is not difficult," they said, "but it requires a willing heart. Call on us, then move into your heart and think of the Net of Light. This will automatically connect you to the Net that surrounds and permeates your planet, that holds every aspect of the world in light and holds you also in light," they said. Then, lifting their palms high, the Grandmothers said, "We bless and thank you for your willing heart."

About the Author

Sharon McErlane has been a teacher and psycho-therapist for more than three decades. She is also an accomplished artist and gardener, creating an environment in her home that many consider sacred space. She is married with two grown children and travels the world, empowering people with the energy of the Feminine Principle and teaching them how to work with the Net of Light.

Closing Note from the Author

Work with the Great Council of the Grandmothers and the Net of Light continues. Whenever the Grandmothers give a new lesson, we pass it on. Now people all over the world are meeting to share these teachings, pass on the Grandmothers' Empowerment into the energy of Yin, and cast and magnify the Net of Light for our beloved planet. As the holiness that lives at the core of these people awakens, they open to their loving connection to one another as well as to the Divine. You will find a listing of Beacons, those who pass on this work as service, at grandmothersspeak.com.

We do not know where the Grandmothers and the Net of Light will take us next, but the pull of this 'work' is irresistible so we will happily go wherever they lead. As the Grandmothers put it, **"There is great joy in being on the ride with us."**

— Sharon McErlane